Christology in the Synoptic Gospels

D1607775

Christology in the Synoptic Gospels

God or God's Servant?

By
Sigurd Grindheim

t&t clark

Published by T&T Clark International
A Continuum imprint
The Tower Building, 11 York Road, London SE1 7NX
80 Maiden Lane, Suite 704, New York, NY 10038

www.continuumbooks.com

Extract from James H. Charlesworth, *The Old Testament Pseudoepigrapha*, vol. 2, (1985), reprinted with permission from Yale University Press.

Sigurd Grindheim has asserted his right under the Copyright, Designs and Patents Act, 1988, to be identified as the Author of this work.

British Library Cataloguing-in-Publication Data
A catalogue record for this book is available from the British Library.

ISBN: HB: 978-0-567-00063-7
        PB: 978-0-567-24657-8

Library of Congress Cataloging-in-Publication Data
A catalog record for this book is available from the Library of Congress.

Typeset by Fakenham Prepress Solutions, Fakenham, Norfolk NR21 8NN
Printed and bound in India

Contents

Abbreviations

1 Chron.	1 Chronicles
1 Cor.	1 Corinthians
1 Kgdms	1 Kingdoms
1 Kgs	1 Kings
1 Sam.	1 Samuel
1 Thess.	1 Thessalonians
1 Tim.	1 Timothy
2 Chron.	2 Chronicles
2 Cor.	2 Corinthians
2 Kgdms	2 Kingdoms
2 Kgs	2 Kings
2 Pet.	2 Peter
2 Sam.	2 Samuel
2 Thess.	2 Thessalonians
2 Tim.	2 Timothy
3 Kgdms	3 Kingdoms
4 Kgdms	4 Kingdoms
AB	Anchor Bible
ABD	Anchor Bible Dictionary
ABRL	Anchor Bible Reference Library
AnBib	Analecta biblica
ATANT	Abhandlungen zur Theologie des Alten und Neuen Testaments
BCE	Before the Common Era
BZNW	Beihefte zur Zeitschrift für die neutestamentliche Wissenschaft
CA	California
CBQ	*Catholic Biblical Quarterly*
CE	Common Era
ConBNT	Coniectanea biblica: New Testament Series
CT	Connecticut
Dan.	Daniel

DE	Delaware
Deut.	Deuteronomy
ed.	edition
ed.	editor(s)
Eph.	Ephesians
ET	English translation
Exod.	Exodus
Ezek.	Ezekiel
Gal.	Galatians
Gen.	Genesis
Gr.	Greek
Hab.	Habakkuk
Heb.	Hebrews
Hebr.	Hebrew
Hos.	Hosea
HTKNT	Herders theologischer Kommentar zum Neuen Testament
HTR	*Harvard Theological Review*
ibid	ibidem (Latin for "in the same place"), used for subsequent references to the same source.
ICC	International Critical Commentary
Isa.	Isaiah
Jas	James
JBL	*Journal of Biblical Literature*
Jer.	Jeremiah
Jn	John
Jon.	Jonah
Josh.	Joshua
JSNT	*Journal for the Study of the New Testament*
JSNTSup	Journal for the Study of the New Testament: Supplement Series
Judg.	Judges
Lam.	Lamentations
Lev.	Leviticus
Lk.	Luke
LNTS	Library of New Testament Studies
LXX	Septuagint
Mal.	Malachi
Mk	Mark

Mt.	Matthew
Mic.	Micah
MT	Masoretic Text
MT	Montana
NAB	New American Bible
Nah.	Nahum
Neh.	Nehemiah
NICNT	New International Commentary on the New Testament
NIGTC	New International Greek Testament Commentary
NIV	New International Version
NJB	New Jerusalem Bible
NovTSup	Novum Testamentum Supplements
NRSV	New Revised Standard Version
NTAbh	Neutestamentliche Abhandlungen
NTS	*New Testament Studies*
Num.	Numbers
p.	page
par.	parallel passage(s)
Phil.	Philippians
pp.	pages
Prov.	Proverbs
Ps.	Psalm
Pss.	Psalms
Rev.	Revelation
Rom.	Romans
SBLDS	Society of Biblical Literature Dissertation Series
SJLA	Studies in Judaism in Late Antiquity
SNTSMS	Society for New Testament Studies Monograph Series
STDJ	*Studies on the Texts of the Desert of Judah*
TDNT	*Theological Dictionary of the New Testament*
Tit.	Titus
tr.	translator(s)
TX	Texas
TynBul	*Tyndale Bulletin*
vol.	volume
vols.	volumes
WBC	Word Biblical Commentary
WUNT	Wissenschaftliche Untersuchungen zum Neuen Testament

How To Read This Book

Inevitably, a New Testament textbook introduces the student not only to the New Testament but also to some scholarly jargon. To facilitate the reading of this book, such terminology appears in **bold** the first time it occurs in a given context. This is done in order to alert the reader to the fact that the term is explained in a glossary that is found at the back of the book. Most of these terms concern the titles of Jewish writings that are cited. In these cases, it will be possible to follow the argument without having to look up the information in the glossary, but the information found there will help give a better understanding of the background.

The Synoptic Gospels share much of the same material. In order to avoid repetition, the later chapters therefore often refer to the previous ones. For the same reason, the length given to a particular subject in Matthew and Luke is not always a good guide as to its importance. Therefore, even though it is possible to read the individual chapters without knowledge of the others, it is recommended that the chapters be read in sequence. This is especially important regarding Chapter 1, which provides a necessary framework for understanding the later chapters.

Introduction

Who was Jesus of Nazareth? For hundreds of years, Christians have answered that he is God's Son, fully God, and also fully man. The classic formulation is found in the Nicene Creed (325 CE), which affirms that he is "of the essence of the Father, God of God, Light of Light of Light, very God of very God, begotten, not made, being of one substance with the Father." The creed goes on to explain that he "came down and was incarnate and was made man."

However, the language of the Nicene Creed is not the language of the Bible. Words such as "essence" and "substance" appear to owe more to Greek philosophers than to the fishermen who were among the first followers of Jesus.

New Testament scholarship seeks to read the Bible in its historical context. This is a challenging task, for no scholar is uninfluenced by his or her own biases and presuppositions. This challenge is even more pressing when it comes to what the New Testament tells us about Jesus. We all think we know what it means when we read that Jesus is the Messiah, the Son of God, Lord, and Savior, but we have 2,000 years of Christian tradition that has taught us to understand these terms in a certain way. What did these terms mean to Jesus' first disciples?

The task of this book is to explain what the first three canonical Gospels teach us about who Jesus is. Even the subtitle of this book, the *Christology of the Synoptic Gospels*, shows the difficulty in undertaking this task without being influenced by the church's theological tradition. The word "Christology" does not occur in the Bible; it is the kind of word one would use for something that is the object of study, not a word one would use with respect to a person one knows well (whether by acquaintance or reputation). The evangelists, Matthew, Mark, and Luke, did not write "Christologies" – they wrote Jesus biographies. Such biographies will, of course, tell us a lot about what the authors believed about what kind of person Jesus was, but to explore those beliefs we need to use a rigorous method. It is necessary to understand the evangelists' terminological and conceptual world. We must understand the context of first-century Judaism. It is also necessary to pay close attention to the way the evangelists tell their story. It is not enough to mine the Gospels for direct statements regarding who Jesus is. Much older scholarship focused almost exclusively on the Christological titles ("Son of God," "Son of Man," "Messiah," and "Lord"), but that approach ignores the "implicit Christology" of the Gospels. In contrast, newer studies usually employ **narrative criticism** and focus on what we can learn about Jesus from the way the Gospel stories unfold. What Jesus says and does, how he interacts with others and how other people react to him are factors that make up the Gospels' portraits of Jesus. Titles play an important role, but they should not be analyzed in isolation. Rather, the various titles are filled with meaning by the way they function in the Gospel story.

When we read the Gospels in this light, we will see that they paint a multi-faceted picture of Jesus.

Israel's Eschatological Expectations

Much of what the Gospels have to say about Jesus has to do with questions such as "Are you the Messiah?" (Mk 14.61) and "Who is this Son of Man?" (Jn 12.34). The Messiah and the Son of Man are only two of the many characters that were expected to have a role in the end times. What Jewish people believed about these characters could also differ greatly.

The evangelists explain that Jesus sometimes conformed to people's expectations and that he sometimes corrected them. For example, the scribes were correct in predicting the birthplace of the Messiah (cf. Mt. 2.3-6), but Jesus' disciples were unprepared for the fact that the Messiah had to suffer and die (Lk. 24.25-7). To understand how Jesus relates to these expectations, we must first get an overview of the different Jewish hopes regarding the end-time saviors they believed that God would send.

The Messiah

Many students of the New Testament ask why so few Jews recognized Jesus as the Messiah. This question is very misleading because it presupposes that Jews had a shared understanding of what the Messiah would be like. That was not the case.

When Forrest Gump was asked if he had found Jesus, he answered: "I didn't know I was supposed to be looking for him, Sir." Many Jews in the first century would probably have said that they didn't know they were supposed to be waiting for the Messiah, and those who were waiting did not agree about what they were waiting for.

The disagreements within early Judaism are matched by the disagreements among modern scholars. Scholars read the same sources, but there is no agreement regarding what texts should be classified as "messianic." Some scholars insist that only those passages that explicitly use the word "Messiah" should be included, whereas others argue that the net should be thrown more widely. The functions and characteristics of a Messiah may be described even if the word is not used. Some scholars include all eschatological characters in the "messianic" category.

2 Christology in the Synoptic Gospels

The New Testament not only identifies Jesus as the Messiah but also sees in him the fulfillment of a number of disparate Old Testament passages. Traditionally, Christians have considered all of these passages to be "messianic." However, most Jews in Jesus' time did not read all of these passages as messianic prophecies.

To understand the New Testament in its historical context, it will not do to identify all the passages that later were applied to Jesus, and call them "messianic." In a historical investigation, that would be to work backwards. Instead, we need to study Israel's eschatological expectations as they emerge within the Old Testament and the literature of Second Temple Judaism. The next step is to discuss how the Gospel authors understood these prophecies in light of the fulfillment in Jesus Christ.

The English word "Christ" comes from the Greek *christos*, which is a translation of the Hebrew *mashiach*, a word that also has become the English term "Messiah." "Messiah" (*mashiach*) means the anointed one. Anointing with oil symbolized holiness. The anointed one was made holy and set apart for God (cf. Exod. 30.25-9), he was chosen by him (1 Sam. 9.16), and equipped with the Holy Spirit for the task that God had given him (Isa. 61.1). As kings (1 Sam. 10.1; 16.13 etc.), priests (Exod. 28.41; 1 Chron. 29.22), and prophets (1 Kgs 19.16; 1 Chron. 16.22; Ps. 105.15) were anointed, they might all be called messiah. In an eschatological context, however, the word "messiah" (*mashiach*) occurs only twice, in Dan. 9.25-26, which refers to "the time of an anointed (*mashiach*) prince", and to "an anointed one (*mashiach*)" that will be cut off. It may come as a surprise to many, but the Old Testament does not provide a definition of the word "Messiah" for our purposes.

Biblical scholars agree that Jewish expectations of a Messiah are rooted in God's promise to David, which is recorded in both 2 Sam. 7.8-16, and in 1 Chron. 17.7-14.[1] In several Old Testament texts, this promise was applied to the king on Israel's throne. But some texts also look to the future for its fulfillment. A few later Jewish texts connect the promise with an eschatological character. In this study, we will therefore define the term "Messiah" as an eschatological figure that is understood as a fulfillment of God's promise to David.

The part of the promise that specifically concerns offspring for David reads as follows:

> When your days are fulfilled and you lie down with your ancestors, I will raise up your offspring after you, who shall come forth from your body, and I will establish

his kingdom. He shall build a house for my name, and I will establish the throne of his kingdom forever. I will be a father to him, and he shall be a son to me. When he commits iniquity, I will punish him with a rod such as mortals use, with blows inflicted by human beings. But I will not take my steadfast love from him, as I took it from Saul, whom I put away from before you. Your house and your kingdom shall be made sure forever before me; your throne shall be established forever. (2 Sam. 7.12-16)

The house that God will build (v. 11b) does not refer to a physical house but to a family. More specifically, it refers to a line of successors to David's throne – a dynasty. The promise appeared to have been fulfilled in David's son, Solomon, who built a temple for the Lord (cf. v. 13). To him, God promises a very special status. God "will be a father to him, and he shall be a son to" God (v. 14). However, there is no reason to conclude that this promise implies that the son will be of divine nature. The whole people of Israel could also be called the son of God (Exod. 4.22-3; Hos. 11.1), and so could angels (Job 1.6; Dan. 3.25). The function of the term "son of God" is to assure that the king rules by divine decree. It also describes a relationship of exceptional intimacy.

Messianic Psalms

A number of Old Testament psalms elaborate on the Davidic promise, even though they may originally have been applied to the current king, not necessarily a future ruler. Two of these psalms repeat the promise concerning divine sonship (Pss. 2.7; 89.26-7). In Ps. 2.7, the psalmist proclaims: "I will tell of the decree of the Lord: He said to me, 'You are my son; today I have begotten you.'" Scholars debate whether this oracle should be understood in terms of adoption or begetting, but, in any case, the expression is metaphorical. The word "today" indicates that the king becomes God's son at his coronation. He is now God's son by virtue of his function as ruler. As such, he has a divinely ordained function and a special relationship with God. His sonship does not refer to his origin or to his nature.

According to Psalm 110, the king receives a very exalted position. In what is likely a prophetic oracle, we are told: "The Lord says to my lord, 'Sit at my right hand until I make your enemies your footstool'" (Ps. 110.1). Upon his enthronement the king, the prophet's lord, takes his place at the right hand of God. Scholars speculate regarding a possible background for this seating. Perhaps the king was enthroned in the Holy of Holies, next to the Ark of the

Covenant, or perhaps the oracle refers to the position of the king's palace relative to the temple. In any case, the Psalm expresses the view that the king's rule is an extension of that of God himself.

This Psalm also ascribes a priestly role to the king, also by solemn divine decree: "The Lord has sworn and will not change his mind, 'You are a priest forever according to the order of Melchizedek'" (Ps. 110.4). In the early days of Israel's monarchy, the king also carried out priestly functions (2 Sam. 6.14, 18; 1 Kgs 8.14), and the Lord now ensures the permanency of his priesthood.

Kingship apparently placed the king so close to God that the king himself could be addressed as God. In a song for a royal wedding, Psalm 45, the psalmist exclaims: "Your throne, O God, endures forever and ever" (Ps. 45.6a). Ideas regarding the divine nature of the king were common in the Ancient Near East, but not in Israel. Many scholars have therefore suggested alternative translations of this text. Several have also concluded that the Hebrew text as we have it must have been corrupted. Consequently, they have proposed various emendations of the text. However, the **Septuagint** and all the ancient versions support the translation that is found in most English bibles, where the king is called "God."[2] The meaning must be similar to what we have seen in Psalm 2: the king's "divinity" has to do with his function as ruler on God's behalf. It does not mean that he is of divine nature. Such an understanding would be quite alien to the Old Testament, which emphasizes the absolute distinction between God and his creatures.

The promises to the exalted monarch concern the divine qualities that he will exercise in his government. Like God, he will rule justly (cf. Pss 45.3, 6-7; 72.1-4, 12-14). His kingdom will be secure and his throne will be permanent (2 Sam. 7.16). Hostile kingdoms will not be able to challenge him (cf. Pss. 2.1-12; 45.4-5; 72.8-11; 89.22-3).

The Prophets

As it turned out, however, the history of Solomon and his successors could be seen as a fulfillment of the negative aspect of the promise: "When he commits iniquity, I will punish him with a rod such as mortals use, with blows inflicted by human beings" (2 Sam. 7.14). In particular, the conquest of Jerusalem by the Babylonians and the demotion of the king to vassal status meant that the king could no longer be seen as the embodiment of the Davidic promise. The failure of Judah's kings gave rise to a hope that a future king would emerge, a king through whom the positive aspect of the promise would materialize:

"Your house and your kingdom shall be made sure forever before me; your throne shall be established forever" (2 Sam. 7.16).

It became one of the tasks of Israel's prophets to apply the Davidic promise to the future and to describe the king that one day would emerge. Like the original promise, so do these prophecies describe a political leader who will bring peace and prosperity to Israel and rule with justice and righteousness.

The prophet Amos looks forward to a day when God "will raise up the booth of David that is fallen" (Amos 9.11). At this time, all the nations will belong to the Lord (Amos 9.12), and it will be a time of such prosperity that "the one who plows shall overtake the one who reaps, and the treader of grapes the one who sows the seed; the mountains shall drip sweet wine, and all the hills shall flow with it" (Amos 9.13). Were these words to be taken at face value, the prophecy presupposes a serious change in the state of the world, perhaps a return to the conditions of Eden with its abundant fertility. But the expression is probably poetic hyperbole.

For the prophet Micah, the Messiah is a ruler who will keep Israel safe from political enemies, chief among whom are the Assyrians (Mic. 5.5a-6). In the days of the Messiah the people "shall live secure, for now he shall be great to the ends of the earth; and he shall be the one of peace" (Mic. 5.4b-5a). The Messiah's rule is universal and peaceful.

Isaiah

Among the Old Testament prophetic books, Isaiah is the one that devotes the most attention to the promise to David. He repeatedly returns to this promise, which to him guarantees a new future for Israel. The immediate background for Isaiah's prophecies is the political situation in Judah at the time. When they were threatened by Syria and Israel, Isaiah announced that God would give king Ahaz a sign, a sign that concerned a child to be born: "Therefore the Lord himself will give you a sign. Look, the young woman is with child and shall bear a son, and shall name him Immanuel" (Isa. 7.14). This son will eat curs and honey (v. 15), which represent abundance (cf. v. 22; Exod. 3.8) and probably indicate that he is a king. His name means "God is with us" and signals that he will be an ideal king, ensuring God's goodwill to Israel.

Since the prophecy refers to the destruction of Israel and Syria (v. 16), which took place soon afterwards, most scholars think the son must have been born around the time of the prophet. The most common proposals include the king Hezekiah and a son of the prophet himself.

In any case, the prophecy informed Israel's future, messianic expectations. The earliest indications of such an understanding of the promise are found in the context in which the prophecy appears in the book of Isaiah. In the following passage, which describes the threat from Assyria, Immanuel is mentioned again. Assyria's army "will sweep on into Judah as a flood, and, pouring over, it will reach up to the neck; and its outspread wings will fill the breadth of your land, O Immanuel" (Isa. 8.8). But the enemy will not prevail. "It shall be brought to naught; speak a word, but it will not stand, for God is with us" (Isa. 8.10). The Hebrew word underlying "God is with us" is "Immanuel" and probably refers both to the promised Immanuel of Isa. 7.14 and the promise of God's presence, which he embodies.

The trend towards a messianic interpretation of Isa. 7.14-17 appears to be reflected in the oldest Greek translation of Isaiah as well. According to the Hebrew text, the one who will give birth to Immanuel is *almah*, which means "a young woman of marriageable age." Usually, such a woman would also be a virgin, but in Hebrew *almah* is not the technical term for virgin. That word would be *betulah*. The **Septuagint**, however, has the word *parthenos* here, which refers more specifically to a virgin (cf. Mt. 1.23). It is therefore possible that the Septuagint translator understood the verse to describe a miraculous birth, but it is difficult to know how much we should read into this word choice.

The Septuagint also refers to the pregnancy of the woman with a future tense. In contrast, the Hebrew does not indicate the time of the pregnancy; it is simply stated with a verbless clause (literally: "the young woman pregnant"). The choice of the future tense in the Septuagint may indicate that the translator envisioned a future fulfillment of the prophecy.

In vv. 15-16 the translator has taken more freedom in his rendering of the text. The Hebrew text mentions a time "before the child knows how to refuse the evil and choose the good" (Isa. 7.16), but does not specify what moral choices the child will make. However, the **Septuagint** leaves no room for doubt and takes this opportunity to emphasize the child's moral superiority: "before he knows or prefers evil things, he shall choose what is good. For before the child knows good or bad, he defies evil to choose what is good, and the land that you fear from before the two kings will be abandoned" (Isa. 7.15b-16 **LXX**).[3] The cumulative weight of these observations gives us good reason to conclude that the Septuagint understood Isaiah's prophecy as referring to an extraordinary future character.

The child to be born features once again in Isaiah 9. Israel's fortunes will be reversed and their oppressors defeated when "a child has been born for us, a son given to us; authority rests upon his shoulders; and he is named Wonderful Counselor, Mighty God, Everlasting Father, Prince of Peace. His authority shall grow continually, and there shall be endless peace for the throne of David and his kingdom. He will establish and uphold it with justice and with righteousness from this time onward and forevermore. The zeal of the Lord of hosts will do this" (Isa. 9.6-7).

This prophecy specifically recalls God's promise to David in 2 Sam. 7.12-16 as the child inaugurates an era of "endless peace for the throne of David and his kingdom" (v. 7).

Most scholars identify this child as king Hezekiah and understand his names as the conventional hyperbole of coronation ceremonies. In the context of the book of Isaiah, however, the child may be seen as the expression of Israel's hopes for a qualitatively different ruler, a ruler whose government demonstrates divine qualities. As the Lord is "wonderful in counsel" (Isa. 28.29), so will the child's name be "Wonderful Counselor." He will even be known by divine names like "Mighty God" (cf. Isa. 10.21), "Everlasting Father" (cf. Isa. 57.15) and "Prince of Peace" (cf. Isa. 2.4).

However, in early Jewish interpretation, the child was less closely associated with God. Perhaps the interpreters were motivated by a concern to maintain the distinction between God and his Messiah. In any case, the **Septuagint** translators understood *el gibbor* (in NRSV translated "Mighty God") to refer to a mighty angel or messenger, which is also a possible meaning for the term. In this version, Isa. 9.6 reads: "because a child was born for us, a son also given to us, whose sovereignty was upon his shoulder, and he is named Messenger of Great Counsel, for I will bring peace upon the rulers, peace and health to him."

To the Aramaic translator responsible for what we know as the *Isaiah Targum*, it is clear that the child is the Messiah. However, the divine names do not belong to the child at all, but to God, in whose presence the child will be named. The relatively free Aramaic translation of Isa. 9.6 is: "The prophet said to the house of David, For to us a child is born, to us a son is given; and he will accept the law upon himself to keep it, and his name will be called before the Wonderful Counselor, the Mighty God, existing forever, 'The messiah in whose days peace will increase upon us.'"[4]

Isaiah's excitement about the messianic times reaches something of a climax in chapter 11. The Messiah is here identified as "a shoot [that] shall come out from the stump of Jesse" (v. 1). He will be equipped with the spirit of the Lord in an exceptional way, so that he is given divine qualifications to rule: "The spirit of the Lord shall rest on him, the spirit of wisdom and under-standing, the spirit of counsel and might, the spirit of knowledge and the fear of the Lord" (v. 2). He can therefore rule with justice, give the poor their right, and judge evildoers (vv. 3b-5). As a result, the world will experience an unprecedented time of peace and harmony:

> The wolf shall live with the lamb, the leopard shall lie down with the kid, the calf and the lion and the fatling together, and a little child shall lead them. The cow and the bear shall graze, their young shall lie down together; and the lion shall eat straw like the ox. The nursing child shall play over the hole of the asp, and the weaned child shall put its hand on the adder's den. They will not hurt or destroy on all my holy mountain; for the earth will be full of the knowledge of the Lord as the waters cover the sea. (vv. 6-9)

This vision embraces not only humanity, but also the animal world, and presupposes a fundamentally new creative act of God. The theme of a new creation is developed further elsewhere in the book of Isaiah (35.1-10; 65.17-25), but this is the only instance where the new creation is associated with the coming of the Messiah.

Jeremiah

For Isaiah, the corruption and injustice of Judah's rulers serve as the background of his prophecies. That is also the case for the prophet Jeremiah, who views the people's leaders as unfaithful shepherds of God's people (23.1). In contrast, God himself will raise up a shepherd for the people. With a name that recalls the shoot "from the stump of Jesse" (cf. Isa. 11.1), Jeremiah identifies the new leader as "a righteous Branch" that God will raise up for David (Jer. 23.5). As a true shepherd, he will ensure that "Israel will live in safety" (Jer. 23.6). His name will be "The Lord is our righteousness" (Jer. 23.6). This name is a play on the name of Israel's king, Zedekiah, which means "My righteousness is the Lord." Zedekiah's name had proven to be ironic, as he had had nothing to do with God's righteousness. In contrast, the righteous Branch "shall reign as king and deal wisely, and shall execute justice and righteousness in the land" (Jer. 23.5).

Ezekiel

The picture of the Messiah as a good shepherd is also the dominant metaphor for the prophet Ezekiel. Since Israel's shepherds have failed, God will give them another shepherd, a new David (Ezek. 34.23–24). Like Isaiah 11, so does Ezekiel also envision a time of bliss in the land. God makes a covenant of peace with the people, Israel will be safe from wild animals, the land will yield its fruit, the people will no longer be troubled by their enemies, and Israel will know the Lord (Ezek. 34.25-31; cf. 37.24-8).

Daniel

The only place in the Old Testament where a future ruler is explicitly called "Messiah" is the prophecy in Dan. 9.24-7. This prophecy describes seventy "sevens" or weeks. These seventy weeks are divided into seven weeks, sixty-two weeks, and one last week. The anointed one, the Messiah, will be put to death after seven plus sixty-two weeks (Dan. 9.25-6). It is usually assumed that each of these "weeks" refers to seven years. If this were to be taken literally, the Messiah would die 483 years after "the time that the word went out to restore and rebuild Jerusalem" (Dan. 9.25). Suggestions regarding the identification of this "word" are many. They range from Jeremiah's prophecy (Jer. 25.12; 29.10), which was spoken in 605 BCE, to the Persian king Artaxerxes' decree to Nehemiah to rebuild the entire city of Jerusalem in 444 or 445 BCE (cf. Neh. 2.1-10). In any case, attempts to coordinate the 483 years of Daniel's prophecy with the crucifixion of Jesus require a good deal of ingenuity, as Jesus' death is dated to 30 or 32 CE. A better interpretation of these numbers takes them as a stylized way of writing history, much like the numbers in the Old Testament genealogies and the numbers in the book of Revelation. The meaning of the numbers would then be that Israel suffers their seventy years of punishment (cf. Jer. 25.11; 29.10) sevenfold (cf. Lev. 26.18, 21, 24, 28).

During this period, God will restore the purity and holiness of Israel and Jerusalem. "Seventy weeks are decreed for your people and your holy city: to finish the transgression, to put an end to sin, and to atone for iniquity, to bring in everlasting righteousness, to seal both vision and prophet, and to anoint a most holy place" (Dan. 9.24).

The Messiah's place in relation to these seventy weeks is a matter of some dispute. Most scholars translate the **Masoretic Text** of Dan. 9.25 more or less like the NRSV: "Know therefore and understand: from the time that the word went out to restore and rebuild Jerusalem until the time of an anointed prince, there shall be seven weeks; and for sixty-two weeks it shall be built again with streets and moat, but in a troubled time." On this translation, a Messiah appears after seven weeks, while v. 26 refers to the death of a Messiah sixty-two weeks later. Many scholars therefore see a reference to two Messiahs in this passage, usually the high priest Zerubbabel or Joshua (cf. Zech. 4.14) and Onias III (cf. **2 Maccabees** 4.34) respectively.

However, the **Septuagint** has a different understanding of the text. In this version, there is no mention of a Messiah, and the seven weeks and the sixty-two weeks make up one time period, a period that leads to the removal of anointing: "after seven and seventy and sixty-two weeks, an anointing will be removed and will not be" (Dan. 9.26). Yet another view is found in the **Theodotion** version. In Theodotion, the Messiah appears after sixty-nine weeks: "from the going forth of the command for the answer and for the building of Jerusalem until Christ the prince *there shall be* seven weeks, and sixty-two weeks" (Dan. 9.25).[5] Some scholars, who find a messianic prophecy in Dan. 9.25, have argued that the Hebrew text should be understood in a similar way.

Early Jewish interpreters were able to find a number of different applications for Daniel's prophecy. The desolations outlined in Dan. 9.26-7 were seen as a description of the atrocities of Antiochus Epiphanes. In 167 BCE, Antiochus conquered Jerusalem, made it illegal to practice the Jewish religion, dedicated the temple to the Greek god Zeus, erected a statue of Zeus in the Holy of Holies, and sacrificed a pig there. This interpretation is mentioned by the Jewish historian **Josephus**, who also saw the prophecy as fulfilled when Titus' Roman army destroyed the Jerusalem temple in 70 CE (*Antiquities of the Jews* 10.276; cf. *Jewish War* 6.94). This interpretation is reflected in the Gospels of Matthew and Mark as well (Mt. 24.15; Mk 13.14).

In one of the **Qumran** scrolls, the Messiah of Dan. 9.25 is identified as the messenger of Isa. 52.7, "the messenger who announces peace, who brings good news, who announces salvation, who says to Zion, 'Your God reigns.'" According to the Qumran scroll, this messenger announces the coming of Melchizedek, who is the savior that will come at the end of time (**11Q13** 2.15-18). On this particular eschatological scenario, Daniel's Messiah is subordinate to Melchizedek (cf. further pp. 21-22).

Even though Daniel's seventy weeks were understood to describe the end times, the Messiah of Dan. 9.25-6 does not play an important role in the surviving literature from **Second Temple Judaism**. The text was applied and interpreted in various ways, but this Messiah did not take centre stage.

Zechariah

As this Messiah is described by Daniel himself, he is associated with atonement for sin (Dan. 9.24) and evidently had a priestly function (cf. also Ps. 110.4). For the prophet Zechariah as well, the Messiah is a priest. The Branch (cf. Jer. 23.5) is compared to the high priest Joshua:

> Now listen, Joshua, high priest, you and your colleagues who sit before you! For they are an omen of things to come: I am going to bring my servant the Branch. For on the stone that I have set before Joshua, on a single stone with seven facets, I will engrave its inscription, says the Lord of hosts, and I will remove the guilt of this land in a single day. (Zech. 3.8-9)

In their high-priestly function, Joshua and his colleagues serve as a foreshadowing of the function of the Messiah. Here, their function is connected with "a single stone with seven facets." Interpreters are divided with respect to what this stone represents. Some favor a reference to a precious stone on the high priest's turban. Like Zechariah's stone, so did this turban carry an inscription: "Holy to the Lord" (Exod. 28.36). Others point to the top stone of the new temple, which is mentioned in Zech. 4.9. If the latter interpretation is correct, the Messiah's priestly function would be associated with the construction of the temple.

In chapter 9 of the book of Zechariah, the prophet looks forward to the judgment of Israel's enemies. Part of this triumphant vision is devoted to the entrance of Israel's king, the Messiah, into Jerusalem:

> Rejoice greatly, O daughter Zion! Shout aloud, O daughter Jerusalem! Lo, your king comes to you; triumphant and victorious is he, humble and riding on a donkey, on a colt, the foal of a donkey. He will cut off the chariot from Ephraim and the war-horse from Jerusalem; and the battle bow shall be cut off, and he shall command peace to the nations; his dominion shall be from sea to sea, and from the River to the ends of the earth. (Zech. 9.9-10)

Considering that this king will be victorious over Israel's enemies, his choice of transportation is highly ironic. Even though it was common in the ancient Near East for a king to be mounted on a donkey, the donkey is not an animal used for warfare. Military warriors used horses and chariots (cf. Zech. 1.8; 6.2, 3, 6). Zechariah's point is that the Messiah's victory is not won by military might; he will destroy the weapons of war. Not with the force of arms but with humility does he bring "peace to the nations" and establish "his dominion from sea to sea."

In chapter 13, Zechariah's prophecy turns to the shepherd of the Lord and his demise: "'Awake, O sword, against my shepherd, against the man who is my associate,' says the Lord of hosts. Strike the shepherd, that the sheep may be scattered; I will turn my hand against the little ones" (Zech. 13.7). As the image is the dispersion of the people, the shepherd in view must be the king (cf. Jer. 23.1-2; Ezek. 34.1-6). Few scholars venture a more precise identification. One suggestion is that the prophet refers to the downfall of the monarchy as such at the time of Israel's exile.

In the **Qumran** community, Old Testament prophecies were often reinterpreted to apply to the community's own history and situation. In Zech. 13.7, they found a description of an eschatological character that was distinguished from the Messiah, who would come later (**CD**-B 19.7-10). Since they also thought that those who revered the shepherd were "the poor ones of the flock," it is quite likely that they identified Zechariah's shepherd as their own leader, the **Teacher of Righteousness**.

Other Prophecies

Apart from the prophetic books, there are two passages from the Pentateuch that must be considered. Scholars debate how they relate historically to the promise in 2 Sam. 7.12-16, but for our present purposes it is more important to note that they were understood messianically by Jewish interpreters.

In Jacob's last words, he announces that a ruler will come from Judah's tribe (Gen. 49.8-12). Judah is likened to a lion (v. 9), a symbol of royalty, and Jacob predicts that "the scepter shall not depart from Judah, nor the ruler's staff from between his feet, until tribute comes to him; and the obedience of the peoples is his" (v. 10). The king from Judah will have an eternal kingdom. Under his rule, there will be such an abundance of resources that this ruler will bind "his foal to the vine" and wash "his garments in wine" (v. 11). In Qumran, this ruler is identified as the royal messiah, "the messiah of righteousness … the branch of David" (**4Q252** 5.3-4).

The wicked prophet Balaam was also forced to prophesy about Israel's future king. He announces: "I see him, but not now; I behold him, but not near – a star shall come out of Jacob, and a scepter shall rise out of Israel; it shall crush the borderlands of Moab, and the territory of all the Shethites" (Num. 24.17). The future Israelite king is now symbolized by a star, which eventually was established as a messianic image (*Testament of Levi* 18.3; *Testament of Judah* 24.1, 6; **CD** 7.18-19; **1QM** 11.6; cf. also **4Q175** 9-13).

The Psalms of Solomon

There are clear references to God's promise to David in the Jewish writings from **Second Temple Judaism** (**Sirach** 47.22; **1 Maccabees** 2.57). One implication of this continued interest in the Davidic promise may be that Jews in this period held out hope that the future would see a new king who would bring these promises to fulfillment. However, most of the surviving writings from this period are not explicit regarding a future Messiah. The most significant exception is the *Psalms of Solomon*, which in chapter 17 contains the classic description of the messianic hope in Second Temple Judaism. The background for this chapter is that Israel is oppressed by Gentiles, a predicament that the author understands to be God's judgment for Israel's sins. Specifically, God "rose up against them a man alien to our race" (17.7). Scholars usually identify this alien as the Roman general Pompey, who conquered Jerusalem in 63 BCE and brought an end to Israel's monarchy.

With the land in ruins (17.11) and the corruption reaching from the palace to the slum (17.20), the psalmist turned to God in prayer for a brighter future:

> [21]See, O Lord, and raise up for them their king,
> the son of David, to rule over your servant Israel
> in the time known to you, O God.
> [22]Undergird him with the strength to destroy the unrighteous rulers,
> to purge Jerusalem from gentiles
> who trample her to destruction;
> [23]in wisdom and in righteousness to drive out
> the sinners from the inheritance;
> to smash the arrogance of sinners
> like a potter's jar;
> [24]To shatter all their substance with an iron rod;
> to destroy the unlawful nations with the word of his mouth;
> [25]At his warning the nations will flee from his presence;
> and he will condemn sinners by the thoughts of their hearts.
> [26]He will gather a holy people
> whom he will lead in righteousness;
> and he will judge the tribes of the people
> that have been made holy by the Lord their God.
> [27]He will not tolerate unrighteousness (even) to pause among them,
> and any person who knows wickedness shall not live with them.

For he shall know them

that they are all children of their God.

[28]He will distribute them upon the land

according to their tribes;

the alien and the foreigner will no longer live near them.

[29]He will judge peoples and nations in the wisdom of his righteousness. Pause.

[30]And he will have gentile nations serving him under his yoke,

and he will glorify the Lord in (a place) prominent (above) the whole earth.

And he will purge Jerusalem

(and make it) holy as it was even from the beginning,

[31](for) nations to come from the ends of the earth to see his glory,

to bring as gifts her children who had been driven out,

and to see the glory of the Lord

with which God has glorified her.

[32]And he will be a righteous king over them, taught by God.

There will be no unrighteousness among them in his days,

for all shall be holy,

and their king shall be the Lord Messiah.

[33](For) he will not rely on horse and rider and bow,

nor will he collect gold and silver for war.

Nor will he build up hope in a multitude for a day of war.

[34]The Lord himself is his king,

the hope of the one who has a strong hope in God.

He shall be compassionate to all the nations

(who) reverently (stand) before him.

[35]He will strike the earth with the word of his mouth forever;

he will bless the Lord's people with wisdom and happiness.

[36]And he himself (will be) free from sin, (in order) to rule a great people.

He will expose officials and drive out sinners

by the strength of his word.

[37]And he will not weaken in his days, (relying) upon his God,

for God made him

powerful in the holy spirit

and wise in the counsel of understanding,

with strength and righteousness.

[38]And the blessing of the Lord will be with him in strength.

and he will not weaken;

[39]His hope (will be) in the Lord.

Then who will succeed against him,

[40]mighty in his actions

strong in the fear of God?

Faithfully and Righteously shepherding the Lord's flock,

he will not let any of them stumble in their pasture.

[41]He will lead them all in holiness

and there will be no arrogance among them,
that any should be oppressed.
[42]This is the beauty of the king of Israel
which God knew,
to raise him over the house of Israel
to discipline it.
[43]His words will be purer than the finest gold, the best.
He will judge the peoples in the assemblies,
the tribes of the sanctified.
His words will be as the words of the holy ones,
among sanctified peoples.
[44]Blessed are those born in those days
to see the good fortune of Israel
which God will bring to pass in the assembly of the tribes. (17.21-44)

This king, who is called "the Lord Messiah" (17.32; cf. 18 heading; 18.5, 7), will be the righteous counterpart to the ungodly alien. Inspired by Isaiah 11, the psalmist explains how he will rule with wisdom and righteousness. He will drive out the Gentiles and sinners from Jerusalem. The people that serve under him will be holy, and there will be no sinners among them. Israel's tribes will be restored to their land. Non-Israelites will have no place in the land, but they will recognize the glory of Jerusalem and be subject to Israel's Messiah.

Scholars discuss whether this Messiah will be a military leader. When the psalmist proclaims that he will "shatter all their substance with an iron rod" (17.24), it appears that he has read about the "rod of his mouth" in Isa. 11.4 and reinterpreted it in a militant sense. But in the following line, the psalmist continues, "to destroy the unlawful nations with the word of his mouth" (cf. also 17.35). Many scholars therefore think that the *Psalms of Solomon* envision a Messiah who has rejected military might. After all, "he will not rely on horse and rider and bow, nor will he collect gold and silver for war" (17.33). Instead, his might is based on the fact that he has "a strong hope in God" (17.34). His strength is in his word, his wisdom, and righteousness.

In any case, the *Psalms of Solomon* describe the Messiah as a political leader who will bring restoration to Israel and ensure that the Gentiles are made subject to them. The most characteristic qualities of this Messiah are his wisdom and righteousness. His righteousness makes him unique among human beings; he is even free from sin. Unique as he is, however, he is no more than a human being. His name is Lord Messiah (Gr: *christos kurios*), but it is very unlikely that the name "Lord" goes back to the Old Testament name for

God, Yahweh. The Greek version of the *Psalms of Solomon* that has survived is almost certainly a translation of an original Hebrew, and the Hebrew name for the Messiah in the original version was most probably *mashiach adon*. *Adon* is used as a royal title.[6] The *Psalms of Solomon* do not develop the idea that the Davidic king is called the son of God (cf. 2 Sam. 7.14; Ps. 2.7). Instead, all of God's people share in divine sonship (17.27). There is a hint that the Messiah is pre-existent (17.21, 42), but the idea is simply that God knows him, like God knows the prophets before their birth (cf. Jer. 1.5), not that the Messiah has conscious pre-existence.

Apart from the **Psalms of Solomon**, later **apocalyptic** works show the greatest interest in the Messiah. However, as apocalyptics are characterized by a sharper distinction between heaven and earth and between this world and the world to come, the most important actor in their eschatological scenarios is God himself. The work of the Messiah is strictly limited and subordinated to the apocalyptic intervention of God. According to *4 Ezra* (100 CE), God announces a future messianic kingdom: "For my son the Messiah shall be revealed with those who are with him, and those who remain shall rejoice four hundred years. After those years my son the Messiah shall die, and all who draw human breath" (7.28-9). The fact that the Messiah is God's son cannot keep him from dying. His rule is clearly distinguished from the end, which will be inaugurated after his death, when the resurrection of the dead and God's final judgment will take place (7.30-44).

Second Baruch (100–120 CE) also includes the Messiah in its eschatological timetable (29.3; 30.1; 39.7). His role is that of a judge. He will convict the last ruler and punish him (40.1-2) and save God's people (70.9). Of all the nations, he will kill some and spare some (72.2). As in *4 Ezra*, his eschatological role is preparatory, preceding the rule of God. "His dominion will last forever," but only "until the world of corruption has ended and until the times which have been mentioned before have been fulfilled" (40.3).

Qumran

The community whose library contained the **Dead Sea Scrolls** is usually referred to as the **Qumran** community. Most scholars are convinced that this community belonged to the Jewish group otherwise known as the Essenes, but this question continues to be discussed. Regardless, the writings of this community demonstrate a keen interest in eschatological events. It is quite natural, therefore, that they contain numerous references to messianic characters. Unfortunately, the interpretation of these scrolls is complicated by a number of factors. Those who discovered the scrolls were able to command a high price when they sold them. Since they got paid per item, some of them also discovered that it would be profitable to cut up the documents into small pieces and sell them separately. We are therefore often left with very small fragments to interpret. The date of the writings is also uncertain. They can be dated based on palaeography, but these analyses can only give us a ballpark figure, accurate to within 50–100 years. In any case, these dates concern the surviving manuscripts, which may be copies of much older originals. It is therefore often difficult or impossible to be certain about the provenance of these writings.

What seems clear, however, is that the community was expecting more than one messiah. In a now-famous passage, the Community Rule affirms that the members 'shall be ruled by the primitive precepts in which the men of the Community were first instructed until there shall come the Prophet and the Messiahs of Aaron and Israel" (**1QS** 9.10-11).[7] Another scroll, 4QTestimonia (**4Q175**), contains quotations from various biblical texts, including Deut. 18.18-19; 33.8-11; and Num. 24.15-17. These biblical passages probably serve as the Scriptural basis for the community's messianic beliefs. Deut. 18.18-19 announces the coming of a prophet like Moses; in Num. 24.15-17, Balaam prophesies regarding a scepter that has arisen from Israel (a royal Messiah, the Messiah of Israel); and Deut. 33.8-11 refers to a pious man who will steward the Urim and Thummim, the priestly tools for knowing the will of God (a priestly Messiah, the Messiah of Aaron).

The Qumran community was obsessively concerned with religious and ritual purity, so it is not surprising that they would give priority to the priestly Messiah. The Messianic Rule explains that the royal Messiah will have to defer to the priestly Messiah (probably a thinly veiled insistence that the political leaders in Jerusalem should defer to the priestly authority of their community):

> When God engenders (the Priest-) Messiah, he shall come with them [at] the head of the whole congregation of Israel with all [his brethren, the sons] of Aaron the Priests, [those called] to the assembly, the men of renown; and they shall sit [before him, each man] in the order of his dignity. And then [the Mess] iah of Israel shall [come], and the chiefs of the [clans of Israel] shall sit before him, [each] in the order of his dignity, according to [his place] in their camps and marches. (**1QSa** 2.11-15)

One of the fragments from Qumran that has commanded the most scholarly attention is the "Son of God" document (**4Q246**, dated 35–1 BCE). Column 2 of this document introduces an intriguing character: "He will be called son of God, and they will call him son of the Most High" (2.1). The text immediately proceeds to describe the enemies of God's people (2.2-3), and it has been argued that "son of God" should be understood as a name for a particularly reprehensible pagan king, possibly Antiochus IV Epiphanes, who desecrated the temple; his son, Alexander Balas, who bribed the high priest for political support; or even the eschatological archenemy of God's people. But it is more likely that the title is intended positively, and that the son of God should be associated with the people of God, who appear on the stage in line 4. The figure could be understood as a guardian angel, a coming Jewish ruler, Israel collectively, or, as is perhaps most likely, an individual that represents the people. This son of God is described in a way characteristic of the Messiah and is probably also inspired by Daniel's vision of the heavenly Son of Man (Dan. 7.13-14). He has an eternal kingdom, is a truthful judge, and brings peace to the earth as he establishes his worldwide rule: "His kingdom will be an eternal kingdom, and all his paths in truth. He will jud[ge] the earth in truth and all will make peace. The sword will cease from the earth, and all the provinces will pay him homage" (4Q246 2.5-7a). He will not do so on his own authority, however: "The great God is his strength, he will wage war for him; he will place the peoples in his hand and cast them all away before him. His rule will be an eternal rule" (4Q246 2.7b-9a).[8] There is no hint that his sonship implies that he is equal to God or divine. The scroll refers to his unique privilege as God's special protégé. A few other texts also refer to the Messiah as a son of God (**4Q174** 1.11; **4Q369** 1.ii.6), but they do not provide any further clues as to how divine sonship is understood.

Several other texts mention the sonship of the Messiah without elaborating on its meaning. The Messianic Rule describes the seating arrangements when God "engenders (the Priest-) Messiah with them" (**1QSa** 2.11-12). In **4Q369**, there is a reference to "a first-born son" (4Q369 1.ii.6), which may indicate a Davidic character as well (cf. Ps. 89.28).

An even more mystifying character is introduced in the "Elect of God" text (**4Q534**). This scroll describes the birth and ascendancy of a character called the elect of God (4Q534 1.10). Like the Messiah (Isa. 11.2), the elect one is distinguished by his wisdom:

> Counsel and prudence will be with him, and he will know the secrets of man. His wisdom will reach all the peoples, and he will know the secrets of all the living.

And all their designs against him will come to nothing, and (his) rule over all the living will be great. His designs [will succeed], for he is the Elect of God. His birth and the breath of his spirit ... and his designs shall be for ever ... (4Q534 1.7-10)

Since the scroll mentions "the breath of his spirit," many scholars have seen an allusion to the messianic prophecy in Isa. 11.4 and identified this elect one as the Messiah. But the majority of scholars follow Joseph Fitzmyer, who thinks the elect one was Noah. Against this view, however, other scholars argue that there is no evidence from this early stage that this title was applied to Noah.

Whoever this elect one is, he is no ordinary human being. Even though the surviving text does not attribute any divine titles to him, he has an exceptional wisdom. This wisdom probably includes knowledge of the works and destinies of all humans. Armed with this wisdom, he has an unassailable power. However, these unmatched qualities are not inherent with him. As a young man, his knowledge was remarkably limited: "In his youth, he will be like ... [like a m]an who knows nothing until the time when he knows the three Books" (**4Q534** 1.4). The members of the Qumran community prided themselves on a unique wisdom that was given to them by divine revelation, and the "Elect of God" excelled in this respect. He did not have knowledge or power that compared to God's; he was uniquely gifted by God.

Conclusion

There was obviously considerable diversity among Jewish expectations regarding the Messiah, corresponding to the diversity of opinion in general among the various groups of Judaism. Some common traits emerge nevertheless. The Messiah would be a human being with a special relationship to God. He would be exceptionally wise and righteous, and therefore preeminently qualified to serve as Israel's king, bring the people back to God, and restore their fortunes. In the process, he would make the nations subject to Israel and their God. There is no evidence that Jews in the first century believed the Messiah would be equal to God.

The angel of the Lord

Because Jewish expectations of the Messiah cannot explain how Christians came to believe in Jesus as God, several scholars have turned their attention to another character that held a more exalted position in Jewish thought, namely the Angel of the Lord.[9] The Angel of the Lord is a most mysterious figure. In Zech. 1.12 he addresses the Lord of hosts and must clearly be understood as a separate character from him. But in a number of passages, the narrative blurs the distinction between the two. A good example is found in Gideon's encounter with the angel of the Lord under the oak at Ophrah. The angel talks to Gideon and Gideon responds (Judg. 6.11-15), but suddenly the narrative changes the identity of Gideon's conversation partner to God himself (Judg. 6.16). Similar accounts are found concerning Abraham (compare Gen. 22.11 and 22.12), Hagar (compare Gen. 16.7, 9, 10, 11 and 16.13), and Moses (cf. Exod. 3.2, 3 and 3.7). Another important text is Exod. 23.20, where God promises to send an angel in front of Israel and says that God's name will be in him. Although the word "angel" is not used, a similar ambiguity can be observed in Genesis 18. The story switches between saying that Abraham met and talked with the Lord (Gen. 18.1, 13) and with three men (Gen. 18.2) who ate Sarah's food (Gen. 18.8).

In later Jewish literature, the term "Angel of the Lord" is less prominent. Instead, there is a heightened interest in the archangels. The description of these angels is sometimes dependent upon the Scriptural traditions regarding the Angel of the Lord, but the ambiguity that is found in these Scriptural accounts has not influenced the picture of the archangel. Instead, these texts typically emphasize the spiritual nature of God and do not portray God as interacting directly with the world. The archangels take the function of communicating with human beings.

The best known archangel is Michael. He is mentioned in Dan. 10.13, 21, where he appears as the guardian angel of Israel and is clearly distinct from and inferior to God. In **Targum Pseudo-Jonathan**, the man that fought with Jacob is identified as the angel Michael (*Targum Pseudo-Jonathan* Gen. 32.25). In contrast to the Hebrew Bible, however, the Targum does not include the comment that Jacob fought with God (Gen. 32.28) or that he saw God face to face (Gen. 32.30). Instead, Michael tells Jacob that he was magnified with the angels of the Lord, and Jacob is stunned that he survived seeing the angels of the Lord (*Targum Pseudo-Jonathan* Gen. 32.28, 30). In some of the **apocalyptic** writings, Michael's function is to punish evil angels (*1 Enoch* 10.11-13; cf. 54.5-6), to fight for his people (**1QM** 17.6), and to take Adam to Paradise (*Apocalypse of Moses* 37.5; *Life of Adam and Eve* 48.1-3).

The late apocalyptic work known as *3 Enoch* (fifth to sixth century CE) chronicles the exploits of an exalted angel called Metatron. Like he did concerning the angel from Exod. 23.20, God declared that his name was in Metatron (*3 Enoch* 12.5). Metatron is also identified as Enoch, the son of

Jared (*3 Enoch* 4.2), is installed as God's vice regent and is given authority over all the angels (*3 Enoch* 4.5; 10.3-6). God also gives him a throne, equal to his own, where Metatron is seated (*3 Enoch* 10.1-2), as well as a number of exalted names such as "Prince of the Divine Presence" (*3 Enoch* 1.4 etc.) and "the glory of the highest heaven" (*3 Enoch* 13.1 etc.). But the name that has biblical scholars salivating is the one Metatron makes known in *3 Enoch* 12.5: "[God] called me, 'The lesser YHWH' in the presence of his whole household in the height, as it is written 'My name is in him.'" Exodus 23.20 is here taken quite literally: Metatron is given God's own name, Yahweh.

It is possible that **3 Enoch** contains several traditions concerning Metatron, and perhaps one of these traditions is critical of the high view that the others give to him. In any case, when 'Aher sees Metatron on the throne and concludes that "there are indeed two powers in heaven" (*3 Enoch* 16.3), 'Aher is punished. He is not allowed to return to God (*3 Enoch* 16.4) and Metatron has to vacate his throne and suffer sixty lashes of fire (*3 Enoch* 16.5).

As exalted as Metatron is, he is not God's equal. He does not act as God acts, but he is consistently on the receiving end of God's actions. His exalted status is given him by God as a reward for his righteousness (*3 Enoch* 4.3; 6.3). God is the one who seats him on the throne (*3 Enoch* 10.2) that God had made for him (*3 Enoch* 10.1). He rules the angels in God's name (*3 Enoch* 10.5), and he judges them on God's authority (*3 Enoch* 16.1). Although Metatron holds the highest position under God in heaven, his status is not entirely unique. Other angels are also known by the name YHWH (eight according to *3 Enoch* 10.3 and sixteen according to *3 Enoch* 18.8-24; cf. 30.1).

Melchizedek

The Metatron traditions are considerably younger than the New Testament. For information about beliefs held in Jesus' days, we turn to the **Qumran** scrolls. A scroll known as 11QMelch (**11Q13**) paints a fascinating picture of the mysterious Melchizedek figure.[10] Scholars are divided regarding the identity of this character. The majority think that "Melchizedek" is another name for the archangel Michael, but other proposals have also been put forward, including the views that he is the Messiah, God himself, or even a second deity. The background for the last two proposals is that Melchizedek is very closely associated with God:

> For this is the moment of the Year of Grace for Melchizedek. [And h]e will, by
> his strength, judge the holy ones of God, executing judgment as it is written

concerning him in the Songs of David, who said, *ELOHIM has taken his place in the divine council; in the midst of the gods he holds judgment* (Psalms lxxxii, I). And it was concerning him that he said, (Let the assembly of the peoples) *return to the height above them; EL (god) will judge the peoples* (Psalms vii, 7-8). As for that which he s[aid, *How long will you] judge unjustly and show partiality to the wicked? Selah* (Psalms lxxxii, 2), its interpretation concerns Belial and the spirits of his lot [who] rebelled by turning away from the precepts of God to … And Melchizedek will avenge the vengeance of the judgments of God … and he will drag [them from the hand of] Belial and from the hand of all the sp[irits of] his [lot]. And all the 'gods [of Justice'] will come to his aid [to] attend to the de[struction] of Belial (11Q13 2.9-14).

The scroll describes Melchizedek as the end-time judge who will punish Belial (Satan) and his minions. Melchizedek is referred to by the Hebrew words *el* and *elohim* (which is the plural form of *el*). These words are usually translated "God," but they may also be used with reference to other heavenly beings. That Melchizedek is called by these names is not unprecedented, if he is an angelic character. The text also describes the "gods (*el*) of Justice" (11Q13 2.14), which must refer to angels. What is more striking is that the author of 11Q13 quotes several Old Testament passages that originally spoke about God and applies them to Melchizedek. Ps. 82.1 speaks of God taking a stand in the assembly of angels, but when this Psalm is quoted in 11Q13 2.10, Melchizedek is the subject. In Ps. 7.7-8, God judges the peoples. Once again, 11Q13 2.12-13 sees Melchizedek as the judge when this Psalm is quoted. The scroll even mentions "the Year of Grace" (11Q13 2.9), which is an allusion to "the year of the Lord's favor" in Isa. 61.2a. In 11Q13 2.9; however, the year of Grace is Melchizedek's.

It would appear, then, that Melchizedek somehow has taken God's place. However, even though Melchizedek is exceptional in Second Temple Judaism in this respect, he remains an agent of God. He is subordinate to God and acts on his behalf. When he executes judgment, the judgments are "the judgments of God" (11Q13 2.13). The picture of Melchizedek in 11QMelch compares to other Jewish ideas regarding angelic beings. Like them, he is given honorific names, but his functions are clearly subordinate to God.

The Son of Man

One of the most intriguing characters in the Old Testament and the literature of **Second Temple Judaism** is the Son of Man. "Son of Man" is a literal translation of the Hebrew term *ben adam*, which corresponds to the Aramaic *bar enosh* and the Greek *huios tou anthropou*. In Hebrew and Aramaic, the meaning of this term is basically "human being" (cf. Ezek. 2.1, 3, 6, 8; 3.1 etc.; Pss. 8.4; 80.17). The expression does not exist in classical Greek, except as a translation of Hebrew or Aramaic. Modern scholars often render this term as "human being," which is quite accurate. Here, the form "Son of Man" will be used, since it is so familiar from its use in most English translations of the New Testament.

The first time a character is identified as a "Son of Man" is in Daniel's vision of four great beasts: one like a lion, one like a bear, one like a leopard, and one that has ten horns and is so gruesome that it looks like nothing else (Dan. 7.2-8). These animals represent the political superpowers of the time (cf. Dan. 7.17), and scholars usually identify them as the empires of the Babylonians, the Medes, the Persians, and the Greeks respectively. The fourth of these kingdoms would inflict terrible suffering upon the people of God, but only for a limited time (Dan. 7.19-20, 23-26). Ultimately, its power will be taken away when the Son of Man appears:

> As I watched in the night visions, I saw one like a human being [like a Son of Man] coming with the clouds of heaven. And he came to the Ancient One and was presented before him. To him was given dominion and glory and kingship, that all peoples, nations, and languages should serve him. His dominion is an everlasting dominion that shall not pass away, and his kingship is one that shall never be destroyed. (Dan. 7.13-14)

This Son of Man is apparently a heavenly being, and he shares several attributes with God. His rule will be universal and eternal, and he comes with the clouds of heaven, like God (Exod. 16.10; 19.9, 16; 24.15-18; 34.5; 40.34-35; Num. 9.18, 22; Deut. 31.15; Ezek. 1.4-28 etc.).

The Son of Man "was given dominion and glory and kingship, that all peoples, nations, and languages should serve him" (Dan. 7.14a), but later we are told that "the kingship and dominion and the greatness of the kingdoms under the whole heaven shall be given to the people of the holy ones of the Most High" (Dan. 7.27a). The kingdom is thus given both to "the people of the holy ones of the Most High" and to the Son of Man. Most scholars therefore conclude that "the holy people of the Most High" and the Son of Man must be one and the same. On this interpretation, the Son of Man is not an individual, but a symbol for God's people. In the same way, the four beasts of Daniel's vision are symbols of the four different worldly kingdoms (Dan. 7.2-8, 15-28).

But there are important differences between the Son of Man and the four beasts. The Son of Man is not given an interpretation like the four beasts are. He also appears separately from them and is included in the vision of the Ancient of Days, which is not merely symbolic but is a vision of God's heavenly throne. It may therefore be best to conclude that the Son of Man also is more than a symbol; he may be the heavenly representative of the people of God. Some scholars suggest that he is the archangel Michael (cf. Dan. 10.13, 21; 12.1).

In any case, some **apocalyptic** writings understand the Son of Man as more than a symbol; he is a heavenly figure. The most elaborate development of this character is found in the **Similitudes** that are preserved in *1 Enoch* (chapters 37–71). There has been much scholarly debate over the relevance of these traditions for the study of the New Testament, as they have often been dated to late in the first century CE. Some scholars have argued that they cannot inform our understanding of the New Testament. But most scholars now date them to late in the first century BCE or early in the first century CE. If so, we cannot rule out their relevance for Jesus and the New Testament.[11]

In the **Similitudes** of *1 Enoch* the Son of Man appears in Enoch's heavenly vision:

> At that place, I saw the One to whom belongs the time before time. And his head was white like wool, and there was with him another individual, whose face was like that of a human being. His countenance was full of grace like that of one among the holy angels. And I asked the one – from among the angels – who was going with me, and who had revealed to me all the secrets regarding the One who was born of human beings. "Who is this, and from whence is he who is going as the prototype of the Before-Time?" And he answered me and said to me, "This is the Son of Man, to whom belongs righteousness, and with whom righteousness dwells. And he will open all the hidden storerooms; for the Lord of the Spirits has chosen him, and he is destined to be victorious before the Lord of the Spirits in eternal uprightness. This Son of Man whom you have seen is the One who would remove the kings and the mighty ones from their comfortable seats and the strong ones from their thrones. He shall loosen the reins of the strong and crush the teeth of the sinners. He shall depose the kings from their thrones and kingdoms. For they do not extol and glorify him, and neither do they obey him, the source of their kingship." (*1 Enoch* 46.1-5)

The reference to the one with a head like white wool is clearly an allusion to the vision in Daniel 7, and the audience is thereby prepared to associate the Enochic "Son of Man" (cf. also *1 Enoch* 48.2; 62.5, 7, 9, 14; 63.11; 69.27, 29;

70.1; 71.14, 17) with the one who appears in Dan. 7.13. In the **Similitudes**, "Son of Man" is only one of the many names by which this character is known. He is initially introduced as the Righteous One (*1 Enoch* 38.2; 53.6), but is most frequently referred to as the Elect One.[12] The name "Elect One" shows that this character was closely associated with the people of God, who are also known as the elect ones in the Similitudes. They have been elected through the impartation of special knowledge, such as the revelation of the name of the Son of Man (*1 Enoch* 69.27). The Similitudes also refer to a Messiah character (*1 Enoch* 48.10; 52.4), and it is clear that he is none other than the Son of Man or the Elect One, as similar descriptions are given to all of them and all these names can be used interchangeably.

Towards the end of the Similitudes, the Son of Man appears to be identified with Enoch (*1 Enoch* 71.14). However, most scholars believe that the last two chapters of the Similitudes were a later addition, and that the author of the earlier version did not intend to identify the Son of Man. The Similitudes of *1 Enoch* are purportedly written by the Enoch who did not die because God took him (*1 Enoch* 37.1; cf. Gen. 5.22), but there is no indication that the author of the Similitudes realizes that the Son of Man is in fact himself. The identification of the Son of Man remains uncertain, therefore.

The main function of the Son of Man is to be the eschatological judge. He will be revealed at the end to execute God's judgment (*1 Enoch* 38.2-3). He will sit on the seat of glory and judge humankind (45.3; 69.27, 29), even the secret things (49.4). Not only humans, but also Azaz'el and his army (55.4) and the angels will be judged by him (61.8). He is distinguished by his exceptional righteousness, and is chosen by God to depose the rulers of this world (46.4-6). For the righteous, the Son of Man is the object of their trust, as he is "the light of the Gentiles" and "the hope of those who are sick in their hearts" (48.4).

What is perhaps most astonishing is that God says that "in those days, (the Elect One) shall sit on my throne" (*1 Enoch* 51.3; cf. 61.8; 62.2). In **Second Temple Judaism**, to sit on the heavenly throne was one of the exclusive prerogatives of God himself. Other creatures, usually angels, could be present at God's throne, but they would be standing in God's presence. They would certainly not be sitting on his throne. The Son of Man's position on God's throne therefore makes him quite unique even among the heavenly and angelic characters that are known from Second Temple Judaism.

The Son of Man's presence on the heavenly throne is in fact so awesome that the very sight of it brings terror and pain to the wicked (*1 Enoch* 62.5; cf.

69.29). As a result, they will worship him (62.6, 9). The worship of the Son of Man is another example of how he encroaches upon God's own role. Among the many religions in the Ancient Near East, the most distinguishing characteristic of Judaism was the fact that the Jews worshipped none other than God alone (cf. Deut. 6.13; Mt. 4.10). Small wonder that the Elect One's "glory is forever and ever and his power unto all generations" (*1 Enoch* 49.2).[13]

It becomes clear, then, that the Son of Man is even more glorious in *1 Enoch* than in Daniel's vision. Whereas, in Daniel, the Son of Man was being presented before the throne of God, Enoch sees him seated on that throne, where he functions as the eschatological judge. This Son of Man is not only exalted to a position comparable to that of God, but he also has functions that are known to belong exclusively to God.

Unlike all the other characters in this survey, this Son of Man manifests several uniquely divine characteristics. His role on God's throne is not merely passive – he also actively takes God's place. Human beings worship him, and he judges both humans and angels. He executes divine judgment by destroying the rulers of this world, and he dispenses divine salvation in his role as the object of hope for the elect.

However, the Son of Man is also distinguished from God and he is seen to be inferior to him. When he and God are both on the scene, the Son of Man is invariably on the receiving end of the works of God. God makes the Elect One dwell on earth among humans (*1 Enoch* 45.4-5). The Son of Man is chosen by God, who has destined him to be victorious (46.3). From eternity, the Elect One is pre-existent with God (48.6), who has given him his name (48.2). In his pre-existence, the Son of Man was hidden by God, who eventually revealed him to the saints (62.7). The supremacy of God is also presupposed when the Son of Man is said to be strong before the Lord of the Spirits (69.29).

The Similitudes also contain several indications that the Son of Man does not have his authority in his own right. His authority is from God, and the Son of Man exercises authority on God's behalf. Although he is a revealer, he does not reveal his own wisdom, but God's (48.7; 51.3). The Elect One has his own throne of glory, but he stands before the Lord of Spirits (49.2). When the Elect One judges Azaz'el and his army, he does so in the name of the Lord of Spirits (55.4). His judgment of the angels is determined by the word and method of God (61.9). While the wicked rulers worship the Son of Man, it is God who will cause them to be frantic, make them flee and be ashamed, and finally deliver them up to punishment (62.10-11). God has also reserved some of his characteristic works for himself. He is the one who transforms heaven and earth (45.4-5). Salvation is in his name (48.7), and in his name the congregation of the Elect One will not be hindered (53.6).

The servant of the Lord

When the New Testament authors paint their picture of Jesus, one of the Old Testament characters that they find most important is the Servant of the Lord from the book of Isaiah. In four songs (Isa. 42.1-9; 49.1-7; 50.4-9; 52.13–53.12), Isaiah describes a figure whom God had chosen. God has equipped him with his Spirit so that he may bring international justice (42.1). He will be "a covenant to the people, a light to the nations" (42.6). God will be glorified in him (49.3), and he will not only bring salvation to Israel, but also to the Gentiles, even to the ends of the earth (49.5-6). He suffers at the hands of evildoers (50.6-7) but is vindicated by the Lord (50.8-9). The fourth song explains that the servant's suffering was also his way to glory (52.13). His suffering is the way in which he brings salvation to his people. He does not suffer for his own wrongdoing, but bore the sins of his people. On behalf of this people, Isaiah confesses:

> Surely he has borne our infirmities and carried our diseases; yet we accounted him stricken, struck down by God, and afflicted. But he was wounded for our transgressions, crushed for our iniquities; upon him was the punishment that made us whole, and by his bruises we are healed. All we like sheep have gone astray; we have all turned to our own way, and the Lord has laid on him the iniquity of us all. (53.4-6)

He was without sin (53.9), but it was God's will to make him suffer (53.10). In this way, the Lord made "his life an offering for sin" so that he could "see his offspring," "make many righteous," and "bear their iniquities" (53.10-11). Through his suffering, he is glorified. God "will allot him a portion with the great, and he shall divide the spoil with the strong; because he poured out himself to death, and was numbered with the transgressors; yet he bore the sin of many, and made intercession for the transgressors" (53.12).

This servant is closely connected with the people of Israel, and God even addresses him as "Israel" in Isa. 49.3. To the translators of the **Septuagint**, the servant had to be understood as a personification of Israel. When the Servant is introduced in Isa. 42.1, the Septuagint inserts a **gloss**, "Israel," to identify him. Applied to Isa. 52.13–53.12, this interpretation would cohere with the

Jewish conviction that no one could die for the sins of anyone but themselves.[14] Many modern scholars follow the Septuagint in this interpretation, but some insist that the servant has to be an individual. A somewhat mediating position is taken by those who argue that the Servant stands for "ideal Israel" and that this ideal eventually is represented by an individual. This individual must then be the Messiah, as the traditional Christian interpretation maintains. One of the arguments for this position is that the Servant must be distinguished from the people, as he suffers in their place and bears their sins.

Within **Second Temple Judaism**, Isaiah's Servant Songs play a surprisingly minor role. The concept of four such songs is a modern scholarly construct, and there is no evidence that these four songs were read together in Second Temple Judaism. The surviving literature contains only a few references to these texts. Some of the clearest allusions occur in the descriptions of the Son of Man in *1 Enoch*. His name, "the Elect One," may very well be based on Isa. 42.1 ("my chosen"), and perhaps the designation "the Righteous One" is inspired by Isa. 53.11. Like the servant (Isa. 49.6), so is the Son of Man "the light of the gentiles" (*1 Enoch* 48.4).

References to the suffering of the servant are even more sparse, and there is no firm evidence that the servant was understood as a suffering Messiah. However, some scholars maintain that there are indications that some Jews may have understood these songs to describe an individual and that this individual may have been seen as a messianic character.[15]

The most important of these indications is found at **Qumran**. Four Isaiah scrolls have been discovered among the **Dead Sea Scrolls**, and one of these betrays significant differences when compared to the **Masoretic Text**. If the scribes responsible for the scroll understood the servant as a messianic character, that understanding may explain some of the changes they made. Whereas the Masoretic Text of Isa. 52.14 refers to the servant's marred appearance, the scroll describes God's anointing of the servant. A possible translation is: "Just as many were astonished at you, so have I anointed his appearance beyond that of any (other) man, and his form beyond that of the sons of humanity" (**1QIsa**ᵃ 52.14).[16] This anointed one may very well be the priestly Messiah of Qumranic eschatological expectation. However, this evidence is inconclusive. That the servant is anointed by God does not necessarily mean that he is the Messiah. In the book of Isaiah, Cyrus is also called the Lord's anointed (Isa. 45.1).

More decisive evidence appears in a later source, the **Isaiah Targum**. Here, the fourth song (Isa. 52.13–53.12) is clearly understood as a prophecy about the Messiah. The targumic version introduces the song in this way: "Behold, my servant, the Messiah, shall prosper, he shall be exalted and increase, and shall be very strong" (*Targum* Isa. 52.13).[17] However, this interpretation is unlikely to stem from pre-Christian times. The version of the Targum that has come down to us is dated between the third and the fifth century CE. Even though some of its traditions may be much older, scholars agree that the interpretation of Isa. 52.13–53.12 is younger than the Christian use of the same text. It is also worth noting that while the Targum has read this song messianically, it has also interpreted the verses about suffering in a way that precludes the idea that the Messiah suffered vicariously. His work will bring forgiveness, not through his vicarious suffering, but because of his intercession:

> Then he will beseech concerning our sins and our iniquities for his sake will be forgiven; yet we were esteemed wounded, smitten before the Lord and afflicted. And he will build the sanctuary which was profaned for our sins, handed over for our iniquities; and by his teaching his peace will increase upon us, and in that we attach ourselves to his words our sins will be forgiven us. (*Targum* Isa. 53.4-5)

To conclude, the use of Isaiah's Servant songs in Second Temple Judaism was eclectic. Certain aspects, such his election, righteousness, and dispensation of the truth, inspired the picture of the Son of Man. His suffering made less of an impact, although Isa. 52.13–53.12 may have been understood to refer to an individual. In Qumran, some members may even have seen these sufferings as those of the priestly Messiah. The aspect that has made the least impression in the available sources is the vicarious nature of the servant's suffering.

The wisdom of God

In contrast to the figures discussed above, the wisdom of God is not understood as a distinct character, nor is it specifically associated with eschatological hopes. Nevertheless, it is very important to be familiar with Jewish wisdom ideas in order to understand the Gospels' picture of Jesus.

In the Old Testament wisdom literature, God's wisdom could be described as a personified entity. The example par excellence is found in Proverbs 8, in a poem where wisdom is the speaker:

> [22]The Lord created me at the beginning of his work,
> the first of his acts of long ago.

> [23]Ages ago I was set up,
> at the first, before the beginning of the earth.
> [24]When there were no depths I was brought forth,
> when there were no springs abounding with water.
> [25]Before the mountains had been shaped,
> before the hills, I was brought forth –
> [26]when he had not yet made earth and fields,
> or the world's first bits of soil.
> [27]When he established the heavens, I was there,
> when he drew a circle on the face of the deep,
> [28]when he made firm the skies above,
> when he established the fountains of the deep,
> [29]when he assigned to the sea its limit,
> so that the waters might not transgress his command,
> when he marked out the foundations of the earth,
> [30]then I was beside him, like a master worker;
> and I was daily his delight,
> rejoicing before him always,
> [31]rejoicing in his inhabited world
> and delighting in the human race. (Prov. 8.22-31)

Here, the personification of wisdom is a literary device. Wisdom is still an attribute of God, not a person. However, as a poetic way of praising the virtues of God's wisdom, this wisdom appears as the speaker. In addition to the conventional task of revealing the will of God (Prov. 8.4-21), wisdom is now also credited with the act of creation. Wisdom was God's agent when he created the world.

In the wisdom literature of **Second Temple Judaism**, the idea of God's wisdom as agent of creation is important. According to the **Wisdom of Solomon**, wisdom is "the fashioner of all things" (Wisdom of Solomon 7.22) and the one "who knows [God's] works and was present when [God] made the world" (Wisdom of Solomon 9.9). The tendency to describe wisdom as its own entity is also taken further than in the Old Testament. "There is in [wisdom] a spirit that is intelligent, holy, unique, manifold, subtle, mobile, clear, unpolluted, distinct, invulnerable, loving the good, keen, irresistible" (Wisdom of Solomon 7.22). Wisdom is "a pure emanation of the glory of the Almighty" (Wisdom of Solomon 7.25), "a reflection of eternal light, a spotless mirror of the working of God, and an image of his goodness" (Wisdom of Solomon 7.26).

The tendency to speak of God's wisdom in this way corresponds to the tendency to think of God as transcendent and removed from this world. In contradistinction to earlier traditions of the Old Testament, where God is frequently portrayed as a human being (anthropomorphism) in his interaction with the world, this literature is concerned to maintain the otherness and exaltedness of God. There is therefore usually at least "one step" between God and his creation, and he is often seen to interact with the world through exalted agents, such as his angels. When God comes into contact with the world, this contact is frequently attributed to his wisdom.

God's election of Israel can therefore be described as God's wisdom coming down to Israel, as when God's wisdom speaks in the Wisdom of Ben Sira (**Sirach**):

> Then the Creator of all things gave me a command, and my Creator chose the place for my tent. He said, "Make your dwelling in Jacob, and in Israel receive your inheritance"… In the holy tent I ministered before him, and so I was established in Zion. Thus in the beloved city he gave me a resting place, and in Jerusalem was my domain. (Sirach 24.8, 10-11)

In the Old Testament, the tabernacle could be understood as the dwelling place of God (Exod. 25.8; 29.46; Lev. 26.11; Num. 5.3). Now, God's wisdom is seen in this role.

Even though the language of the wisdom literature may give the impression that there are two entities within the Godhead, that implication was not drawn. The oneness and uniqueness of God were not called in question. The purpose of the statements regarding God's wisdom was different. That God performed his actions through his wisdom meant that he had no need for outsourcing: "And there is no adviser and no successor to my creation. I am self-eternal and not made by hands. My thought is without change. My wisdom is my adviser and my deed is my word. And my eyes look at all things" (*2 Enoch* 33.4). The point of distinguishing between God and his wisdom was not to envision God's wisdom as an entity of its own, but to safeguard the transcendence of God. Nevertheless, these traditions provided the literary tools to make distinctions within the Godhead, without jeopardizing the oneness of God. Jesus and the first Christian theologians would exploit these possibilities and take them to an entirely new level.

Conclusion

Jewish eschatological expectations were nothing if not diverse. Different characters, both angelic and human, were expected to play a part in the eschatological scenario. Of these characters, the royal Messiah receives the most attention. He is a political ruler who will restore the kingdom of Israel. Under his leadership, Israel will be delivered from their enemies. More importantly, however, Israel will turn away from sin and be faithful to their God. The Messiah will rule with divine justice. He may be more than a normal human being, and may even be called a son of God. However, he is divine only as far as his exercise of divine functions. His divinity does not pertain to who he is.

Some Old Testament passages also attribute priestly functions to the Messiah. These elements have left the strongest traces in Qumran. This community expected two messiahs, one priestly and one royal. The royal messiah would be subordinate to the priestly one.

In some texts, the Messiah is also identified as the Son of Man, the heavenly character from Daniel's vision. In these sources, the Messiah appears as an angelic figure, and he may be compared to other angels that are attributed with important eschatological functions. One of them is Melchizedek, who will exercise God's judgment in the end times.

Little attention is given to the Servant of the Lord. There is clear evidence that this character was understood as a corporate symbol for Israel, but there are also some indications that he was identified as the Messiah. The suffering of this Servant may also have been read as the suffering of the Messiah, but there is no evidence that he was understood to suffer vicariously for the sins of others.

Notes

1   For the development of messianic ideas, see especially Sigmund Mowinckel, *He That Cometh*, tr. G. W. Anderson (New York: Abingdon, 1954); James H. Charlesworth, ed., *The Messiah: Developments in Earliest Judaism and Christianity* (Minneapolis: Fortress, 1992); John J. Collins, *The Scepter and the Star: The Messiahs of the Dead Sea Scrolls and Other Ancient Literature*, ABRL (New York: Doubleday, 1995); Stanley E. Porter, ed., *The Messiah in the Old and New Testaments*, McMaster New Testament Studies (Grand Rapids: Eerdmans, 2007).

2   For a discussion of the translation of Ps. 45.6, see Murray J. Harris, "The Translation of *Elohim* in Psalm 45:7–8," *TynBul* 35 (1984): 65–89.

3   Quotations from the **Septuagint** are taken from *A New English Translation of the Septuagint and*

the Other Greek Translations Traditionally Included Under that Title, ed. Albert Pietersma and Benjamin G. Wright (New York: Oxford University Press, 2007).

4   Translation taken from Bruce D. Chilton, *The Isaiah Targum*, The Aramaic Bible 11 (Wilmington, DE: Glazier, 1987).

5   Translation taken from Lancelot Charles Lee Brenton, tr., *The Septuagint Version of the Old Testament* (London: Bagster and Sons, 1844).

6   It is also possible that *christos kurios* is a mistranslation and that the original Hebrew should be understood as a genitive construction. If so, the name would be "the Lord's Messiah."

7   Quotations from the Dead Sea Scrolls are taken from Geza Vermes, tr., *The Complete Dead Sea Scrolls in English* (New York: Penguin, 1997).

8   Quotations from 4Q246 are taken from Florentino García Martínez and Eibert J. C. Tigchelaar, ed., *(1Q1–4Q273)*, vol. 1 of *The Dead Sea Scrolls Study Edition* (Leiden: Brill, 1997).

9   See, among others, Alan F. Segal, *Two Powers in Heaven: Early Rabbinic Reports About Christianity and Gnosticism*, SJLA 25 (Leiden: Brill, 1977); Jarl E. Fossum, *The Name of God and the Angel of the Lord: Samaritan and Jewish Concepts of Intermediation and the Origin of Gnosticism*, WUNT 36 (Tübingen: Mohr Siebeck, 1985); Margaret Barker, *The Great Angel: A Study of Israel's Second God* (London: SPCK, 1992); Darrell D. Hannah, *Michael and Christ: Michael Traditions and Angel Christology in Early Christianity*, WUNT II/109 (Tübingen: Mohr Siebeck, 1999).

10 For a comprehensive overview of Melchizedek traditions, see Eric F. Mason, *"You Are a Priest Forever": Second Temple Jewish Messianism and the Priestly Christology of the Epistle to the Hebrews*, STDJ 74 (Leiden: Brill, 2008), 138–90.

11 For a discussion of the traditions regarding the Son of Man and their relevance for the New Testament, see Gabriele Boccaccini, ed., *Enoch and the Messiah Son of Man: Revisiting the Book of Parables* (Grand Rapids: Eerdmans, 2007).

12 *1 Enoch* 39.6; 40.5; 45.3, 4, 5; 48.6; 49.2, 4; 51.3, 4; 52.6, 9; 53.6; 55.4; 61.5, 8, 10.

13 For the characteristics of Jewish monotheism, see especially Richard Bauckham, *Jesus and the God of Israel: God Crucified and Other Studies on the New Testament's Christology of Divine Identity* (Grand Rapids: Eerdmans, 2008).

14 In Isa. 52.13–53.12, the translators have also made some subtle changes. Joseph Ziegler, who prepared the scholarly edition of the Septuagint version of Isaiah, concluded that the manuscript tradition in Isa. 53.2 was corrupt. Instead of the reading that is attested in the manuscripts, *anengeilamen* ("we announced"), he suggests reading *aneteile men* ("he sprang up"). See Joseph Ziegler, ed., *Isaias*, Vetus Testamentum Graecum. Auctoritate Academiae Scientiarum Gottingensis Editum 14 (Göttingen: Vandenhoeck & Ruprecht, 1983). The value of such scholarly conjectures will of course always be disputed, but if Ziegler's emendation is accepted, Isa. 53.2 may be translated "for he sprang up before him as a child." This phrase is perhaps an allusion to the messianic prophecy in 11.1: "A shoot shall come out from the stump of Jesse, and a branch shall grow out of his roots." Cf. Martin Hengel, with the collaboration of Daniel P. Bailey, "The Effective History of Isaiah 53 in the Pre-Christian Period" in *The Suffering Servant: Isaiah 53 in Jewish and Christian Sources*, ed. Bernd Janowski and Peter Stuhlmacher, tr. Daniel P. Bailey (Grand Rapids: Eerdmans, 2004), 134–5.

Other changes in the Septuagint amount to a downplaying of the vicarious suffering of the servant. Whereas the **Masoretic Text** of Isa. 53.10 probably refers to the servant's life becoming "an offering for sin," the Septuagint asserts: "If you give an offering for sin, your soul shall see a long-lived offspring."

15 See Hengel, "Effective History of Isaiah 53."

16 Translation taken from ibid., 104.

17 Translations of the Isaiah Targum are taken from Chilton, *The Isaiah Targum*.

2

God's Coming: Christology In Mark's Gospel

The Synoptic Gospels make heavy use of Jewish traditions regarding the Messiah and other eschatological characters. They also modify these traditions and move beyond them. But most importantly, Mark and the other evangelists show that Jesus fills an even bigger role: that of God himself.

In Mark's Gospel, Jesus takes on God's role by fulfilling Old Testament prophecies that concern God's own coming to earth. He comes as God's servant because he is the Messiah who comes to suffer in obedience to God. As the Son of God, he is both God's servant and God's equal.

Jesus in the role of God

"Gospel"

The very title of Mark's work, "the beginning of the gospel of Jesus Christ" (1.1), gives an indication of what Mark thought about Jesus. The word "gospel" (Gr.: *euangelion*) has a profound meaning. To appreciate it fully, we must know its Hebrew background. There is no Hebrew equivalent to the noun *euangelion* in the Scriptures, but the **cognate** verb *euangelizomai* corresponds to the Hebrew verb *basar*. This verb has both a secular and a religious meaning. In the book of Isaiah, a form of *basar* (participle) is used for the messenger who proclaims the eschatological victory of God, the reality of his salvation, and the onset of his visible rule (Isa. 40.9; 41.27; 52.7; cf. Nah. 1.15; Pss. 40.9; 68.11). In later Jewish sources, this messenger is sometimes identified as a messianic character (**11Q13** 2.15-19), but that is not always the case (***Psalms of Solomon*** 11.1). Even later still, he is thought to be Elijah, who would return in the end times (***Pesiqta Rabbati*** 35.4). One source even attests to the expectation that there would be many such messengers (***Midrash Psalms*** 147.1). Regardless of who the messenger is, however, the content of the glad tidings is always the mighty works of God himself.

Mark qualifies this "gospel" as "the gospel of Jesus Christ." The grammar allows for this phrase to be interpreted in two different ways: either as "the good news proclaimed by Christ Jesus" (subjective genitive) or as "the good news concerning Jesus Christ" (objective genitive). Mark mentions "the gospel" again in 1.14, where he reports that Jesus proclaims the gospel of the kingdom of God. If the heading in 1.1 is interpreted in light of 1.14, then it must refer to the gospel proclaimed by Jesus Christ (subjective genitive), as he comes and proclaims the kingdom of God. But it is also possible to reverse the logic and read 1.14 in light of 1.1. If so, the gospel concerning Jesus Christ (objective genitive) is also the gospel of the kingdom of God, the new reality that Jesus brings.

The latter interpretation is preferable. Mark later uses the word "gospel" and Jesus' name in parallel statements, implying that the two terms are synonymous (Mk 8.35; 10.29; cf. 13.10). He also understands the anointing of Jesus for his death as an essential element of the gospel message (14.9). More importantly, the actual contents of Mark's Gospel have little to do with what Jesus proclaimed but very much to do with the person of Jesus. If one asks for the content of "the gospel of the kingdom of God" (1.14) according to Mark, the answer will have to be closely tied to the person of Jesus. Mark's "good news" is the good news about Jesus Christ, although he may have intended his heading to play on the ambiguity of the expression. In any case, Mark is evidently capable of understanding Jesus not only as the proclaimer but also as the content of the gospel (8.35; 10.29; 13.10; 14.9).

When we read this usage of the term "gospel" against its Jewish background, we see that Mark has placed Jesus where Jewish eschatological expectations saw God himself. Whereas Isaiah's messenger merely proclaimed the good news of God (Isa. 40.9; 41.27; 52.7; 61.1), Mark sees Jesus as the content of the message. Jesus does not merely take the place of the messenger – he takes the place of God.

Against this interpretation, one may object that Jesus is elsewhere identified as the eschatological messenger (Mt. 11.5 par.; Lk. 4.18). As we shall see, the Gospels portray Jesus in a number of different roles that are known from the Old Testament. One of our challenges is to do justice to all of them and not play them against each other in such a way that we end up prioritizing one element of the tradition and ignore other elements. As far as Mark's heading is concerned, we note that Jesus is not the messenger – he is the message.

The Prologue

By defining the gospel as the message of Jesus Christ, Mark has indicated that Jesus is connected with the eschatological victory of God. Mark then connects his gospel with the prophetic words of Israel's Scriptures: "As it is written in the prophet Isaiah, 'See, I am sending my messenger ahead of you, who will prepare your way; the voice of one crying out in the wilderness: "Prepare the way of the Lord, make his paths straight"'"(Mk 1.2-3).

As Rikk Watts has shown, Mark draws heavily on Israel's expectations of a new exodus, especially as these expectations were known from the book of Isaiah. Modeled upon God's mighty acts at the exodus from Egypt, these expectations concern the coming of Israel's God to deliver Israel from exile, defeat her enemies, and lead her back to Jerusalem. Israel's God, Yahweh, is seen as the divine warrior who destroys his enemies and his people's enemies, and he is seen as the king who establishes his unopposed rule. Mark's picture of Jesus is in significant ways modeled after this picture of Yahweh.[1]

But before we get to Mark's use of Isaiah, we must note that his quotation is actually taken from at least three different passages in the Old Testament. In addition to Isa. 40.3, he also quotes from Exod. 23.20 and Mal. 3.1.

"See, I am sending my messenger ahead of you" (Mk 1.2b) is taken from Exod. 23.20, which refers to an angel that God will send in front of Israel. The Hebrew word *melek* and the Greek word *angelos* may be translated both "angel" and "messenger." In the context of Exodus 23, this angel's function is to guard Israel when they are on their way to the Promised Land. God warns Israel against disobeying the angel's voice. They will not be forgiven for such disobedience. If Israel obeys the angel, however, God will be with them as the warrior who stands against their enemies.

The next phrase in Mk 1.2 ("who will prepare your way") is a quotation from Mal. 3.1, which also describes an angel or messenger that prepares the way before the Lord. After the angel has come, the Lord himself will come to his temple with judgment.

Finally, Mark quotes from Isa. 40.3: "the voice of one crying out in the wilderness: 'Prepare the way of the Lord, make his paths straight'" (Mk 1.3). In its original context, this verse describes the great act of salvation when the Lord will come with great might and deliver his people from captivity. As a preparation for his intervention, a voice calls for the preparation of the way of the Lord (v. 3).

The voice from Isa. 40.3 as well as the angels or messengers of Exod. 23.20 and Mal. 3.1 all have their role *vis à vis* God. They announce or prepare for his coming. Mark combines all these images and applies them to John the Baptist. In v. 4 John is introduced as appearing in the wilderness, which is Mark's way of identifying him as the voice of Isa. 40.3. John's role is to prepare the way for Jesus. In the course of Mark's story this becomes clear when Jesus is introduced immediately after John has announced the coming of the one more powerful than himself (Mk 1.7, 9). Through his introductory Scripture quotations, Mark is interpreting the coming of Jesus onto the public scene as the fulfillment of the promises regarding God's own coming to his people. The Scriptures Mark quotes lead us to believe that "the one who is more powerful" than John is God, whereas the progress of Mark's story shows us that the more powerful one is Jesus.

Because he understood the prophecies about God's coming as speaking of the coming of Jesus, Mark has taken some liberties in quoting the texts. Whereas the prophet Isaiah announces the making straight a path "of our God" (Isa. 40.3), Mark simply refers to "his" path (Mk 1.3). The pronoun "his" refers back to "the Lord" in the first part of the verse. By avoiding the mention of "God," Mark makes the text more ambiguous. It is not clear whether "the Lord" is God or Jesus. The original context of Mark's quotations indicates that the Lord is God, but the context of Mark's story leads to the conclusion that "the Lord" is a title for Jesus.

When Mark identifies John the Baptist as the preparing messenger, he thereby also identifies him as the eschatological Elijah (cf. also Mk 9.11-13). In Mal. 4.5, God announces that "I will send you the prophet Elijah before the great and terrible day of the Lord comes." This announcement matches the prophecy regarding the messenger in Mal. 3.1. In the context of the book of Malachi, the messenger and the prophet Elijah are therefore one and the same. This prophecy forms the basis for a Jewish expectation of an eschatological Elijah. A number of Jewish eschatological texts refer to the coming of Elijah (e. g. **Sirach** 48.10-11; **4Q558** 1.ii.4). According to many scholars, Elijah was expected to be a forerunner of the Messiah. However, none of the pre-Christian texts describe him as such. We cannot conclude that he was a forerunner of the Messiah just because he would appear in the end times. Jesus and the Gospels identified John the Baptist as Elijah, and since Christians saw Jesus as the Messiah, they concluded that Elijah was a forerunner of the Messiah. But the reason that Elijah was seen as Jesus' forerunner was that he was the one who would prepare for the coming of God himself.[2]

The Kingdom of God

When Jesus is introduced, Mark summarizes his preaching as a message that "the time is fulfilled, the kingdom of God has come near: repent, and believe in the good news" (Mk 1.15). The prophecies are now being fulfilled and the kingdom of God is at hand.

The Greek term *basileia tou theou*, which is usually translated "kingdom of God," refers both to the territory where God rules and to God's ruling activity. The translation "kingdom of God" is not wrong, but it captures only half of the meaning of the Greek term. Another translation might be "the kingly rule of God."

In the Old Testament, God's kingdom or kingly rule is the universal kingdom of God himself. It relates to the idea that God is the king of heaven and earth, which must be distinguished from the idea of the Messiah as the king of a renewed Israel.

The "kingdom of God" is not mentioned frequently in the Hebrew and Aramaic text of the Old Testament (only once, in 1 Chron. 28.5). But the Old Testament often explains that God rules as king. God is the king of the entire universe. He rules over all the nations (1 Chron. 29.11-12; Pss. 47.2, 8-9; 96.10; 99.1-5; Jer. 10.7, 10). His rule is eternal (Pss. 29.10; 145.10-13; Jer. 10.10) and reaches both to heaven and earth (1 Chron. 29.11-12; Ps. 103.19).

The kings of this world are in rebellion against God and his rule (cf. Ps. 2.1-3). God's kingdom is therefore in conflict with earthly kingdoms. But there will come a day when God will establish his unopposed rule over the world. That is the day when Israel will experience salvation (Zeph. 3.15-20), "and the Lord will become king over all the earth; on that day the Lord will be one and his name one" (Zech. 14.9). That will be the day when all other powers will disappear. There will only be one name left: the name of the Lord.

This will be the day when God's enemies will be defeated once and for all.

> On that day the Lord will punish the host of heaven in heaven, and on earth the kings of the earth. They will be gathered together like prisoners in a pit; they will be shut up in a prison, and after many days they will be punished. Then the moon will be abashed, and the sun ashamed; for the Lord of hosts will reign on Mount Zion and in Jerusalem, and before his elders he will manifest his glory. (Isa. 24.21-23)

That the sun and the moon will be ashamed is a metaphorical way of saying that all other powers will pale when God comes with his kingdom.

This is the time of eschatological salvation. It is the time when

> the Lord of hosts will make for all peoples a feast of rich food, a feast of well-aged wines, of rich food filled with marrow, of well-aged wines strained clear. And he

will destroy on this mountain the shroud that is cast over all peoples, the sheet that is spread over all nations; he will swallow up death forever. Then the Lord God will wipe away the tears from all faces, and the disgrace of his people he will take away from all the earth. (Isa. 25.6-9)

If death is to disappear, the world as we know it will have to be completely changed. What Isaiah describes is the new creation, the new earth.

There are several Jewish writings from the time between the Old and the New Testament that give us a picture of how these prophecies were understood. Many Jews were waiting for God to come to earth, put an end to the devil, and establish his kingdom. The clearest expression of this expectation is found in the *Testament of Moses* (first century CE): "Then his kingdom will appear throughout his whole creation. Then the devil will have an end. Yes, sorrow will be led away with him" (10.1).

The way that Mark introduces Jesus and his teaching is evocative of grand themes from the Old Testament and **Second Temple Judaism**: God himself coming to earth to defeat the devil, to establish his unopposed rule, to bring the new creation, and to save his people.[3]

Eschatological Fulfillment through the Divine Warrior

Mark's opening lines set the stage for an understanding of the gospel as the fulfillment of Isaiah's new exodus and of the teaching of Jesus as the establishment of God's kingdom. Mark then proceeds to describe how the ministry of Jesus manifests God's decisive victory over evil and his liberation of Israel. In his understanding of God's victory, Mark stands in the tradition of the Jewish **apocalyptic** writings. Whereas the prophets focused on Israel's political enemies, the apocalyptic writings gave more attention to the spiritual powers that were believed to stand behind the powers of this world.[4]

Jesus begins to form the nucleus of the kingdom community by calling his first disciples (1.16-20). The next four stories are all located in or around Capernaum on a Sabbath and the following day. These stories provide a snapshot of Jesus' ministry, a ministry consisting of casting out evil spirits (1.21-28, 34, 39), healing (1.29-34), proclamation (1.35-39), and cleansing of skin diseases (1.40-44). Jesus not only announces the presence of the kingdom (1.15), but brings it through his own person. Through him, God's victory is won over his cosmic enemies, the demons. The new world order, where there are no longer any diseases (cf. *Jubilees* 23.29-30; *1 Enoch* 96.3; **4 Ezra** 8.53) or any impurities (cf. Isa. 35.8; 52.1), is now a reality.[5]

Defeating the Evil Army

In describing the new eschatological reality, Mark pays a lot of attention to Jesus' encounters with evil spirits. The first detailed account of Jesus casting out a demon occurs in Mk 1.21-28, and Mark's story emphasizes Jesus' total superiority. There is no battle between Jesus and the demons in Mark's account; Jesus casts them out because they are already defeated by him. As soon as Jesus approaches, the demon concedes defeat and submissively addresses him as Jesus of Nazareth and the Holy One of God (1.24). The title "Holy One of God" is not very specific; in the Scriptures of Israel it is used for Aaron (Ps. 106.16), Samson (Judg. 16.17), and Elisha (2 Kgs 4.9). Here, it identifies Jesus as a special agent of God. Mark's description of Jesus' handling of the demon, however, shows Jesus to be more than a servant of God and places him in the role of God. Mark succinctly describes his encounter with the demon: "But Jesus rebuked him, saying, 'Be silent, and come out of him!' And the unclean spirit, convulsing him and crying with a loud voice, came out of him" (Mk 1.25-26). The Greek word that is usually translated "rebuke," *epitimao* (Mk 1.25; cf. 4.39; 9.25), corresponds to the Hebrew verb *ga'ar*. *Ga'ar* and *epitimao* are unusual words to use in connection with an exorcism. They are not found in known exorcism stories from **Josephus**, **Greek Magical Papyri**, and **Rabbinic literature**.

When *ga'ar* occurs in the Hebrew Bible, it is normally rendered "rebuke" or "threaten" in modern versions. But as Howard Clark Kee has shown, in most cases this is an inadequate translation. The word is often used in the context of God's subjugation of his enemies. The NRSV translates Ps. 9.5: "You have rebuked (*ga'arta*) the nations, you have destroyed (*ibadta*) the wicked; you have blotted out (*machita*) their name forever and ever." As the parallelism shows, the translation "rebuke" is quite anemic. The verse describes a complete annihilation. Another illustrative verse is Isa. 54.9, where God's act of *ga'ar* is compared to the flood at the time of Noah. Frequently, *ga'ar* and its derivatives are used for God's judgment – not merely his warning – of sinners (Deut. 28.20; Isa. 30.17; 51.20; 54.9; Mal. 2.3; Ps. 119.21) and the enemies of God and his people (Isa. 17.13; 66.15; Pss. 9.5; 68.30; 76.6; 80.16). Often the object of God's *ga'ar* is the sea and the waters, seen as the powers of chaos (2 Sam. 22.16; Isa. 50.2; Pss. 18.15; 104.7; 106.9; Job 26.11). In the later prophets, the enemy can be personified, as in Mal. 3.11, and identified with Satan, as in Zech. 3.2. In the context of God's conflict with his enemies, *ga'ar* has connotations of complete domination and victory.[6]

Kee's findings are confirmed by the evidence from the **Dead Sea Scrolls**. Among these writings, the verb *ga'ar* belongs naturally in the War Scroll (**1QM**), with its portrayal of the eschatological war between God's people and the armies of Belial (another name for Satan). When God hands his people the definitive victory over the evil forces, the War Scroll praises him for having chased away (Hebr.: *ga'artah*) Belial's spirits (**1QM** 14.10). Elsewhere, *ga'ar* also describes God's destruction of his people's enemies.[7] Other writings from the **Second Temple** period evince a similar use of the Greek equivalent, *epitimao* (**Wisdom of Solomon** 3.10; *Psalms of Solomon* 2.23).

In the Genesis apocryphon (**1QapGen**), *ga'ar* occurs in connection with Abraham's prayer for Pharaoh that the evil spirit may depart from him (1QapGen 20.28-29). Abraham is not the agent of the verb *ga'ar*, however; the verb is in the passive (itpaal) form. The presumed agent of the subjection is God. Abraham's role is to pray.

When the Greek word *epitimao* is understood against its Jewish background it becomes clear that it does not merely describe an exorcism. Its connotations are of God's victory over his enemies and the enemies of his people. It paints a picture of God as the divine warrior whose superior force eliminates his adversaries. It does not describe the authority of God's agent but the power of God himself. For Mark, it is therefore an apt term to use when he portrays the ministry of Jesus as God's own coming to earth to defeat his cosmic enemies, the army of Satan. Tellingly, the same term is used when Jesus affirms his authority over the sea (4.39).

In Mark's first account of Jesus' encounter with evil spirits, the spirit understands what is about to happen. There is no indication that more than one spirit is involved (contrast 5.9), but the spirit uses the plural in his question to Jesus: "Have you come to destroy us?" (1.24). Not only the spirit's personal downfall is imminent, but the destruction of the whole evil army. When Jesus' ministry has such cosmic ramifications, it is indicative of who he is. He is no mere human being.

Similarly, the Greek word *ekballo*, which Mark uses in his summary statements about Jesus' exorcisms (1.34, 39), is not a common word for exorcism.[8] It is, however, frequently used in the old Greek translations of the Old Testament, not in connection with exorcisms, but with God's driving out Israel's enemies.[9]

The setting in which Jesus is casting out demons also indicates the completeness of Jesus' victory over evil forces. Turning to Mark's second detailed account, set in the country of the Gerasenes, the man with an unclean spirit lived among the tombs (Mk 5.1-3). This note has strong connotations of uncleanness, as contact with the dead brought uncleanness for seven days (Num. 19.11; cf. Lev. 21.1, 11; Isa. 65.4). To top it off, a herd of swine, the most notoriously unclean animals, was feeding in the vicinity (Mk 5.11). But Jesus still exercises complete control over the unclean spirit (Mk 5.6-13). His superiority is equally unchallenged in Gentile territory and in a context replete with uncleanness.

At this point, it will be useful to compare Mark's portrait of Jesus with the teaching of the Jewish sect whose library has been discovered in **Qumran** by the Dead Sea. In their understanding, all of life was determined by the conflict between the spirit of Light and the spirit of Darkness (**1QS** 3.15-24; **1QM** 13.11-12). The children of light could be free from the influence of the spirit of Darkness by participation in the community and observation of their rigorous rules of purity (**1QS** 4.2-6). In contrast, Mark shows the universality of Jesus' victory. It does not extend merely to a restricted space, such as the Qumran community, where strict purity is observed; Jesus claims his rule everywhere, even in the midst of the most flagrant uncleanness. In the worldview of the Qumran community, the final demise of the spirit of Darkness does not take place until God's eschatological judgment (**1QS** 4.26). While there is no reason to assume that **Qumran**'s doctrine of the two spirits serves as the direct background for the account in Mk 5.1-20, it does provide a snapshot of how one Jewish group understood the conflict with the domain of evil spirits. In contrast, there is a distinct finality to the exercise of Jesus' rule in Mark's story. The reason is apparently that he understands Jesus' presence to constitute God's eschatological coming to earth.

The totality of Jesus' victory is also underscored by the fact that the Gerasene does not only have one unclean spirit but a Legion (Mk 5.9). A Legion was the principal division of the Roman army, consisting of approximately 6,000 men. The word has strong military overtones and fills in the picture of Jesus as the divine warrior, subduing the army of Satan.

The significance of Jesus' encounter with the demons is spelled out in Mk 3.22-27:

> And the scribes who came down from Jerusalem said, "He has Beelzebul, and by the ruler of the demons he casts out demons." And he called them to him, and spoke to them in parables, "How can Satan cast out Satan? If a kingdom is divided against itself, that kingdom cannot stand. And if a house is divided against itself, that house will not be able to stand. And if Satan has risen up against himself and is divided, he cannot stand, but his end has come. But no

one can enter a strong man's house and plunder his property without first tying
up the strong man; then indeed the house can be plundered."

Jesus here explains his expulsions of the demons as the consequence of a
previous encounter with Satan (cf. 1.13). He has already tied up Satan (3.27)
and thus handed him his ultimate defeat. Mark's emphasis in this story falls
upon Jesus as the one who ties up the strong man (Gr.: *ischuros*; 3.27) and
thereby shows himself to be the stronger one. Mark's choice of words recalls
the message of John the Baptist, who announced the coming of the stronger
one (Gr.: *ho ischoroteros*; 1.7). As John the Baptist was introduced as the one
preparing the way for the Lord (1.3), the stronger one is naturally identified
as the Lord himself in Mark's narrative. When Jesus emerges as the stronger
one, Mark has implicitly connected Jesus' expulsion of the demons with the
coming of God himself.

A Teacher with Authority

Mark ties Jesus' demon-expelling activity closely to his activity as a teacher.
He displays considerable interest in the teaching activity of Jesus, but very
little about his actual teaching is revealed.[10] Mark's concern is with the person
of Jesus and the authoritative manner of his teaching. When Mark focuses
on Jesus as a teacher it is just another way for him to reveal something about
Jesus' character. The content of the teaching is the teacher himself.[11]

The first time Mark refers to Jesus' teaching is in the synagogue in
Capernaum, but we are not told what Jesus was teaching (1.21). Instead, Mark
reports the bewilderment of the audience, as Jesus taught with authority
(1.22). Mark proceeds to tell about the casting out of an evil spirit (1.23-26),
but it is clear that he wants the audience to connect this scene with the note
about Jesus' teaching. Both the time indicator ("just then;" Gr.: *euthus*) and the
place ("in the synagogue") closely tie this event to the scene of Jesus' teaching.
Mark also repeats the reference to the authoritative nature of Jesus' teaching
towards the end of this story. The bystanders were asking one another: "What
is this? A new teaching – with authority! He commands even the unclean
spirits, and they obey him" (1.27). The first example of Jesus' teaching is
actually the expulsion of an evil spirit, and its novelty is the authority of the
teacher.

It is not until he retells some of Jesus' parables that Mark finally gets around
to elaborating on the actual contents of Jesus' discourse. But not even in this
case does Mark provide anything remotely comparable to the Sermon on the

Mount (Mt. 5–7) with its discussion of the Mosaic law. Mark's parables are also overwhelmingly self-referential. Their point is typically that it is important to heed their message and that the power of the message is enormous (cf. 4.1-9, 13-20, 26-29, 30-32; 12.1-12).

While Jesus' authority is not associated with the content of this teaching, it is clearly linked to his forgiveness of sins (2.10). To explain the significance of Jesus' act of forgiveness (2.5), Mark provides an insight into the thoughts of the scribes that were present. They were "questioning in their hearts, 'Why does this fellow speak in this way? It is blasphemy! Who can forgive sins but God alone?'" (2.6b-7). They consider Jesus' words to be blasphemous because he is encroaching upon the uniqueness of God.[12] According to the Old Testament and Jewish tradition, only God could forgive sins (Exod. 34.7, 9; Num. 14.20; 30.5; 1 Kgs 8.30; Ps. 103.3; Isa. 55.7; Jer. 31.34; Mic. 7.18). In the Greek text, the words of the scribes ("but God alone;" Gr.: *ei me heis ho theos*) are an allusion to the Shema, the Jewish creed: "The Lord is our God, the Lord alone" (Deut. 6.4).[13] Mark thus shows that Jesus takes the role of God.

Following the teaching of Jesus, the disciples are sent out and authorized by him (Mk 6.7). Their function is summed up as what "they had done and taught" (6.30). Mark again says nothing beyond "repentance" to describe what they taught. His interest apparently lies elsewhere: as teachers, the disciples have shared in Jesus' authority over unclean spirits (6.7), and they were enabled to cast out demons and heal the sick (6.13).

Although he does not develop the theme in the way that Matthew does, Mark also shows that Jesus has an authority that stands above that of the Old Testament law. Like Matthew and Luke, so does Mark include Jesus' saying about uncleanness and the human digestive system: "Whatever goes into a person from outside cannot defile, since it enters, not the heart but the stomach, and goes out into the sewer" (Mk 7.18-19). Only Mark, however, provides his own commentary on Jesus' words: "Thus he declared all foods clean" (Mk 7.19). Whereas Matthew and Luke leave it more open as to whether Jesus really contradicts the Mosaic law, Mark leaves no room for doubt; Jesus abolishes the food laws. By so doing, Mark's Jesus implicitly claims an authority that is even greater than that of the Old Testament, which was understood to rest on God's authority.

Healing

In addition to being able to forgive, cast out demons, and abolish the food laws, Jesus' authority is also an authority to heal. Mark's portrayal of Jesus' healing activity follows the same pattern of presenting Jesus in the role of God. His healing miracles are the fulfillment of Isaiah's prophecy regarding God's own eschatological acts: "Then the eyes of the blind shall be opened, and the ears of the deaf unstopped; then the lame shall leap like a deer, and the tongue of the speechless sing for joy" (Isa. 35.5-6a). Here, it is important to note that this and similar prophecies were not associated with the Messiah. The Messiah was not expected to be a healer. Rather, the prophecies regarding healing concerned the coming of God himself and the establishment of the new world order, where death and disease would cease to exist (*Jubilees* 23.26-30; *1 Enoch* 96.3; *4 Ezra* 8.52-54; *2 Baruch* 29.7). The so-called Messianic Apocalypse from Qumran also attributes these acts to God: "And the Lord will accomplish glorious things which have never been as [He ...] For He will heal the wounded, and revive the dead and bring good news to the poor" (**4Q521** 2.11-12).[14]

The clearest connection with the prophecy from Isaiah 35 is perhaps found in the story about the healing of the deaf-mute (Mk 7.31-37). Using the Greek word *mogilalos*, Mark explains that the man has a speech impediment. Mk 7.32 is the only verse where this word occurs in the New Testament. In the **Septuagint** version of the Old Testament it also only occurs once, namely in the above quoted prophecy regarding the new creation, Isa. 35.6. Mark's subtle allusion to new creation themes is strengthened in the crowd's response to Jesus' miracle: "He has done everything well; he even makes the deaf to hear and the mute to speak" (7.37). The first phrase echoes the comment on God's creation from Gen. 1.31, and the second phrase again recalls the prophecy from Isa. 35.5-6 (cf. also Isa. 29.18; 32.4). It was common in Jewish thought to see a connection between the first creation (protology) and the new creation (eschatology). By alluding to both Gen. 1.31 and Isa. 35.5-6, Mark makes use of this connection and shows that Jesus acts as God in restoring creation to its perfect order.

When we have observed the connection between Jesus' healing miracles and the theme of the new creation, we may also consider whether some of the other healing stories in Mark should also be read in this light and be taken as fulfillment of Isa. 35.5-6. This prophecy mentions the opening of the eyes of the blind, the hearing of the deaf, the speaking of the mute, and the walking of the lame. It may appear that Mark has modeled his picture of Jesus' healing activity after this Isaianic prophecy. The healing of the blind plays an important role in Mark's Gospel. Not long after the healing of the deaf-mute, Mark includes his first account of a blind man who receives his sight (8.22-26), and the second follows immediately before Jesus' entry into Jerusalem (10.46-52). We have already seen that Mark connects the healing of the deaf-mute (Mk 7.31-37) with Isaiah's prophecy. With the report of Jesus making a lame man walk (2.1-12), Mark has completed the picture of Jesus' fulfilling Isa. 35.5-6.

Theophany on the Sea of Galilee

Most of the healing miracles discussed above occur after Jesus has been rejected by the Pharisees, the Herodians (3.6), and the people of his home town (6.1-6a). In the following sections, Mark sharpens his focus on the disciples. They are provided with a crescendo of experiences that reveal Jesus' identity. As the Messiah was expected to duplicate Moses' feeding miracles (*2 Baruch* 29.8; *Midrash Rabbah Ecclesiastes* 1.28), Jesus' messianic identity is more than hinted at through the multiplication of the loaves and the fish in 6.30-44.

But the disciples get to see even greater things. The next passage shows Jesus walking on water (Mk 6.45-52), a scene that can be described as an **epiphany**. Its background is found in stories of deliverance from peril at sea, a danger from which only God can save (Exod. 14.13-31; Jon. 1.1-16; Pss. 89.9-10; 107.23-32; Job 26.11-12; *Testament of Naphtali* 6.1-10). In the Jewish tradition, especially in **Qumran**, such stories were sometimes reapplied to their own time (**1QH**[a] 11.6, 13-18; 14.22-25; 15.4-5). Mark stands in this tradition when he couches his account of Jesus in phrases known from the stories about God's mighty works at sea.[15]

As God was known to trample the waves of the sea (*peripaton hos ep edafous epi thalasses*, Job 9.8 **LXX**), so did Jesus approach the disciples walking on the sea (*peripaton epi tes thalasses*, Mk 6.48; cf. also Hab. 3.15; Pss. 65.7; 77.19 [76.20 LXX]; Isa. 43.16; 51.9-10; **Wisdom of Solomon** 14.1-4). The theme of passing by (Mk 6.48) is also familiar from **theophanies** in Israel's Scriptures. Yahweh's passing by was part of his revelation to Moses (Exod. 33.19, 22; 34.6) and to Elijah (1 Kgs 19.11). A closer parallel is found in Amos 7.8; 8.2, where God warns that he will no longer pass by Israel. The meaning is that he will no longer spare them. "To pass by" is thus an alternative way of referring to

God's salvation. Jesus' address to the disciples, "take heart, it is I; do not fear" (Mk 6.50), has close parallels in the way God addresses the exiles of Israel in Isa. 43.1-7. He repeatedly identifies himself with the words "I am" (vv. 2, 3, 5; cf. vv. 10, 11) and comforts his people: "Do not fear" (vv. 1, 5).

Since Mark's story is so rich in allusions to the known actions of God, many scholars have concluded that Jesus' self-identification should be understood as an appropriation of the divine name, "I am," from Exod. 3.14. The Greek version of this name (*ego eimi* in the Septuagint) is identical to Jesus' words to his disciples in Mk 6.50 (the Greek *ego eimi* is here usually translated "it is I"). But in Greek this phrase may also be innocuously self-referential. It is probably best to understand Mark's story as intentionally ambiguous and mysterious, heightening the sense of wonder that his story created around Jesus' character. In typical Markan fashion, the disciples fail to perceive the significance of the revelation. In contrast to Matthew's account (14.33), Mark includes no confession on the part of the disciples.

As far as the available evidence goes, the scene on the Sea of Galilee shows Jesus in a role that is unparalleled among the mighty agents of God. Instead, Jesus takes the place of God himself.

Jesus in God's Place

The scene on the Sea of Galilee may be the first time that Mark shows that the disciples were given a **theophany** where Jesus took on the role of God. But the audience of his Gospel was from the outset introduced to Jesus as the fulfillment of the prophecies regarding God's own coming to earth. They might have been able to understand several details in Mark's story in this light. In the story of the healing of the paralytic (2.1-12), Mark recounts the hidden thoughts of some of the scribes that were present (2.6-7). In line with Mark's understanding of who Jesus is, he attributes him with a miraculous insight into what the scribes were thinking (v. 8), thoughts they are explicitly said to harbor in their hearts (v. 6). The precedent for such knowledge is the knowledge of God himself, who knows the hearts of human beings (1 Sam. 16.7; 1 Kgs 8.39; 1 Chron. 28.9; Pss. 7.9; 139.23; Jer. 11.20; 17.10; **Sirach** 42.18; *Psalms of Solomon* 14.8).

In the discussion about fasting (Mk 2.18-22), Jesus refers to himself as bridegroom: "The wedding guests cannot fast while the bridegroom is with them, can they? As long as they have the bridegroom with them, they cannot fast. The days will come when the bridegroom is taken away from them, and then they will fast on that day" (Mk 2.19-20).

The bridegroom metaphor is a stock theme in the Old Testament and in Jewish literature. It is used to describe God's relationship to his people (Hos. 2.19-20; Isa. 54.5-6; Ezek. 16.8; *Midrash Rabbah Deuteronomy* 3.16; *Pirqe Rabbi Eliezer* 41; *Mekilta* Exodus 15.2; 19.1, 17), but there are no clear examples of it being used for the Messiah. The earliest known example in Jewish sources of the bridegroom as a reference to the Messiah is from *Pesiqta Rabbati* 15.14-15, which is dated to the sixth or the seventh century. Jesus' use of this metaphor is consistent with the picture that has already emerged from Mark's Gospel: Jesus understands himself to take God's place.[16]

When Mark later focuses on the theme of discipleship, Jesus assumes a role of such authority that it is only paralleled by the authority of Yahweh. In the Scriptures of Israel, human beings were said to perform a diverse range of activities in God's name. They spoke in his name (Exod. 5.23; Deut. 18.19; 2 Chron. 33.18; Jer. 26.16; 44.16; Zech. 13.3), prophesied in his name (Jer. 11.21; 26.9), walked (Mic. 4.5), set up banners (Ps. 20.5), conquered the enemy (Pss. 44.5; 118.10-12; cf. 1 Sam. 17.45), ministered (Deut. 10.8; 18.7), blessed (Deut. 10.8; 21.5; 2 Sam. 6.18; 1 Chron. 16.2), and cursed in God's name (2 Kgs 2.24). Viewed in this light, the disciples' failure to do anything in God's name is surprising. Instead, Jesus' name has completely taken over. In his name, the disciples are authorized to receive small children (Mk 9.37), throw out demons (Mk 9.38), and perform powerful deeds (Mk 9.39). Even false prophets will claim to come in his name (13.6). The relationship that Jesus expects from his disciples is modeled upon that between God and faithful Israel in the Scriptures. As it was demanding to be faithful to God in the Old Testament, so are the costs of following Jesus dire. It will result in persecution "for my sake" (Gr.: *heneken emou*, Mk 13.9; cf. 8.35; 10.29). This expression may allude to Ps. 44.22. There, it refers to suffering for the Lord's sake (44.23 **LXX**: *heneken sou*). Jesus goes even further and assures his disciples that they will be hated by everyone for his name's sake (Mk 13.13). From the Scriptures of Israel one knows that the faithful remnant suffers in a similar way; being hated for the Lord's name's sake (Isa. 66.5).

Jesus' instructions to the disciples about the future, his Olivet discourse (Mk 13), also assures them that suffering will not be the end. Things will change when "the sun will be darkened, and the moon will not give its light, and the stars will be falling from heaven, and the powers in the heavens will be shaken" (Mk 13.24-25). Here Jesus alludes to Isa. 13.10 and 34.4. The context of both verses is the judgment of God. In Isaiah 13, the prophet announces cosmic judgment on the day of the Lord (v. 6). The oracle is introduced as pertaining to Babylon (v. 1), but Babylon is not mentioned until v. 19. Instead the prophecy takes on the proportions of universal judgment, with its condemnation of the sinners on earth (v. 9), on the day when "the sun will be dark at its rising, and the moon will not shed its light" (v. 10). In the first stanza, an army from a distant land is summoned to execute God's anger (vv. 3, 5). But this army quickly disappears from view, and the focus is on God himself, who will destroy his enemies.[17] Isaiah 34 evokes a similar cosmic scenario. It introduces God's rage against the nations (v. 2), which will be unleashed when "all the host of heaven shall rot away, and the skies roll up like a scroll" (v. 4). Beginning with the following verse, the focus narrows to the Edomites (v. 5). Throughout, God is acting alone, as the one who wields his sword to slaughter the land of Edom (v. 6).

Instead of proceeding to the image of God's judgment, however, the Markan Jesus next links to Dan. 7.13 and the picture of the Son of Man coming in clouds. The cryptic Son of Man, who first appeared as an enigmatic self-reference in Mk 2.10, is now directly tied to the vision of Daniel. But as Jesus identifies himself with this figure, he also goes beyond the description in Daniel 7. Whereas the Son of Man in Dan. 7.13 represents the people of God and their vindication by him (cf. Dan. 7.27), in Mk 13.26 he is an agent of judgment.[18] He has now taken God's place. First, the Son of Man emerges at the point in Jesus' discourse when his biblical allusions have prepared the audience for the appearance of God himself in judgment. Second, the Son of Man is attributed with characteristics that are not found in Daniel 7. The Son of Man is now coming "with great power and glory" (Mk 13.26). Power and glory were among the stock characterizations used for God in the Jewish tradition.[19] In the Scriptures of Israel, "power and glory" as a dual description is only used of God (Ps. 63.2).[20] Third, Jesus also claims for himself two distinctive acts of God: sending out angels and gathering his elect.[21] His claim that the elect belong to him is especially noteworthy, as he has just clarified that the elect were chosen by the Lord (v. 20). The image in Mk 13.27 may be dependent on the prophecy from Zech. 14.5, which declares: "then the Lord my God will come, and all the holy ones with him." Here, the Son of Man takes God's place, and his coming represents the fulfillment of the day of the Lord and God's coming to earth in judgment.

To assure the disciples of the certainty of his promises, Jesus goes on to state that his words will never pass away, not even upon the dissolution of the universe as we know it (13.31). The Scriptures of Israel know of only one character who makes such claims: Yahweh himself (Isa. 40.6-8; cf. 51.6; 54.10;

Ps. 102.26-27). If Jesus' saying is read as an allusion to Isa. 40.8, he claims even more for himself than what the relevant passage of Scripture claimed for Yahweh. Whereas Isa. 40.6 mentions the prospective passing away of the grass and the flower, Jesus makes the claim absolute by mentioning heaven and earth instead. His authority is second to none, not even that of God.

Lord

Mark understands Jesus to be on the same level as God the Father. This is confirmed when we observe Mark's use of the title "Lord." This title is introduced in Mk 1.3, where the referent is ambiguous. Mark quotes Isa. 40.3: "prepare the way of the Lord, make his paths straight." In its original context, this Lord is God. In the context of Mark's Gospel, however, the Lord appears to be Jesus (cf. pp. 37-38). The next time the title occurs is in the story of the Gerasene demoniac (5.1-20). Jesus instructs the man to tell his friends about what the Lord has done for him (5.19). In this verse, "Lord" is most naturally understood as referring to God, but in the next verse Mark tells us that the man went and told people what Jesus had done for him. This ambiguity is explicable if Mark thought of Jesus as God's agent, and if he meant that the man told people what God had done through Jesus. But Mark's language also leaves open the possibility that "Lord" could be understood as a title for Jesus.

In connection with Jesus' entry into Jerusalem, the title "Lord" takes on special significance. Jesus instructs the disciples to go to the village ahead of them, where they will find a colt that has never been ridden. If anyone asks them why they are taking it, they shall say: "Its Lord needs it" (*ho kurios autou chreian echei*, Mk 11.3). Many interpretations have been offered to explain this statement. Some scholars suggest that this "Lord" refers to the actual owner of the colt, but he does not appear in the story and is not seen to need the colt. Others maintain that the Lord must be God, who is the Lord of everything. This interpretation is equally unable to do justice to the story, as God does not demonstrate any need for the colt, either. The Lord must be Jesus, and since we have no reason to believe that he was the actual owner of the colt, the word "Lord" must be intended at another level. In itself, Jesus' brief statement does not clarify what kind of Lord he is, but the reader who has received the information Mark has provided in the prologue and the hints he has given along the way, may be prepared to see that Jesus is the Lord of creation. The way Mark tells the story of the triumphal entry confirms this interpretation. Jesus is presented as having specific knowledge of future events (11.2-3), so that he can predict the disciples' finding a male colt that has never been ridden.

Since Mark has developed the "Lord" title in this way, his audience may be in a better position to understand Jesus' enigmatic discussion about the Messiah and David in Mk 12.35-37: "While Jesus was teaching in the temple, he said, 'How can the scribes say that the Messiah is the son of David? David himself, by the Holy Spirit, declared, "The Lord said to my Lord, 'Sit at my right hand, until I put your enemies under your feet.'"' David himself calls him Lord; so how can he be his son?' And the large crowd was listening to him with delight." Jesus here uses Ps. 110.1 to show that the Messiah is more than David's son – he is also his Lord. Jesus does not explain how the Messiah can be David's Lord, but Mark's audience knows by now that "Lord" is a title for Jesus the Messiah, a title he shares with God the Father.

Jesus as God's servant

Mark's portrait of Jesus as God's equal and sharing the name Lord is balanced by his description of Jesus as subject to the Father. The Markan Jesus does not know the time of the end (13.32), and he is not at liberty to assign the seats on his right and his left (10.40). He prays to the Father (1.35; 6.46; 14.32, 39), and submits completely to him, even to the point of death (14.36). For Mark, Jesus is God's servant.

Messiah

Mark makes it clear right off the bat that Jesus is the Messiah (Mk 1.1). As his story proceeds, however, there is more and more reason to ask if this is indeed an appropriate title for Jesus. For one thing, Jesus never uses the title for himself, even though he does refer to his disciples as those who belong to Christ (Mk 9.41). What is more, when Peter speaks on behalf of the disciples and ventures that Jesus is the Messiah (Mk 8.29), Jesus says nothing to indicate his approval. All Mark tells us is that Jesus "sternly ordered them not to tell anyone about him" (Mk 8.30). Mark's version of this story differs dramatically from that of Matthew, who has included the famous words where Jesus praises Peter and promises to build his church "on this rock" (Mt. 16.17-19).

Finally, when he is questioned by the high priest, Jesus affirms that he is the Messiah. In response to the question "'Are you the Messiah, the Son of the Blessed One?' Jesus said, 'I am, and "you will see the Son of Man seated

at the right hand of the Power" and "coming with the clouds of heaven" ' "
(Mk 14.61-62). Jesus' answer includes a profound elaboration on the Messiah
title (more on this below on p. 69). It appears, therefore, that Mark wants us
to know that Jesus is the Messiah, but that we must be careful how we understand the title.

The first time we encounter the title in Mark's narrative (after the introductory line in 1.1) is in Peter's confession (Mk 8.29).[22] The story of Peter's
confession is immediately followed by Jesus' first prediction of his suffering
and death (Mk 8.31). He did not allow Peter and the disciples to tell anyone
that he was the Messiah (Mk 8.30), but he has no objection when blind
Bartimaeus addresses him as "son of David" outside Jericho (Mk 10.47–48).
The title "son of David" identifies Jesus as the one who would fulfill God's
promises to David. It is therefore a messianic title (cf. *Psalms of Solomon*
17.21). Within Mark's narrative, Bartimaeus' cry represents a turning point,
because it is the first time Jesus publicly accepts being identified as the
Messiah. The passage immediately following is the story of Jesus' triumphal
entry into Jerusalem (Mk 11.1-11). This story is steeped in messianic imagery.
Jesus enters Jerusalem on a donkey, an animal that is closely associated with
the Messiah in Israel's Scriptures. Jacob's promise to Judah describes the future
king of Judah, who will be "binding his foal to the vine and his donkey's colt
to the choice vine" (Gen. 49.11a). The prophecy in Zech. 9.9 announces to
Jerusalem: "Lo, your king comes to you; triumphant and victorious is he,
humble and riding on a donkey, on a colt, the foal of a donkey." As he enters,
the crowds greet him with words from Ps. 118.25-26: "Hosanna! Blessed is the
one who comes in the name of the Lord!" (Mk 11.9). Psalm 118 is one of the
psalms that were used in connection with the major festivals in Israel, when
the people made pilgrimage to Jerusalem. Verses 25-26 contain the greeting
that met the king when he led a procession of pilgrims to the temple. The
verses were not originally used in connection with a future Messiah, therefore,
but when the crowds greet Jesus in this way, their words have messianic
overtones. The messianic nature of their expectations becomes explicit in the
following verse, where the crowds continue: "Blessed is the coming kingdom
of our ancestor David!" (Mk 11.10). Jesus' triumphal entry is therefore the
occasion when Jesus actively associates his own ministry with messianic
expectations.

As it turns out, however, Jesus' triumphal entry becomes his entry into
his trial, conviction and death, as he also repeatedly has predicted (Mk 8.31;
9.31; 10.33-34). By tying the announcement of Jesus' messiahship to his

entry into Jerusalem, Mark thereby ties Jesus' messiahship to his suffering and death. It is therefore appropriate that when Jesus explicitly accepts the title, it is at his trial, when the high priest asks him if he is "the Messiah, the Son of the Blessed One" (Mk 14.61-62). Having crafted the story the way he did, Mark shows a Messiah whose mission is to die. He thereby interprets messiahship in a radically different way from the common expectations of a political leader who would restore the kingdom of Israel. This interpretation of messiahship may also, at least partly, explain Jesus' reluctance in accepting the title and his many exhortations to people not to talk about him (Mk 1.25, 34, 44; 3.12; 5.43; 7.24, 36; 8.26, 30; 9.9, 30). He is indeed the Messiah, but not the Messiah of popular expectation. He was not a Messiah that would put other people to death, but, as we shall see, a Messiah that would die in their place.

It is therefore clear that Mark's picture of Jesus as the Messiah is intended to correct alternative views of messiahship. The New Testament scholar Theodore Weeden has emphasized this point very strongly and presented a proposal regarding Mark's Gospel that is widely discussed in New Testament scholarship, although rarely accepted. He argues that Mark's Gospel was written to correct a certain Christological thinking that was popular among Hellenistic Christians. These **Hellenistic** Christians, he maintains, viewed Jesus as a divine man. The term "divine man" refers to a perceived Hellenistic category of miracle workers and men that were thought to exercise divine powers. According to Weeden, the first of half of Mark's Gospel presents a Christology along such lines, where Jesus is portrayed as a miracle-working Son of God. Weeden's point is that Mark disapproves of this "divine man" Christology, just as Jesus dismisses Peter's confession of Jesus as the Messiah (Mk 8.30). In the rest of the Gospel, Jesus is therefore shown as the Son of Man that has to suffer and die (Mk 8.31).[23]

Later studies have shown, however, that there was no coherent and unified "divine man" concept in the ancient Greco-Roman world.[24] This term, which was so popular during much of the twentieth century, is therefore only rarely used by scholars today. There is broad agreement that Weeden is correct in emphasizing the significance of suffering in Mark's portrait of Jesus, but he has overstated his case. True, Mark's Gospel contains statements about Jesus that Mark does not necessarily accept. Herod's conclusion, that Jesus is the resurrected John the Baptist (Mk 6.15), is obviously incorrect. When the people say that Jesus is a prophet, Mark as a story-teller gives us no indication that this is an adequate understanding of who Jesus is. There is therefore good reason to ask if we should believe the demons when they address Jesus as the Son of God (Mk 3.11; cf. 5.7). The lack of commendation of Peter's confession also raises the question of how Mark assesses its value.

To find Mark's point of view, however, we need to turn to the voices in his narrative that he certainly would have considered authoritative. Chief among these are the Scriptures and the voice of God. In his prologue, Mark hints at Jesus' divine nature with his use of Scripture, and the divine voice that sounds at Jesus' baptism and transfiguration confirms that he is the Son of God. A leading narrative critic such as Jack Dean Kingsbury therefore concludes that Son of God is the most important of all the titles in Mark's Gospel.[25]

It is unwarranted, therefore, to conclude that Mark disapproves of the view of Jesus as a powerful miracle-working Son of God. Mark's genius is rather that he combines this image of Jesus with the necessity of his suffering. It is precisely as the glorious Son of God that Jesus the Messiah has to suffer. As Jesus moves towards Jerusalem, his miraculous knowledge continues to be a key element in Mark's story (11.2-6; 14.13-16, 30, 41-42), and his unique authority as a teacher propels the plot towards his execution (11.27–12.44).

When he is talking with the Jewish leaders, Jesus indicates that their understanding of the Messiah is not fully correct. He reminds them that David called the Messiah "lord" and explains that the Messiah therefore must be greater than David, even though David is his forefather (Mk 12.35-37). When the high priest asked Jesus if he were the Messiah, he answered affirmatively (Mk 14.62). Then he continued to describe himself with a quotation from Dan. 7.13 and Ps. 110.1. The point is that the Messiah is also a heavenly being who shares God's authority.

Son of Man

When Jesus makes statements about his own authority, he often refers to himself as "the Son of Man" (2.10, 28; 8.38; 13.26; 14.62). This term goes back to the expression *bar enosh* in Aramaic, which was the language Jesus spoke. Like the Hebrew equivalent, *ben adam*, this term may mean "a human being" (cf. Ezek. 2.1, 3, 6, 8; 3.1 etc.) or humankind in general (cf. Pss. 8.4; 80.17). The problem is that in the Gospels the term appears to be a title, and it refers exclusively to Jesus Christ.

In order to explain this discrepancy, Maurice Casey has argued very well for the thesis that the meaning of this term changed as a result of the translation of Jesus' words from Aramaic to Greek. In Casey's view, Jesus originally used the term as a way of referring to human beings in general or to a group of human beings, even though he often made statements that applied more specifically to himself. As an example of this general usage, he refers to Jesus' defence of the disciples plucking grain on the Sabbath, where Jesus says: "The sabbath was made for humankind, and not humankind for the sabbath; so the Son of Man is lord even of the sabbath" (Mk 2.27-28). As long as Jesus' words circulated in Aramaic, it was possible to understand his words as having both a general reference and a more specific reference to himself. When his sayings were translated to Greek, however, it was impossible to preserve this ambiguity. The translators had to choose between the specific and the general and opted for a translation that could be understood as a Christological title: *ho huios tou anthropou* ("the Son of Man"). Casey also turns this explanation into a criterion for judging which sayings are authentic. Only those Son of Man sayings that can be translated back to Aramaic and make sense as a general reference can go back to the historical Jesus. Those passages where "Son of Man" can only be understood in a titular sense (e.g., Mk 13.26) must be the creation of the early church.[26]

Casey's views remain controversial, not least because he postulates such a great divide between the historical Jesus and the final form of the Gospels. In Mark's Gospel (as in Matthew and Luke), Jesus' portrait of himself as the Son of Man is clearly derived from Daniel's vision of "one like a human being (son of man) coming with the clouds of heaven" (Dan. 7.13). The clearest example is found in Jesus' Farewell Discourse, where he teaches the disciples about the future: "Then they will see 'the Son of Man coming in clouds' with great power and glory" (Mk 13.26). Many scholars have therefore understood "Son of Man" as a title that refers to the heavenly character from Daniel's vision. This view seems to be confirmed by the evidence from some of the Jewish **apocalyptic** writings. A character that is referred to as "Son of Man" appears both in *1 Enoch* and *4 Ezra*, and this character is clearly inspired by Daniel's vision as well. As Casey and others have shown, however, the mere expression "son of man" is not automatically a title and does not necessarily invoke the Danielic character. In those cases where there is such a connection, the Son of Man character is always introduced with an allusion to Dan. 7.13. That is the case in Mk 13.26 as well. It is not the term "son of man" in itself but the words "coming in clouds" that enable the audience to make the connection with Daniel's vision. It is therefore questionable whether we are justified in reading a reference to Dan. 7.13 into every occurrence of the term "Son of Man" on

Jesus' lips, especially in those sayings that otherwise have no connection with the prophet Daniel.

A closer look at the New Testament evidence also shows us that "Son of Man" does not function as a well-defined title. Unlike the titles "Son of God," "Lord," and "Messiah," "Son of Man" is never used in early Christian confessions. There is no evidence that early Christians ever confessed that "Jesus is the Son of Man." In fact, with one exception that is clearly an echo of one of Jesus' own sayings (Acts 7.56; cf. Lk. 22.69), Jesus is the only one who uses the term "the Son of Man" in the New Testament.[27] What is more, there is no evidence in the New Testament that anyone understood Jesus as appropriating an exalted title when he talked about himself as the Son of Man. The scribes, for example, deemed it blasphemous when Jesus forgave sins (Mk 2.7), but they do not appear to have had any problem with Jesus' use of the term "Son of Man" (Mk 2.10). In the Gospel of John, we also find evidence that the term was cryptic and that people did not understand what Jesus meant. According to Jn 12.34, the crowd told Jesus: "How can you say that the Son of Man must be lifted up? Who is this Son of Man?" (cf. also Mt. 16.13).

The fact that his contemporaries found it difficult to understand Jesus' use of the term "Son of Man" may be an indication that Jesus used this term in an unusual way. Richard Bauckham has argued that there was something innovative about Jesus' use of the term "Son of Man." Specifically, Bauckham suggests that Jesus used the term "Son of Man" in an indefinite sense as a roundabout way to refer to himself, very much like the use of the English pronoun "someone." An author of a seminary textbook may say something like "someone has written an article about this passage," although "someone" is none other than the author. As an example of a similar use of language, Bauckham points to 2 Cor. 12.2, where the apostle Paul refers to himself as a person he knows in Christ.[28]

Bauckham's explanation is able to account very well both for the Aramaic evidence and for the New Testament usage.[29] We are then led to the conclusion that "Son of Man" is in itself a modest self-reference. Literally, the term means "human being," but Jesus uses it to say something about himself. However, some of the things that Jesus has to say about himself as this Son of Man are anything but modest. It is as the Son of Man that Jesus forgives sins (Mk 2.10), is lord of the Sabbath (Mk 2.28), and will come again to judge the living and the dead (Mk 8.38; 13.26-27; 14.62). However, it is also as the Son of Man that Jesus announces that he has to die (Mk 8.31; 9.9-12, 31; 10.33, 45; 14.21, 41).

It has been common to divide the Son of Man sayings into three groups: 1) those focusing on his authority during his earthly life; 2) those concerning his suffering, death, and resurrection; and 3) those focusing on his future glory. The theme that unites all the sayings is the question of authority. The earthly Jesus demonstrates his authority (1); his authority is rejected, which leads to his suffering (2); but his authority is vindicated and he returns in glory (3).

In the context of Mark's Gospel, the term "Son of Man" functions very much like the parables are said to function: they cause outsiders to become even more hardened, but they reveal the secret of the kingdom of God to insiders (Mk 4.10-12). Similarly, the authority of the Son of Man is rejected by outsiders, who see him as a mere human being. On the other hand, insiders accept his divine authority, as Daniel's vision portrayed him: "To him was given dominion and glory and kingship, that all peoples, nations, and languages should serve him. His dominion is an everlasting dominion that shall not pass away, and his kingship is one that shall never be destroyed" (Dan. 7.14).

According to Dan. 7.27, "the kingship and dominion and the greatness of the kingdoms under the whole heaven shall be given to the people of the holy ones of the Most High." This parallelism between the Son of Man and the people of the holy ones shows that there is a close connection between the Son of Man and this people, so close that the Son of Man may be understood as a personification of or, probably better, as a representative of this people. As Daniel 7 has a lot to say about the suffering of God's people, and since Jesus ties the vision of the Son of Man so closely to the prospect of suffering and death, his idea seems to be that he suffers on behalf of his people. That Jesus understands his suffering in this way becomes clear when we observe how he draws on yet another Old Testament character in order to explain his own role, namely that of Isaiah's suffering servant.

The Servant of the Lord

In the most specific of Jesus' predictions of his death, Mk 10.33-34, he envisions that the Gentiles "will mock him, and spit [Gr.: *emptusousin*] upon him, and flog him [Gr.: *mastigosousin*], and kill him." These words echo Isa. 50.6, where God's servant says: "I gave my back to those who struck me (**LXX**: *mastigas*), and my cheeks to those who pulled out the beard; I did not hide my face from insult and spitting (LXX: *emptusmaton*)."

Isaiah 50.4-9 is one of four passages in the book of Isaiah that describes a character identified as the Lord's servant (cf. also Isa. 42.1-9; 49.1-7; 52.13–53.12). In modern scholarship these passages are often referred to as the Servant songs (cf. pp. 27-29). The echoes from Isaiah's songs in Jesus' words indicate that he understood his own role in light of the picture of this servant of the Lord. When he maintains that it is "written about the Son of Man, that he is to go through many sufferings and be treated with contempt" (Mk 9.12; cf. 14.49), the background is most probably the Servant songs in Isaiah. The Greek word that is translated "treated with contempt" (*exoudenethe*) is not used in the **Septuagint** version of Isaiah 53. However, a different form of this verb occurs in all three other early Greek translations, **Symmachus**, **Theodotion**, and **Aquila**. In Isa. 53.3 (NRSV: "he was despised"), these versions have the form *exoudenomenos*. If Mark knew a translation of Isa. 53.3 that was similar to the ones we find in these versions, it is possible that Mk 9.12 was meant as an allusion.

One of the most debated verses in Mark's Gospel is also the only verse where Jesus explains the purpose of his death, namely in Mk 10.45: "For the Son of Man came not to be served but to serve, and to give his life a ransom for many." Part of the discussion concerns whether there is an allusion to Isaiah 53 here. Some scholars argue that there is not, as none of the words in Mk 10.45 are clearly derived from Isa. 52.13–53.12. Even though there are no clear verbal links, however, the conceptual links are significant. That Jesus comes to "serve" (*diakonesai*) recalls the character of the servant (**LXX**: *doulos/pais*), who "is serving many well" (Isa. 53.11 LXX: *eu douleuonta pollois*). That he will "give his life" (*dounai ten psuchen autou*) mirrors the servant about whom the prophet says: "When you make his life an offering for sin" (Isa. 53.10 LXX: *ean dote peri hamartias*) and "he poured out himself to death" (Isa. 53.12 LXX: *paredothe eis thanaton he psuche autou*). That his life is a ransom (*lutron*) corresponds to the idea that the servant's life is made "an offering for sin" (Isa. 53.10). Finally, that he gives himself "for many" (*anti pollon*) echoes the prophecy that says the servant will "make many (LXX: *pollois*) righteous" and that he "bore the sin of many" (LXX: *pollon*). In themselves, these verbal similarities are unimpressive, but the conceptual overlap is decisive.[30] The Markan Jesus understands his mission as a fulfillment of the prophecies regarding the suffering servant. Specifically, he will give his life on behalf of his people, to set them free from God's punishment. (Compare Exod. 30.16, where the ransom money frees the people of Israel from the wrath of God following the census.)

Many scholars also find a connection to the Servant songs in Jesus' words at his Last Supper with the disciples. As he gave them to drink, he told them: "This is my blood of the covenant, which is poured out for many" (Mk 14.24). The background for this statement is often sought in Isa. 53.11-12:

> Out of his anguish he shall see light; he shall find satisfaction through his knowledge. The righteous one, my servant, shall make many righteous, and he shall bear their iniquities. Therefore I will allot him a portion with the great, and he shall divide the spoil with the strong; because he poured out himself to death, and was numbered with the transgressors; yet he bore the sin of many, and made intercession for the transgressors.

The terminological link is even weaker here than in Mk 10.45. Between the Greek text of Mk 14.24 and the **Septuagint** version of Isa. 53.11-12, the only word that recurs is the word for "many" (*pollon*). The connection to Isaiah 53 is at the most general level; like the suffering servant dies for the people, so does Jesus give his life for them.

Son of God

So far, we have seen that there is considerable tension between what Mark has to say about Jesus as God's servant and his picture of Jesus as God's equal. Mark allows both of these aspects of Jesus' person to stand, and he does not provide an explanation or an explicit resolution of the tension. A concept that combines these aspects is the idea that Jesus is the Son of God. The "Son of God" title is the most important title for Jesus in the Gospel of Mark. Jesus' identity as the Son of God is announced twice by God himself, at Jesus' baptism (1.11) and at his transfiguration (9.7). The unclean spirits know his identity (3.11; 5.7), and Jesus accepts the title at his trial (14.61-62). As the Gospel reaches its climax with Jesus' crucifixion, his identity is so compellingly revealed that it is being called out by a Roman centurion (15.39).

Ironically, the importance of this title in Mark's Gospel makes it difficult to know whether or not Mark included it in the opening line of his work (1.1). The surviving manuscripts are divided between the reading "The beginning of the good news of Jesus Christ, the Son of God" and "The beginning of the good news of Jesus Christ." Did Mark want to state as succinctly as possible the identity of Jesus from the very beginning? Or did he intend to allow the truth about Jesus to emerge as his story proceeded? If Mark omitted the words, a scribe might have been moved to clarify the purpose of the Gospel by expanding the title. On the other hand, if Mark included them, they may have been omitted by a scribe as a result of oversight, but it is unlikely that a scribe would skip the name of God occurring in the first verse.[31] In any case, whether secondary in 1.1 or not, the Son of God title is the most significant title for Jesus in Mark's Gospel.

The son of God title is used quite broadly in Jewish tradition. Angels, Israel, the king, and the Messiah could be known as sons of God (cf. p. 3). What the title means to Mark must be determined from the way he uses it in his narrative.

The Baptism

Apart from the Gospel heading, Mark's first identification of Jesus as God's Son follows immediately after his implicit identification as the Lord of Israel's Scriptures. "In those days Jesus came from Nazareth of Galilee and was baptized by John in the Jordan. And just as he was coming up out of the water, he saw the heavens torn apart and the Spirit descending like a dove on him. And a voice came from heaven, 'You are my Son, the Beloved; with you I am well pleased'" (Mk 1.9-11). The tearing apart of the heavens (1.10a) indicates an **apocalyptic** event and a revelation from God (cf. Ezek. 1.1; *Testament of Levi* 2.6; 5.1; *2 Baruch* 22.1). Perhaps the specific background for this spectacular occurrence is Israel's prayer for God's renewed intervention in Isa. 63.15–64.12. In Isa. 64.1, Israel prays that he will "tear open the heavens and come down" to rescue his people. This phraseology may also point forward to the tearing of the temple curtain and the centurion's proclamation of Jesus' identity in Mk 15.38-39.

The descent of the Holy Spirit in the form of a dove (Mk 1.10b) recalls the first creation event, where the Spirit of God, water, and the image of a bird (implied in the verb "hovering") also occur together. Jesus' baptism is portrayed in such a way that it has connotations of an eschatological event and of the new creation. The presence of the Holy Spirit provides a further legitimization of Jesus: his ministry is Spirit-endowed. In the Old Testament, prophets (Num. 11.29) as well as the Messiah (Isa. 11.2) and the Servant of the Lord (Isa. 42.1; cf. 61.1) were known to have a special endowment by God's Spirit. However, Mark's picture is so different from these antecedents that we cannot conclude that he intends to portray Jesus as a specific character. Rather, his description of Jesus draws on a number of Old Testament images and combines them.

Having thus alerted the reader that a pivotal heavenly revelation will take place, Mark reports the voice from heaven, announcing to Jesus: "you are my Son, the Beloved; with you I am well pleased" (Mk 1.11). In later **Rabbinic** texts such heavenly messages are known as *bat qol* ("daughter of a voice"), and *Tosefta Soṭa* 13.3 explicitly distinguishes such messages from the voice of the Holy Spirit. But in the older tradition, no such distinction is made, even though the speaker may be both the Angel of the Lord (Gen. 21.17; 22.11, 15) and God himself (Exod. 19.19; Deut. 4.10-12; 1 Kgs 19.13-15). In Mark's worldview, God's voice is the most authoritative of all, and this statement must therefore be taken as an ultimately reliable declaration of who Jesus is. The announcement appears to be another **conflated** quotation from the Scriptures of Israel, combining Ps. 2.7; Gen. 22.2, 12, 16 and Isa. 42.1.

The first part of the divine declaration, "you are my son," is taken from Ps. 2.7b: "you are my son; today I have begotten you." In tune with the divine warrior theme that Mark has already invoked (cf. pp. 37, 40-44), Psalm 2 portrays the conflict between the nations on earth on one side and God and his anointed on the other (vv. 1-3). The nations are no match for God (v. 4), however, and he ensures the supremacy of his anointed one, as long as he depends on him (v. 8). Originally, the Psalm may have referred to the Davidic king in Jerusalem (v. 6), but subsequent interpretation saw in the Psalm a description of future, eschatological events, when God would bring salvation to his people. A messianic interpretation is found in *Psalms of Solomon* 17.21-25. This passage draws on the picture of the anointed one of Psalm 2 and describes a future Messiah who will shatter the rulers of the nations. The messianic interpretation is not the only one we find in Jewish sources, however. According to 4QFlorilegium (**4Q174**), the **Qumran** community appears to have found a reference to themselves in the mention of "the anointed one." In their understanding, Ps. 2.1 describes "the elect ones in Israel in the last days" (**4Q174** 1.18-19). Their understanding is firmly rooted in Jewish tradition. Apart from the instance in Ps. 2.7, there is ample evidence in Jewish sources that God refers to the people of Israel as his son (Exod. 4.22; Deut. 1.31; Hos. 11.1; **Wisdom of Solomon** 18.13), firstborn (Jer. 31.9) or sons (*Psalms of Solomon* 17.27).

The epithet "beloved" is sometimes traced back to Isa. 42.1a: "here is my servant, whom I uphold, my chosen, in whom my soul delights." The adjectives "beloved" and "chosen" appear to be interchangeable in some cases (compare Mt. 12.18 with Isa. 42.1 and Lk. 9.35). This affinity of the two words may be the result of a Christian development, however. It is far from obvious that Isa. 42.1 lies behind the use of "beloved" in Mk 1.11. In the **Septuagint**, the Hebrew word *bachir* ("chosen"), which is used in Isa. 42.1, is never translated as *agapetos* ("beloved"), which is the word that is used in Mk 1.11. A closer terminological match is found in Gen. 22.2, 12, 16 where Isaac is called Abraham's beloved son. In the Isaac narrative, it is a crucial point that Isaac is Abraham's only son. The meaning of the word "beloved" becomes close to that of "unique."

The conclusion of the saying in Mk 1.11, however – "with you I am well pleased" – seems to be drawn from the description of the Lord's servant in Isa. 42.1a. This servant will bring justice, not only to Israel, but to the whole earth (v. 4).

Rather than identify one specific character, the voice from heaven combines images of several of God's agents. Jesus is the ultimate divine servant in whom all God's purposes on earth crystallize. In other words, any one character from Scripture is in itself insufficient to explain who Jesus is. The way the Son of God title is introduced thus indicates that it transcends expectations connected with it. Mark expands its connotations and gives it a fuller meaning. The picture of the messianic king helps the audience to see Jesus' as the one who brings the peaceful restoration of Israel. Isaac invokes the example of unbridled obedience and willing sacrifice as well as the realization of the promise to Abraham. Isaiah's Servant promises the establishment of God's unopposed rule on earth with international justice. By combining all of these ideas, the baptism account paints the picture of a Son of God who transcends human categories. As Mark has already indicated that Jesus represents the eschatological coming of God to earth, so does his picture of the Son of God show a character who brings a new world order.

Many scholars, especially in the German tradition, have read the voice from heaven as an adoption formula, indicating that the baptism was the moment when Jesus was understood to become the Son of God.[32] One of the arguments for this interpretation is that the voice quotes from Psalm 2, which originally may have been used in connection with the coronation of a king. The king's divine sonship was connected with his function as king. He apparently received this status when he became king, as the oracle reads: "today I have begotten you" (Ps. 2.7b).

But even though this may have been the original function of Psalm 2, it is unwarranted to read the voice from heaven as an adoption formula, indicating that the baptism was the moment when Jesus was understood to become the Son of God. Omitting the phrase "today I have begotten you" in his quotation, Mark does not directly address the question of when Jesus became the Son of God. Mark has also changed the word order. Whereas the oracle in Ps. 2.7 has the words "my son" at the beginning (both in the **MT** and the **LXX**), Mark begins with "you." The function of Mark's word order is to provide a simple identification. As Eduard Norden has shown, the Greek expression *su ei* ("you are") is not natively Greek, but goes back to a Semitic predication formula, correctly paraphrased by Matthew (3.17): "This is my Son ..." (Gr.: *houtos estin ho huios mou* ...).[33] Mark demonstrates no interest in the biography of Jesus before he appears on the public scene and is baptized by John. His concern is to show who this man is, not when or how he became such a man. If the analogy with John the Baptist is brought to bear on the question, Mark's single interest is to present him as the forerunner, not when he became the forerunner. This interpretation is confirmed when it is observed that the heavenly oracle not only alludes to Ps. 2.7 and Isa. 42.1 but also to Gen. 22.2. Gen. 22.2 does not refer to any "becoming" on Isaac's part. It states what he already is. There is no reason, therefore, to read a "becoming" or "investiture" into the declaration of the heavenly voice. This is all the more so when it is observed that, in Mark's story, the coming of Jesus has already been introduced as the coming of God (1.2-3).

If the baptism announces Jesus as the Son of God who will bring a new world order, this announcement is bad news for God's cosmic enemies, the evil spirits. It comes as no surprise, therefore, that they respond to Jesus with despair as they recognize him as God's Son (3.11; 5.7). As spiritual beings, they have an insight that human beings lack. Their awareness of Jesus as God's Son is directly connected with Jesus' indisputable authority to cast them out (3.11). Jesus' sonship must therefore partly pertain to his supreme power over the demons, a power that is not of this world. In the mouth of the demons, the Son of God title is not merely a messianic title; it identifies Jesus as the divine warrior who deals the army of Satan their final defeat.

The Glory of the Father (Mk 8.38)

A further indication of the nature of Jesus' sonship comes in the context of his first explicit prediction of his suffering (8.31). As he prepares his disciples to take their crosses up and follow him (8.34), he assures them that "those who are ashamed of me and of my words in this adulterous and sinful generation, of them the Son of Man will also be ashamed when he comes in the glory of his Father with the holy angels" (8.38). With this warning, Jesus also provides a profound statement about his own identity. As the Son of Man, he is also the Son of God, as he refers to God as his father. What is more, he claims that the glory of the Father also belongs to him. In the Bible the word "glory" (Gr.: *doxa*) is used to describe the divine radiance and "to express the 'divine mode of being.'"[34] According to Dan. 7.13-14, the Son of Man would be presented before the Ancient One and be given glory. By combining Dan. 7.13-14 with Zech. 14.5, however, Mk 8.38 envisions Jesus as the Son of Man in a way that transcends the expectations of Daniel. In Mk 8.38, the Son of Man is not coming to God, but is coming from heaven. He is not receiving glory from the Father – his glory is now explicitly the Father's own glory. The purpose is not his own vindication: his coming results in the judgment of the unfaithful. This brief description therefore presupposes both that Jesus is a person distinct from the Father and that he shares the characteristic that sets the Father apart from human beings, his glory.

The Transfiguration

This statement about Jesus' glory leads naturally into the transfiguration account (Mk 9.2-8), which provides a revelation of Jesus' heavenly glory.[35] This story also complements the various human assessments of Jesus by providing an authoritative pronouncement in the form of a heavenly voice: "This is my Son, the Beloved; listen to him!" (9.7b). Again, motifs where Jesus is seen as God's eschatological agent are combined with motifs where he takes the place of God himself. Most obviously, Jesus is described as the new Moses, the eschatological prophet of Deut. 18.15-19. The parallels between the transfiguration and the Sinai event have long been noticed: the reference to six days (Mk 9.2; cf. Exod. 24.16), the three companions (Mk 9.2; cf. Exod. 24.1, 9), the climbing of the mountain (Mk 9.2; cf. Exod. 24.9, 12–13, 15, 18), the transfiguration (9.2-3; cf. Exod. 34.29), God's voice from the cloud (Mk 9.7; cf. Exod. 24.16), and the awe of the bystanders (Mk 9.15; cf. Exod. 34.30). Although the parallel is not exact, it is reasonable therefore to find an allusion to Deut. 18.15 in the second part of the heavenly oracle: "Listen to him!" (Mk 9.7).

The heavenly oracle combines Moses imagery with that of other special agents of God. As in 1.11, both the king of Ps. 2.7 and Isaac, whom Abraham was ready to sacrifice, are invoked with the phrase "This is my Son, the Beloved."

At the same time, however, the transfiguration transcends agency categories and Moses **typology**. When Moses appears with Jesus, he is not commissioning or authorizing him (as in the case of Elijah and Elisha, 1 Kgs 19.16-21; 2 Kgs 2.1-15). As a character in the Gospel, Moses is clearly subordinate to Jesus. Jesus is the only one whose appearance is described and he is the focus of the **theophany**. Offering to build three tents (9.5), Peter understands Elijah and Moses to be at the same level as Jesus. This misunderstanding may be at least part of the reason that Mark disapproves of his statement (9.6). Moses and Elijah are the only individuals who were said to have spoken with God on Mount Sinai, but now Jesus takes God's place as the one with whom they converse. When God does speak, he confers the full authority of the eschatological revelation to his Son, Jesus (9.7). The overshadowing cloud signals a theophany.[36] The reference to this cloud therefore sets the reader up to expect a climax in a series of theophanies that include those involving Elijah and Moses. It is therefore somewhat surprising that God does not appear. Moses was allowed to see God's glory when all God's goodness passed before him and he could see God's back (Exod. 33.17-23). Elijah also witnessed God passing by when he heard sheer silence (1 Kgs 19.11-18). In Mark's transfiguration account, however, the presence of Jesus alone replaces the appearance of the Lord (Mk 9.8).

The traditions regarding Elijah and Moses both include unusual circumstances regarding their exit from this world. Elijah was taken up to heaven (2 Kgs 2.1-12), and Moses' grave was never found (Deut. 34.6). Moses was sometimes thought to have escaped death as well (**Josephus**, *Antiquities of the Jews* 4.326; *Testament of Moses*; *Babylonian Talmud Soṭah* 13b). In Mark's story they are present as heaven-dwellers (cf. *Apocalypse of Zephaniah* 9.4-5). Mark mentions Elijah before Moses (Matthew and Luke reverse the order), probably to highlight the eschatological nature of the transfiguration event. Elijah was the expected eschatological messenger (Mal. 4.5; **Sirach** 48.10-11; **4Q558** 1.ii.4-5), and in the closing verses of the book of Malachi he appears together with Moses (4.4-6), who is credited with an eschatological role alongside Elijah in later Jewish sources (**Midrash Rabbah Deuteronomy** 3.17). The presence of Elijah and Moses may therefore serve to announce the presence of God's eschatological intervention on earth. Many interpreters understand the transfiguration account as the fulfillment of Jesus' promise in 9.1, that some of the bystanders will see God's kingdom coming with power. If so, the overtones of God's eschatological intervention are even stronger.

Jesus' transformation (Gr. *metemorfothe*) has been compared to **Hellenistic** accounts of gods who appeared in human form and later were re-transformed to their divine glory. Mark's story is quite different in that it does not portray a god that has temporarily put on a veneer of human appearance, but a human being whose appearance is temporarily changed to that of a heavenly being. Mark explains that Jesus' transformation meant that his clothes became dazzling white (9.3). There is no indication, therefore, that the transformation is of an internal kind. Rather, it concerns specifically the changing of his external appearance.

But Mark, who otherwise delights in colorful detail, is remarkably reticent in describing this transformation. Unlike Matthew and Luke, he makes no reference to Jesus' face, but is content to note the extraordinary whiteness of Jesus' clothes. Commentators have compared this element to the radiance of the righteous in God's eschatological judgment, but the relevant evidence does not mention white clothing, with which Mark is so fascinated.[37] The high priest was also known for his splendid robe (**Sirach** 50.11), but his glory is related to the sparkling stones on his breastplate (***Letter of Aristeas*** 97; ***Liber Antiquitate Biblicarum*** 26.9; **Josephus**, *Antiquities of the Jews* 3.216-217), not the whiteness of his clothes. Closer parallels to the transfiguration scene are found in Daniel's vision of the Ancient One (God), whose clothes were white as snow (Dan. 7.9; cf. ***1 Enoch*** 14.20), as well as in the common pictures of angels wearing white clothing (**2 Maccabees** 11.8; *1 Enoch* 71.1; *Liber Antiquitate Biblicarum* 64.6; cf. Mk 16.5; Mt. 28.3; Jn 20.12; Acts 1.10). Mark's comment that no bleacher on earth can make clothes so white may of course be rhetorical hyperbole, but in the context of a heavenly revelation, it may just as well be an indication that Jesus is a heavenly being.

Mark's transfiguration narrative thus juxtaposes images where Jesus takes God's place in the eschatological scenario with the more clearly drawn distinction between Jesus and the Father, where God acknowledges him as his Son who speaks for him.

The Wicked Tenants

The next reference to Jesus' sonship is found in the parable of the wicked tenants (12.1-12), which follows the controversy with the Jewish leaders over Jesus' authority (11.27-33). The parable describes a vineyard owner who leased his property to tenants and later sent his slaves as well as his son to collect fruit from his vineyard. At the level of Mark's narrative, the parable functions as an allegory, and the meaning is straightforward. The vineyard is Israel, drawing on the image that is familiar from Isa. 5.1-7. The man is God, and the tenants are the Jewish leaders. The slaves are the prophets, who were rejected and mistreated by the Jewish elite. As the story moves towards its climax, the owner of the vineyard turns to his "beloved son." This term echoes God's address to Jesus at his baptism (1.11) and the transfiguration (9.7), which are the only two other instances where the Greek word *agapetos* ("beloved") occurs in the Gospel of Mark. The demise of the beloved son anticipates the execution of Jesus, initiated by the Sanhedrin. Psalm 118.22 is then invoked to show that God will vindicate his son and exact vengeance on the Jewish authorities.[38]

Spoken in the temple (11.27), the parable is Jesus' first public proclamation of himself as the Son of God. When he makes this proclamation, it is in the context of predicting his death, signaling that his divine sonship entails his suffering and crucifixion.

But there is a further Christological significance to this parable. It presents Jesus as the ultimate agent of God, bringing the ministry of the prophets to its culmination. An important distinction is made, however, between Jesus and God's messengers in the past. The latter are likened to the slaves of the vineyard owner, whereas Jesus is likened to the son. Implicitly, Jesus announces that he is more than a prophet. The difference between him and the prophets cannot be understood as a difference in function, because their functions are not any different – they are all messengers. Jesus is killed, but so is one of the previous messengers. The difference lies instead in their relationship to God. Jesus, as son, has a closer relationship to the Father. The language that Mark uses shows that the Son of God title belongs exclusively to Jesus. He is introduced in the parable with language that sets him apart. In Mk 12.6 the word "one" (Gr.: *hena*) is placed before the verb for emphasis (*eti hena eichen hion agapeton*).

Taken by itself, the parable does not enable us to say in what sense Jesus' relationship to God is unique. But in the narrative context, the Son of God title has been established as the most authoritative title for Jesus (cf. pp. 55, 60). The narrative has also established Jesus as the one who appears in the role of God, yet is subordinate to him. In this narrative context, it may be warranted to see in the parable's son metaphor a metaphor that is able to explain the unique relationship between Jesus and God. In the parable, the son is distinct from the owner and clearly subordinate to him, as the owner is the one who sends him. As the owner's only son, he is the heir (v. 7) and therefore the one who one day will take the place of the owner. The son metaphor may thus explain how Jesus can be simultaneously subordinate and equal to God.

Jesus' prayer in Gethsemane also shows that sonship is associated with obedience and willingness to die: "Abba, Father, for you all things are possible; remove this cup from me; yet, not what I want, but what you want" (14.36). In this prayer, which is the only prayer of Jesus found in the Gospel of Mark, Jesus expresses his complete submission to his father's will, even to the point of death.

The High Priest's Question

As the Jewish Sanhedrin is about to hand Jesus over to his death, the High Priest brings up the question of Jesus' sonship again. He asks: "Are you the Messiah, the Son of the Blessed One?" (14.61). "The Blessed One" must here be understood as a Jewish circumlocution for God, and the two titles "Messiah" and "Son of the Blessed One" qualify each other. The question then concerns whether Jesus is the royal Messiah, who could also be named Son of God.

Jesus answers in the affirmative, but provides a further elaboration of his own: "I am; and 'you will see the Son of Man seated at the right hand of the Power', and 'coming with the clouds of heaven'" (14.62). With this quotation from Ps. 110.1 and Dan. 7.13, Jesus gives an **apocalyptic** interpretation of his messiahship and sonship. He is a heavenly son of God. In Daniel 7, the Son of Man represents the vindication of the people of God, and in the context of Jesus' trial the connotations of vindication are obvious. Here, not only vindication is in view, but also the thought of Jesus as the ultimate judge. The image of the heavenly Son of Man is combined with the image from Ps. 110.1, of the one seated at the right hand of the Lord. In the context of Mark's Gospel, Jesus has recently described the coming of the Son of Man as the eschatological judge (13.26-27). As a response to the council that is about to pass judgment on him, therefore, Jesus' statement in effect turns the tables on them: you are not the ultimate judge of me; I am the heavenly judge that you will have to acknowledge.

The idea of a human character seated at the right hand of God is rare in **Second Temple Judaism**. The angels normally stand before God's throne, but Moses (**Ezekiel the Tragedian** 68-82) and David (**4Q504** 1-2.iv.5-8) can be envisioned as seated on heavenly thrones. These thrones, however, are symbolic of their earthly rule, not eschatological thrones that are superior to any earthly throne, as Jesus describes here. The closest parallel to Jesus' statement is found in the **Similitudes** of *1 Enoch*, where the Son of Man is seated on God's throne (*1 Enoch* 51.3; 55.4; 61.8).[39]

Jesus' only affirmation of his sonship in Mark's Gospel therefore confirms the picture that has already emerged. The Son of God is the Messiah, but his sonship also goes beyond conventional ideas of messiahship (cf. Mk 12.35-37). That something more than messiahship is implied is confirmed by the reaction of the high priest. He tears his clothes and concludes that Jesus is guilty of blasphemy (14.63-64). A claim to be the Messiah is unlikely to have provoked this reaction, as such a claim was not considered blasphemous. Jesus must have been understood to be overstepping the divine–human divide. In his answer to the high priest, Jesus appears in unprecedented proximity to God and stands in God's place in his interaction with the world.

The Roman Centurion

As is widely recognized, the climax of Mark's description of Jesus' identity is the confession of the Roman centurion: "Truly this man was God's Son!" (15.39). This confession follows immediately after the tearing of the temple curtain (15.38), a dramatic event that recalls the tearing apart of the heavens at Jesus' baptism (1.10). In Jewish tradition, the temple curtain came to represent heaven (**4Q405** 15.ii-16.3-5; **Josephus**, *Jewish War* 5.214).[40] As the tearing of the heavens at Jesus' baptism prepared for the heavenly voice to identify him as his Son, so does the tearing of the veil enable the centurion to identify Jesus as God's Son. The revelation of Jesus' identity is now complete, and this revelation is so compelling that it is spontaneously comprehended by an outsider, a Gentile. Significantly, the centurion's confession takes place at the time of Jesus' death. Mark thereby ties the true identity of Jesus specifically to the cross. Jesus' divine sonship means unwavering obedience to the Father's will (Mk 14.36) and is defined by his suffering and death.

As Frank Matera has shown, in Jesus' death the Son of God title has significant royal messianic overtones. There is a narrative contrast between the confession of the centurion (15.39) on the one hand and the mockery by the soldiers (15.16-20), the criminals on the cross (15.27-32), and the bystanders (15.35-36) on the other. As the soldiers and the criminals both mock Jesus as king, so must the confession of the centurion pertain to Jesus' kingship. Mark has already connected sonship and messiahship at Jesus' trial (14.61), and in Mark's crucifixion account Jesus is called king of the Jews or king of Israel no fewer than six times (15.2, 9, 12, 18, 26, 32).[41]

However, Mark's narrative also points beyond a messianic sense. Mark does not merely tie the centurion's conviction to the fact that Jesus died. It was the specific way in which Jesus expired ("in this way," Gr.: *houtos exepneusen*; Mk 15.39). In Mark's account, Jesus expired with a loud cry (15.37). As he was hanging on a cross, Jesus' death may have been caused by shock caused by blood loss and dehydration, or by asphyxiation.[42] In such a state, he would not have been able to make a loud cry. This cry is another element of Mark's story that shows Jesus' powers to be more than merely human. The tearing of the temple curtain that was effected by the cry (15.38) and the note about darkness at noon (15.33) make the same point. Darkening of the sun was a well-known **apocalyptic** image for God's own intervention.[43] When the centurion recognizes that Jesus is God's Son, his recognition is caused by the demonstration of powers that have no natural explanation. In Mark's account, Jesus' sonship is not merely a predication of his privileged relationship or his unique mission. His sonship pertains to his powers, powers that are not of this world. It is inadequate, therefore, to see the centurion's exclamation as prompted merely by Jesus' radical obedience.

It is no wonder that the Son of God title is the chief title for Jesus in Mark's Gospel. In the Son of God all the expectations regarding God's eschatological agent are crystallized. It is also as the Son of God that Jesus defeats the cosmic evil forces and brings the new world order. This title shows Jesus as more than a human being. As Son, Jesus shares the glory of the Father and emerges as his equal.

Privilege is not the primary connotation of Jesus' sonship, however. As the only Son, Jesus corresponds to Isaac in his willingness to be sacrificed. As the only Son, Jesus is rejected and killed by the leaders of Israel. The meaning of Jesus' sonship is therefore inextricably tied to his death, and only recognized by human beings in light of his ultimate sacrifice on the cross.

"The Messianic secret"

In Mark's telling of the story of Jesus, Jesus' true identity is known by the demons and by God in heaven. By reporting what the heavenly voice and the demons said to Jesus, the narrator is able to communicate this knowledge to the audience. But the human characters in the Gospel do not share this knowledge.[44] Mark thus juxtaposes two perspectives on Jesus: from above and from below. Mark's audience is given privileged information with which to interpret the events that unfold in the narrative. They can understand the acts of Jesus as the acts of God's Son and therefore need not be surprised when Jesus casts out demons, forgives sins, knows the unspoken thoughts of others, stills the storm, heals the sick, and raises the dead.

Even though Jesus' identity remains hidden to the human beings in Mark's story, the demons betray a clear awareness of who he is (Mk 3.11; 5.7). Jesus' sonship, then, is concealed from human beings, but announced by God and frighteningly perceived by demons. As spiritual beings, they have an insight that human beings lack.

The human characters in Mark's story, on the other hand, are not so privileged. Jesus' identity therefore remains a riddle to them (cf. Mk 1.22, 27; 2.7; 4.41; 6.2-3, 14-15; 8.27-28). Corresponding to this focus on the ignorance of the crowds, Mark has made extensive use of the theme of secrecy: Jesus repeatedly withdraws to lonely places and he frequently urges that his activities and identity be kept secret. Since the influential work of William Wrede, first published in German in 1901, this so-called messianic secret is one of the most debated issues in New Testament scholarship.[45] According to Wrede, there are four themes in Mark's Gospel that are interrelated and must be explained together: 1) Jesus' commands to silence (1.25, 1.34, 43-45; 3.12; 5.43; 7.24, 36; 8.26, 30; 9.9, 30); 2) his statement that the meaning of the parables remains hidden to outsiders (4.10-12); 3) the disciples' lack of understanding (4.13; 6.52; 7.18; 8.17, 21; 9.32); and 4) Jesus' tendency towards withdrawal (1.35, 45; 3.7, 13; 5.37, 40; 7.33; 8.23). Wrede argued that all of these themes were a creation of the early Christian community (even before the composition of the Gospels) and that they were all meant to explain why none of those who had met Jesus remembered that he had claimed to be the Messiah. Wrede also thought that Jesus never claimed to be the Messiah, but that the early church recognized him as the Messiah when they believed he had been resurrected.[46]

When we focus on the context of Mark's Gospel, there is now broad agreement that the messianic secret motif must be understood as a literary device, but there is disagreement as to what the purpose is and whether all the examples of the motif have the same function. There is also relatively broad agreement that it is misleading to group all of Wrede's four themes together. The dullness of the disciples and the significance of the parables are best treated as independent ideas, even though they may be related to the secrecy motif.

As for the commands to silence and Jesus' tendency towards withdrawal, several scholars have observed that the "messianic secret" is something of a misnomer. In most of these cases, Jesus' messiahship is not in view. Instead, the secret concerns Jesus' identity and specifically actions that reveal his identity. It would therefore be better to discuss it as the secret of Jesus' identity.[47]

Perhaps the most popular explanation for the secrecy motif is what Heikki Räisänen calls the "theology of the cross" interpretation: Jesus' messiahship could only be understood correctly in light of the cross, hence the commandment to wait until after the resurrection to announce it (9.9). As we have seen above (pp. 53-54), suffering is essential to messiahship, and Jesus may have kept a low profile in order not to be associated with inadequate expectations of the Messiah. In the context of Mark's Gospel, however, this interpretation cannot fully account for the commands to silence. True, Jesus' messiahship becomes increasingly public as he goes to Jerusalem, but the commands to silence do little to keep his identity a secret up to this point. On the contrary, some of these commands are disobeyed and rather enhance than restrict the spread of Jesus' fame (Mk 1.43-45; 7.36). Moreover, Jesus' identity is never kept secret; it is revealed through his actions, such as his casting out demons (1.21-28) and his forgiveness of sins (2.1-12). At the literary level, therefore, the "theology of the cross" interpretation alone cannot explain the secrecy motif.

Many scholars agree that the secrecy motif at least partly functions to highlight the extraordinary nature of Jesus' works.[48] Jesus did not seek fame, but his popularity could not be contained. Even though Jesus withdrew from the crowds, the crowds sought him out and came to him (6.31-33; 7.24). He instructed people not to tell anyone about what he had done for them, but these commands were frequently disobeyed. The point is similar: even though Jesus did not want his actions to be known, people could not help themselves, and his fame spread everywhere (1.43-45; 7.36). The nature of his works was such that his fame could not be restricted.

In Mark's story, however, not all the commands to silence are disobeyed. There is broad agreement that the commands that are disobeyed serve to heighten the impression of the spectacular nature of Jesus' ministry. But there is less agreement concerning the commands that are obeyed. This book will put forward the proposal that their literary purpose can be understood in broadly the same way as the commands that are disobeyed.

All the commands to silence that are disobeyed concern the actions of Jesus, but the commands that are obeyed all concern his identity. The demons are not allowed to speak because they know Jesus to be the Son of God (1.25, 34; 3.12). The disciples are commanded not to tell anyone that he is the Messiah (8.30), and they are prohibited from telling others about the heavenly voice that identified Jesus as his Son (9.9). Before his entrance into Jerusalem, Jesus is never identified to the public. The only statement regarding his identity that is not silenced is the heavenly voice at his baptism (1.11). But in Mark's story the voice addresses Jesus, not the bystanders.[49] The commands to silence that are obeyed therefore serve to remind the audience that the crowds are ignorant with respect to Jesus' identity.

Nevertheless, people consistently respond to Jesus with wonder, awe, and fear.[50] To Mark, this reaction is appropriate, but it is not sufficient. Its value depends on whether it is coupled with genuine faith, as in the case of the hemorrhaging woman (5.33-34), or not. In and of itself, fear is neither viewed exclusively positively nor exclusively negatively, therefore. What is important for our present purposes, however, is that this kind of fear is the way people are known to respond when they are faced with the numinous. Mark thus shows that even otherwise unwitting characters are compelled to respond to Jesus as one would respond to the divine.

In Mark's literary context, the commands that were obeyed also show what an extraordinary person Jesus was. Jesus' silencing command to his disciples takes place after Peter's confession of him as the Messiah (8.30). The next event in Mark's Gospel is the transformation on the mountain (9.2-8). This story is followed by yet another command to silence (9.9). After a brief conversation between Jesus and the disciples regarding the role of Elijah (9.11-13), the crowd comes to gather around them (9.14). Before any form of interaction has taken place, "when the whole crowd saw him, they were immediately overcome with awe" (9.15). The word Mark uses here (Gr.: *exethambethesan*) is the strongest expression he has for astonishment. It is quite unusual in the Greek dialect in which the New Testament is written (Koine). Mark only uses this word on two other occasions: to describe Jesus' anguish in Gethsemane (14.33) and the women's reaction after the resurrection (16.5, 6). The word is particularly appropriate to describe the reaction to a **theophany**. What is so striking about Mark's usage in 9.15 is that it is prompted by the mere appearance of Jesus. The crowd has not witnessed any miracles and there is no indication that there are any lingering effects of the transfiguration. Mark thus presses the point that the mere presence of Jesus compels even outsiders to respond to him as they would respond to an encounter with God. Just as the commands to silence that are disobeyed show the extraordinary character of Jesus' works, so do the commands that are obeyed show the extraordinary character of Jesus' person.

The blind Bartimaeus also has an extraordinary way of responding to Jesus. In the literary context of Mark's Gospel, Bartimaeus is the first human being to address Jesus publicly with a messianic title: "son of David" (Mk 10.47). But the way he phrases his address to Jesus implies that Jesus is more than a son of David. The cry "have mercy on me" was frequently directed to God, but very rarely addressed to human beings.[51]

Although the crowds are faced with the Son of God and in some ways even respond accordingly, they still do not recognize him for who he is. His identity remains elusive to them. The Jewish authorities are more apt at perceiving what Jesus claims for himself (2.7), but they outright reject him. Both in their own way, the crowds as well as the Jewish leaders fulfill the dictum of 4.11b-12: "for those outside, everything comes in parables; in order that 'they may indeed look, but not perceive, and may indeed listen, but not understand; so that they may not turn again and be forgiven.'"

Their failure to perceive is not for lack of proof, however. The Gospel of Mark reports time and again how Jesus demonstrates who he is, and the Gospel can to some extent be seen as a demonstration of the compelling nature of Jesus' sonship. As Jesus' sonship is fully revealed on the cross, the climax of the Gospel is reached when the Roman centurion confesses him to be God's Son (15.39). At that point, Jesus' divine sonship is so compelling that it is recognized by a complete outsider, a Gentile executioner of Jesus.

Conclusion

Jesus' identity, which only slowly and gradually becomes known to the characters in Mark's Gospel, is revealed to Mark's audience from the very beginning. Mark hints at it by using the term "gospel" for his Jesus biography and by invoking the picture of God's eschatological coming to earth. Jesus' ministry then unfolds as the eschatological fulfillment of Old Testament prophecies, defeating the evil army and establishing the new creation. When Jesus appears in a **theophany** at the Sea of Galilee, it is clear that Jesus' ministry represents the coming of God to earth. With clever ambiguity, Mark also shows that Jesus shares the name of the Lord.

Even though Jesus is God's equal, he is also God's servant, as Mark shows by painting him as the Messiah and the Servant of the Lord. As the Son of God, Jesus submits to his Father and obediently goes to the cross. But the Son of God is also the divine warrior who defeats God's cosmic enemies and brings the new world order. He has a relationship with the Father that is an essentially different relationship from that of everyone else; he even shares the Father's glory and is his sole heir, and can therefore take the Father's place. The tension between Jesus' equality with and subordination to the Father is never fully resolved in Mark's Gospel, even though the sonship metaphor is able to combine both ideas.

With a careful use of the theme of secrecy, Mark also shows the compelling nature of Jesus' person. His fame could not be contained and people had to respond to him as to the divine – even unwittingly. Mark's secrecy theme also links Jesus' identity inextricably to his sacrifice. Only in light of the cross can human beings know him as the Son of God.

Notes

1   Rikk E. Watts, *Isaiah's New Exodus in Mark*, WUNT II/88 (Tübingen: Mohr Siebeck, 1997).

2   See further Sigurd Grindheim, *God's Equal: What Can We Know About Jesus' Self-Understanding?* LNTS 446 (London: T & T Clark, 2011), 53–8.

3   See further ibid., 6–39.

4   Cf. Isa. 27.1; 51.9; Ps. 74.13-14; *1 Enoch* 54.4-5; 60.7-10; *Sibylline Oracles* 3.71-74; *Testament of Levi* 18.12; *Testament of Dan* 5.10-13; *Testament of Zebulon* 9.8; **Testament of Simeon** 6.6; *Testament of Moses* 10.1, 3; *2 Baruch* 29.4; 1QS 3.20-22; 1QM 1.1. Mark's story of the Gerasene demoniac (Mk 5.1-20) gives us a good example of his perspective. The conflict is described with military terminology, most clearly in the name of the demon, which is "Legion" (5.9). The connection between the demons and the swine may be an indication that Mark associates the demons with idolatry, as swine were connected with idol worship (**1 Maccabees** 1.47). Demons were commonly understood as the reality that stood behind idolatry (Deut. 32.17; Ps. 106.37; Isa. 8.19; 19.3; Ps. 96.5; Isa. 65.3, 11 **LXX**; **Baruch** 4.7; *Jubilees* 1.11; 11.4-6; 12.20; 22.17; *1 Enoch* 19.1; 99.6-10; cf. 1 Cor. 10.20; Rev. 9.20). Whereas Isaiah saw idolatrous nations as the enemies of Israel, Mark may have seen demonic forces as the real enemies. See further Watts, *Isaiah's New Exodus in Mark*, 157–60.

5   In his prologue, Mark may be providing a preview of Jesus as the divine warrior who ushers in the new creation. The temptation account shows him engaged directly in conflict with Satan. He is also set in the wilderness with wild beasts, evidently unharmed (1.13). In Mark, the Greek expression *eimi meta tinos* normally refers to friendly association (3.14; 5.18; 14.67; cf. 4.36). Plausibly, therefore, the note is meant to invoke the picture of the new world order as portrayed in Isa. 11.6-9; 65.25; Hos. 2.18 (cf. *Sibylline Oracles* 3.788-795; *2 Baruch* 73.6; **Philo**, *On Rewards and Punishments* 87-90). Cf. Richard Bauckham, "Jesus and the Wild Animals (Mark 1:13): A Christological Image for an Ecological Age," in *Jesus of Nazareth: Lord and Christ: Essays on the Historical Jesus and New Testament Christology*, ed. Joel B. Green and Max Turner (Grand Rapids: Eerdmans, 1994), 14–19; Joel Marcus, *Mark 1–8: A New Translation with Introduction and Commentary*, AB 27 (New York: Doubleday, 2000), 168–70.

6   See further Howard Clark Kee, "The Terminology of Mark's Exorcism Stories," *NTS* 14 (1968): 235–41.

7   See **1Q16** 9-10.2; **1QH**[a] 22.6; **4Q169** 1-2.3; **4Q463** 2.3; **4Q491** 8-10.i.7. In all the instances where *ga'ar* occurs in the **Qumran** Scrolls, the translation "eradicate" or something very similar will be appropriate.

8   According to Graham Twelftree, Lk. 11.20/Mt. 12.28 represents the earliest use of the Greek word *ekballo* for exorcism (*Jesus the Exorcist: A Contribution to the Study of the Historical Jesus*, WUNT II/54 [Tübingen: Mohr Siebeck, 1993], 109).

9 See the **Septuagint**'s translation in Exod. 23.28-30; 33.2; 34.11, 24; Deut. 11.23; 29.27 (ET: 29.28); 33.27; Josh. 24.12, 18; Judg. 6.9; 2 Sam. 7.23; 1 Chron. 17.21; Pss. 43.3 (ET: 43.2); 77.55; 79.9 (ET: 79.8). Cf. Twelftree, *Jesus the Exorcist*, 110.

10 With Jesus as the agent or subject, the verb *didasko* ("to teach") occurs 15 times in Mark's Gospel, compared to only 10 times in Matthew and 15 times in Luke, both of which are considerably longer than Mark. Similarly, the noun *didache* ("teaching") is used five times about Jesus' teaching in Mark, compared to only twice in Matthew and once in Luke.

11 See further Edwin K. Broadhead, *Teaching with Authority: Miracles and Christology in the Gospel of Mark*, JSNTSup 74 (Sheffield: JSOT Press, 1992), 59.

12 See further Darrell L. Bock, "Blasphemy and the Jewish Examination of Jesus," in *Key Events in the Life of the Historical Jesus: A Collaborative Exploration of Context and Coherence*, ed. Darrell L. Bock and Robert L. Webb. WUNT 247 (Tübingen: Mohr Siebeck, 2009), 589–667.

13 See also Marcus, *Mark 1–8*, 222. Many scholars refer to one of the **Dead Sea Scrolls**, the *Prayer of Nabonidus* (**4Q242**), for an example of a Jewish text that shows that a human being could forgive sins. This scroll is fragmentary, and its interpretation is very uncertain. It is possible that it refers to an exorcist that forgave the sins of Nabonidus, but the differences between this text and Mk 2.1-12 are considerable. The surviving text of the *Prayer of Nabonidus* focuses exclusively on the healing of Nabonidus, not on his forgiveness. The word "sin" therefore functions as a synonym for "sickness" (by **metonymy**). Whereas "forgiveness" is simply another word for "healing" in the *Prayer of Nabonidus*, Mk 2.1-12 makes a decisive distinction between these two acts. See further Grindheim, *God's Equal*, 71–3.

14 See further Grindheim, *God's Equal*, 43–53.

15 See especially John Paul Heil, *Jesus Walking on the Sea: Meaning and Gospel Functions of Matt 14:22–33; Mark 6:45–52 and John 6:15b–21*, AnBib 87 (Rome: Biblical Institute Press, 1981).

16 See further Grindheim, *God's Equal*, 124–7.

17 The image of the darkening of the sun and the moon also occurs in Ezek. 32.7-8; Joel 2.10, 31; 3.15; Amos 8.9; *Sibylline Oracles* 3.801-803; *Testament of Moses* 10.5; *Testament of Levi* 4.1 in connection with the day of the Lord and the judgment that God will bring upon sinners. It becomes a stock image of God's eschatological intervention (Adela Yarbro Collins, *Mark: A Commentary*, Hermeneia [Minneapolis: Fortress, 2007], 614; Joel Marcus, *Mark 8–16: A New Translation with Introduction and Commentary*, AB 27A [New Haven: Yale University Press, 2009], 906–8).

18 Mark 13.27 is the clearest example from Mark's Gospel that Jesus will have the function of the eschatological judge. Jesus also refers to his function in the last judgment in 8.38, but it is not clear what this role will be. Jesus' cursing of the fig tree (Mark 11.13-14, 20-21) is also a symbolic act of judgment. However, these themes are toned down in Mark's Gospel compared to the important place they take in the Gospel of Matthew (see pp. 91-92).

19 Pss. 29.3-4; 63.2; 145.11; 1 Chron. 29.11; *1 Enoch* 63.3; *Apocalypse of Moses* 43.4; **1QS** 10.12; **1QH**[a] 13.20; 17.16-17; 18.10-11; 19.8; **4Q403** 1.i.37-38.

20 In a list together with other attributes, power and glory are also applied to king Nebuchadnezzar (Dan. 2.37; 4.30).

21 The angels were normally sent by God (Gen. 24.7, 40; Exod. 33.2; Num. 20.16; Ps. 78.49; 1 Chron. 21.15; 2 Chron. 32.21; Dan. 3.28; 6.22; *Jubilees* 5.6; *1 Enoch* 10.1; *2 Enoch* 21.3; 36.2; *2 Baruch* 6.6;

3 Baruch 1.3-4; 4.15; *Testament of Simeon* 2.8; *Testament of Levi* 5.3; *Life of Adam and Eve* 9.4; 31.2-3; 36.2; 40.3; 41.1; **4Q381** 29.2; **11Q11** 4.5; **Josephus**, *Antiquities of the Jews* 5.280). However, the archangel Michael is also known to send out angels (*1 Enoch* 60.4). The elect were chosen by God (Gen. 18.19; Deut. 4.37; 7.6-7; 10.15; 14.2; Isa. 41.8-9; 43.10, 20; 44.1-2; 45.4; 65.9, 15, 22; Ezek. 20.5; Pss. 33.12; 105.6, 43; 106.5; 135.4; 1 Chron. 16.13; *1 Enoch* 48.9; 56.6; 62.11-12; *Jubilees* 2.19; *Psalms of Solomon* 9.9; *Testament of Moses* 4.2; 1QpHab 9.12; 4Q534 1.10).

22 Jesus' feeding miracles (Mark 6.30-44; 8.1-10) may also play on messianic themes. There was an expectation among Jews that God in the messianic times would miraculously provide food (*2 Baruch* 29.8; **Mekilta** *Exodus* 16.25; **Midrash Rabbah Ecclesiastes** 1.28), as he had brought manna from heaven in the time of Moses (Exod. 16.1-36). If Mark's accounts should be read in light of these ideas, it is probably significant that Jesus on both of these occasions dismisses the crowds and disappears in a boat (Mark 6.45; 8.10). He did not seek public acclaim as the Messiah.

23 Theodore J. Weeden, *Mark – Traditions in Conflict* (Philadelphia: Fortress, 1971), 52–70.

24 Carl R. Holladay, Theios Aner *in Hellenistic-Judaism: A Critique of the Use of This Category in New Testament Christology*, SBLDS 40 (Missoula, MT: Scholars Press, 1977); Barry Blackburn, Theios Anēr *and the Markan Miracle Traditions: A Critique of the* Theios Anēr *Concept as an Interpretative Background of the Miracle Traditions Used by Mark*, WUNT II/40 (Tübingen: Mohr Siebeck, 1991).

25 Jack Dean Kingsbury, *The Christology of Mark's Gospel* (Philadelphia: Fortress, 1983). However, it is important to let all the titles contribute to our view of Jesus. Cf. Elizabeth Struthers Malbon, *Mark's Jesus: Characterization as Narrative Christology* (Waco, TX: Baylor University Press, 2009).

26 Casey has presented his research in a number of books and articles. This work is most fully developed and most helpfully available in Maurice Casey, *The Solution to the "Son of Man" Problem*, LNTS 343 (London: T & T Clark, 2007). For a critique of his conclusions, see especially the essays in Larry W. Hurtado and Paul L. Owen, ed., *Who is This Son of Man? The Latest Scholarship on a Puzzling Expression of the Historical Jesus*, LNTS 390 (London: T & T Clark, 2010).

27 In the book of Revelation, the appearance of Jesus is likened to a son of man (1.13; 14.14). "Son of man" is used without the definite article, and it is not a title. The article is also in lacking in Heb. 2.6, which quotes from Ps. 8.4 (NRSV translates "What are human beings that you are mindful of them").

28 Richard J. Bauckham, "The Son of Man: 'A Man in My Position' or 'Someone'," *JSNT* 2 (1985): 23–33.

29 For a more detailed account of my own assessment, see *God's Equal*, 190–99.

30 For a detailed discussion of the parallels, see Rikk E. Watts, "Jesus' Death, Isaiah 53, and Mark 10:45: A Crux Revisited," in *Jesus and the Suffering Servant: Isaiah 53 and Christian Origins*, ed. William H. Bellinger and William R. Farmer (Harrisburg, PA: Trinity Press International, 1998), 125–51; Craig A. Evans, *Mark 8:27–16:20*, WBC 34B (Nashville: Thomas Nelson, 2001), 120–22.

31 Internal criteria support the shorter reading, therefore, but external criteria favor the longer reading with the inclusion of the title. Whereas the first hand of Sinaiticus has the shorter reading, the longer reading is attested both in the Alexandrian (Vaticanus), Western (Bezae Cantabrigiensis and many Latin witnesses) and Byzantine tradition. For an insightful discussion, see especially

Peter M. Head, "A Text-Critical Study of Mark 1.1: 'The Beginning of the Gospel of Jesus Christ,'" *NTS* 37 (1991): 621–9.

32 For example Rudolf Bultmann, *History of the Synoptic Tradition*, tr. John Marsh (Oxford: Blackwell, 1963), 250–51; Ferdinand Hahn, *The Titles of Jesus in Christology: Their History in Early Christianity* (New York: World, 1969), 733–341; Adela Yarbro Collins, "Mark and His Readers: The Son of God Among Jews," *HTR* 92 (1999): 395.

33 Eduard Norden, *Agnostos Theos: Untersuchungen zur Formengeschichte religiöser Rede*, reprint, 1913 (Darmstadt: Wissenschaftliche Buchgesellschaft, 1974), 177–88.

34 Gerhard Kittel in Gerhard Kittel and Gerhard von Rad, "δοκέω κτλ," in *TDNT* 2.247.

35 For a detailed study of the transfiguration account, see especially John Paul Heil, *The Transfiguration of Jesus: Narrative Meaning and Function of Mark 9:2–8, Matt 17:1–8 and Luke 9:28–36*, AnBib 144 (Rome: Editrice Pontificio istituto biblico, 2000).

36 Cf. Exod. 16.10; 19.9, 16; 24.15-18; 34.5; 40.34-35; Num. 9.18, 22; Deut. 31.15; Ezek. 1.4-28.

37 See Dan. 12.3; *1 Enoch* 62.15-16; *4 Ezra* 2.39; *2 Enoch* 22.8; *2 Baruch* 51.1-3; **Martyrdom and Ascension of Isaiah** 9.9; **Apocalypse of Abraham** 13.14. In the book of Revelation the righteous are also given white robes (7.9, 13-14; cf. 3.4-5, 18; 6.11), but the theme of clothes washed in the blood of the Lamb is clearly a later Christian development.

38 On this parable, see especially Klyne Snodgrass, *The Parable of the Wicked Tenants: An Inquiry into Parable Interpretation*, WUNT 27 (Tübingen: Mohr Siebeck, 1983).

39 See further Martin Hengel, "'Sit at My Right Hand!' The Enthronement of Christ and the Right Hand of God and Psalm 110.1," in *Studies in Early Christology* (Edinburgh: T & T Clark, 1995), 175–214; Richard Bauckham, *God Crucified: Monotheism and Christology in the New Testament* (Grand Rapids: Eerdmans, 1999), 19–20.

40 The curtain that is in view here is most likely the one separating the Holy Place from the Holy of Holies, rather than the one covering the entrance to the temple building. For a discussion of the symbolic meaning of the veil in Jewish texts, see Daniel M. Gurtner, *The Torn Veil: Matthew's Exposition of the Death of Jesus*, SNTSMS 139 (Cambridge: Cambridge University Press, 2007), 72–96.

41 *The Kingship of Jesus: Composition and Theology in Mark 15*, SBLDS 66 (Chico, CA: Scholars Press, 1982), 135–45. Matera also points out that messiahship is a possible meaning of the son of God title in Judaism and that the title has a messianic sense at Jesus' baptism and transfiguration. At the baptism and the transfiguration, however, the title has much broader connotations than merely messiahship (cf. pp. 61-67).

42 Cf. the discussion in Raymond E. Brown, *The Death of the Messiah: A Commentary on the Passion Narratives in the Four Gospels*, vol. 2, ABRL (New York: Doubleday, 1994), 1088–92.

43 Ezek. 32.7; Joel 2.10, 31; 3.15; Amos 8.9; **Sibylline Oracles** 3.801-802; **Testament of Moses** 10.5; **Testament of Levi** 4.1.

44 Mark emphasizes that the demons know Jesus (1.24, 34). This information would be meaningless unless it is presupposed that the other characters in the story do not know him. Cf. William Wrede, *The Messianic Secret*, tr. J. C. G. Greig (Cambridge: James Clarke, 1971), 34.

45 Ibid.

46 For a discussion of the claims of the historical Jesus, see Grindheim, *God's Equal.*

47 Heikki Räisänen, *The "Messianic Secret" in Mark's Gospel*, tr. Christopher Tuckett, Studies of the New Testament and Its World (Edinburgh: T & T Clark, 1990), 48; Christopher M. Tuckett, "Messianic Secret," in *ABD* 4.798–99.

48 Hans Jürgen Ebeling suggested all the references to secrecy and the incomprehension of the audience served to show the profundity of the divine mystery (*Das Messiasgeheimnis und die Botschaft des Marcus-Evangelisten*, BZNW 19 [Berlin: Töpelmann, 1939], 168). No one has accepted this theory, but many scholars have followed Ebeling in seeing the motif as a device to exalt the gospel message. Adela Yarbro Collins understands the messianic secret as a literary device intended to show that Jesus' identity was both revealed and concealed (*Mark*, 172).

49 Note that Mark's version reads "with you I am well pleased" (Mark 1.11; so also Lk. 3.22), whereas Matthew has the voice address the audience: "with whom I am well pleased" (Mt. 3.17).

50 Mark 1.22, 27; 2.12; 3.21; 4.41; 5.15, 20, 33, 42; 6.2, 20, 50, 51; 7.37; 9.15; 10.32; 11.18; 12.17; 15.5.

51 For this prayer being addressed to God, see Isa. 30.19; 33.2; Pss. 6.2; 9.13; 25.16; 26.11; 27.7; 31.9; 41.4, 10; 51.1; 56.1; 57.1; 67.1; 86.3, 16; 119.29, 58, 132; 123.3; **Judith** 6.19; **Sirach** 36.1, 11 **LXX** (ET: 36: 1, 17); **Baruch** 3.2; *3 Maccabees* 6.12. I am only aware of one example where this petition is addressed to a human being (**2 Maccabees** 7.27). For this observation, I am grateful to my colleague Bulti Fayissa.

3

God's Presence: Christology in Matthew's Gospel

Whereas Mark introduces Jesus as the fulfillment of prophecies regarding God's coming to earth, Matthew uses his infancy narrative to show the significance of Jesus' person. Matthew dwells on the names that were given to the child: Jesus and Emmanuel. The latter introduces the theme of Jesus as the presence of God, a theme that Matthew continues to emphasize throughout his Gospel. He shows that Jesus promises to be eternally present with his disciples, effectively replacing God's own presence with his people. However, this exalted view of Jesus does not hold Matthew back from portraying Jesus as God's agent, filling the role of God's great servants: the Messiah, Israel, Moses, Israel's shepherd, and the Servant of the Lord. Matthew also has a broader repertoire than Mark with which to fill in the picture of Jesus as the Son of God, a theme he combines with ideas from the Jewish wisdom tradition.

The presence of God and the names of Jesus

Jesus

When Matthew describes the annunciation of Jesus' birth, the main emphasis falls on the names that will be given to the child. An angel conveniently explains the events to Joseph, and this angel tells him to name the child Jesus (Mt. 1.21). This name is a Greek rendering of the Hebrew Jeshua, a later form of Joshua. According to popular etymology, the meaning of this name was "Yahweh saves" or "Yahweh is salvation." The angel in Matthew's story explains the significance of Jesus' name accordingly: "he will save his people from their sins" (1.21).

Matthew's explanation of the name is striking. He does not say that Jesus' name meant that God would save his people, but that Jesus would save his people. The act of salvation would be attributed to God according to the popular etymology of the name. But Matthew gives this role to Jesus himself. Jesus – not Yahweh – is now the agent of salvation.

In the Scriptures of Israel, the one who saves the people of Israel is normally God.[1] But there are exceptions. The judges (Judg. 3.9, 15, 31; 6.14; 8.22; 10.1; 13.5; Neh. 9.27), Saul (1 Sam. 9.16), and David (1 Sam. 23.2, 5) are all credited with the salvation of Israel. The story of Gideon, however, explains that God is the one who saves, and that Gideon is merely a tool in his hand (Judg. 6.36, 37; 7.2, 7). Nevertheless, Gideon is said to save the people of Israel (Judg. 8.22).

In the biblical story of Joshua, the focus is even more sharply on God's sovereign intervention. The Lord is the one who defeats the inhabitants of the land (Josh. 3.10; 6.2; 8.1; 10.8; 11.6). But later tradition is more forthright in highlighting Joshua's personal role. According to the Hebrew text of **Sirach** 46.1, Joshua became a "great salvation for his [God's] elect." The Greek text, however, may be seen to safeguard against a direct identification of Joshua as Israel's savior. It reads instead that Joshua became, according to his name, "great for the salvation of his [God's] elect."[2]

This brief survey of the background material is enough to show that the predominant tendency was to distinguish between God as the ultimate savior and the human agent of this salvation. But it is not completely unprecedented to speak unguardedly about human characters as saviors. It is possible, therefore, that Mt. 1.21 should be understood along similar lines as the Hebrew text of **Sirach** 46.1 and that Jesus is introduced as the new Joshua, God's agent of salvation.

The immediate context in Mt. 1.21, however, militates against such an interpretation. The child is given the name Jesus, not only because he will be a savior, but because he will save his people from their sins. The people in question are God's people, but Matthew refers to this people as Jesus' people. We are here faced with a distinctly Matthean focus. A comparison with Luke is illuminating. Luke also uses his infancy narrative to announce the salvific function of the newborn child (1.69; 2.11). In connection with Jesus' birth and in a statement quite similar to Mt. 1.21, Luke has Zechariah say that the Lord will "give knowledge of salvation to his people by the forgiveness of their sins" (1.77). Whereas the pronoun "his" in Luke clearly refers to God and the people thus are seen as God's people, Matthew announces that Jesus will save his own people. The qualification of Jesus' saving act as a salvation from sins also sets him apart from human saviors in Israel's past. Joshua, the judges, and David could save from hostile nations, but salvation from sin is the prerogative of the Lord (Ps. 79.9; Ezek. 37.23), the only savior (Isa. 43.11; 45.21).

When Jesus is made both the subject of the verb "to save" and the referent of the pronoun "his" in "his people," Matthew's description transcends that of human agents in the history of Israel. As savior, Jesus takes God's own place.

Emmanuel

This point is strengthened in the second name that Matthew gives to Jesus, based on the prophecy in Isaiah 7.14. According to Matthew, Jesus' birth "took place to fulfill what had been spoken by the Lord through the prophet: 'Look, the virgin shall conceive and bear a son, and they shall name him Emmanuel, which means, "God is with us"'" (Mt. 1.22-23). Matthew's translation of the name Emmanuel consists of a clause without any verb: "God with us" (Gr.: *meth hemon ho theos*; English translations often supply the verb "is"). If his translation is understood strictly literally, the prepositional phrase "with us" should be taken as an adjective that modifies the noun, God. The meaning is then that Jesus is God with us. In other words, he is called by God's name, much like in Jn 1.1; 20.28. However, this is not the only possible interpretation. In Greek, the verb is often implied, even if it is unexpressed. We may therefore be justified in supplying the verb "is" and translating "God is with us." The name will then express the hope or conviction that God is with his people.

Scholarly opinion is divided between these two options. The case against the "God with us" interpretation is summarized by John Nolland, who lists five arguments against it: 1) in the Scriptures of Israel, names given from heaven denote the actions of God; 2) a different word order would have been expected for the translation "God with us;" 3) the two names Jesus and Emmanuel both signify what God will do; 4) Matthew's argument in this context is that Jesus comes from the house of David and an assertion that he is God would be out of place; 5) it is too early in the narrative to make such a grand statement about Jesus.[3]

The first argument carries little weight, as it is the Matthean context that is decisive for the meaning in Matthew. As for the third argument, the parallel with the name Jesus actually serves as an argument in favor of the adjectival interpretation. As I have shown above, the giving of the name Jesus draws attention to Jesus' own work of salvation, directed at his own people. Nolland's fourth and fifth arguments are based on his understanding of the progress of Matthew's story. In response, I will argue below that Matthew's story unpacks the meaning of the name Emmanuel and shows that Jesus brings the presence of God. In 1.23, Matthew introduces a name that can only be fully understood in light of the whole Gospel. Although the material in Matthew 1 serves to situate Jesus within Israel and connect him with the Davidic promises, the naming account also leads into the story about the magi, a story that shows the significance of Jesus beyond Israel and even may show him being worshiped.

Nolland's second argument is based on grammar.[4] In response, it should be noted that Matthew's order is determined by the fact that he is providing a word-for-word translation of the Hebrew *immanu el*. He may also be alluding to Isa. 8.8, 10, where Isaiah provides a play on the name of the child, assuring that "God is with us" (*meth hemon ho theos* in the **Septuagint**). In borrowing Isaiah's language, Matthew has changed its meaning. The phrase is no longer an assurance of God's presence – it is the interpretation of the child's name.[5]

W. D. Davies and Dale C. Allison, who have written the leading English commentary on the Gospel of Matthew, present two theological arguments. The first argument is that the New Testament rarely calls Jesus God and that, apart from Mt. 1.23, Matthew never does so. But evidence cannot be dismissed merely based on the observation that it is unique. The second argument is that Matthew still may have seen Jesus as "the fullest embodiment or vehicle of the divine purpose and love and yet have perceived him as less than God." This argument amounts to a claim that it is possible that Matthew would not have called Jesus God.[6]

However, the discussion above only goes to show that the translation "God is with us" is not the only possible one. The positive arguments in favor of translating "God with us" are based on **narrative criticism**.[7] The interpretation of Jesus' name in Matthew's introduction (1.23) corresponds to Jesus' promise of his own constant presence with his disciples at the very end of the Gospel (28.20).[8] If these verses are read together, 28.20 explains the presence of God in 1.23 as the presence of Jesus. Such an interpretation is consistent with the general outlook of Matthew's Gospel. God is not described as being present with the disciples; he is in heaven (18.10, 19; 23.9). In contrast, there is a strong focus on Jesus' presence with his disciples throughout Matthew's Gospel (10.40; 18.20; 25.31-46; 28.20). These facts should be coupled with the observation that Matthew typically uses the preposition *meta* in the sense "in the company of" rather than "on behalf of."[9] That makes it unlikely that Matthew would speak of the Father being *meta* his people. One might object that this interpretation would have demanded a lot of the readers or audience of Matthew's Gospel. However, if the Gospel of Matthew were intended for **catechetical** use, repeated hearings may have helped the audience to understand the beginning in light of the thought world of the Gospel as a whole. They may then have recognized the connection between 1.23 and 28.20.

If Matthew invested the name with such significance, the reason for his mention of Jesus' virginal conception becomes clear. Matthew introduces the quotation from Isa. 7.14 to explain that Jesus' conception by the Holy Spirit was in fulfillment of Scripture. Unlike Luke, however, Matthew does not connect Jesus' miraculous conception with the fact that he was the Son of God. Rather, he connects it with the name Emmanuel. Through a miraculous, creative act of the Holy Spirit, God's dynamic presence on earth is now in the person of Jesus.

As W. C. van Unnik has shown, the Scriptural formula "God is with you" implies more than mere presence. It is a dynamic concept, denoting God's active assistance in a tangible way. Specifically, it may imply protection, deliverance, showing favor, blessing and success, assurance against fear, and exhortation to courage. It is not normally predicated of the whole people, but of select individuals, such as Joseph, Moses, the judges, Saul, and David, who were endowed with the Holy Spirit.[10] Against this background, Matthew proclaims that as God previously was dynamically present by his Spirit, so is he now present in Jesus. In contrast to Luke and John, Matthew prefers to speak of Jesus' own continued presence with his disciples, rather than the presence of the Spirit. Especially noteworthy is the explicit connection in the **Septuagint** between "God being with" and salvation (Gen. 35.3; Deut. 20.4; Jer. 15.20; 49.11 (ET: 42.11); 2 Chron. 32.8). Matthew's two names for Jesus therefore reinforce each other and make the same point: as God has been with his chosen ones in the past to save them, so is the presence of God now found in Jesus, who is with his people to save them.

In 18.20, Jesus promises his constant presence with his disciples, a promise that contrasts somewhat with statements anticipating his absence (25.14, 19; 26.11). This presence can therefore hardly be explained as a continuation of the resurrection appearances, but is best understood as a parallel to the idea of God's presence with his people.

Much scholarly discussion has centered around the relationship between Mt. 18.20 and a statement from the **Mishnah**. Regarding God's presence, the **Shekinah**, Rabbi Hananiah ben Teradion says: "But two who are sitting, and words of Torah do pass between them – the Presence is with them" (**Mishnah Avot** 3.2).[11] As Rabbi Hananiah ben Teradion died ca 135 CE, it is uncertain whether this tradition is older than the Gospel of Matthew.

Nevertheless, the similarities between his saying and Mt. 18.20 have led many scholars to conclude that the same tradition inspired both Matthew and Rabbi Hananiah. If Jesus' words were without precedence in Jewish tradition, it becomes difficult to explain the origin of Hananiah's statement. It is possible that *Mishnah Avot* 3.2 is dependent upon the Jesus tradition and that this important Jewish concept originated as anti-Christian polemic. But that is considered unlikely. Most scholars think it is more likely that the Christian tradition has substituted Jesus for the Shekinah. In any case, whether or not there is dependence one way or the other, the similarity is an indication that Mt. 18.20 speaks of Jesus' presence in a way that Jews could have spoken of God's presence.

Jesus' Eternal Presence with His Disciples

The understanding of Jesus' presence as the divine presence also underlies the last words that Jesus speaks to his disciples in the Gospel of Matthew: "all authority in heaven and on earth has been given to me. Go therefore and make disciples of all nations, baptizing them in the name of the Father and of the Son and of the Holy Spirit, and teaching them to obey everything that I have commanded you. And remember, I am with you always, to the end of the age" (Mt. 28.18b-20).

The clearest Scriptural echo in this Great Commission is from Daniel's vision of the Son of Man. As the Son of Man was given dominion and glory and kingship (Dan. 7.14), so does Jesus proclaim that all authority in heaven and on earth has been given to him (Mt. 28.18b). Jesus' claims transcend the Danielic image, however. Whereas the Danielic Son of Man was given authority so that "all peoples, nations and languages should serve him" (Dan. 7.14), Jesus explicitly claims authority not only on earth but also in heaven (Mt. 28.18b). Whereas the Danielic Son of Man is presented before the Ancient One (Dan. 7.13), Jesus is not primarily seen on the receiving end, but as the one commissioning his disciples.

The structure of the commission has some affinities with other commissions in the Scriptures of Israel. The most similar ones include the commissioning of Joshua (Deut. 31.23; Josh. 1.1-9), of Solomon (1 Chron. 22.6-16), and of Jeremiah (Jer. 1.1-10). All of these accounts include the commandment to observe everything that God has commanded (Josh. 1.7; Jer. 1.7; 1 Chron. 22.13). All of them also give the promise of divine presence (Deut. 31.23; Josh. 1.9; 1 Chron. 22.16; Jer. 1.8).

Dale C. Allison has pointed out a number of important parallels between Jewish Moses traditions and Matthew's picture of Jesus. He stresses that the elements that are specifically Matthean – and not derived from tradition – are all evocative of Moses' commissioning of Joshua. As Matthean elements he includes the mountain scene, the instruction to go and make disciples, the command to observe everything and the promise of perpetual divine presence.[12] However, the Mosaic parallels regarding the theme of going are superficial. Joshua is promised the divine presence wherever he may go (Josh. 1.9). He is not given any commandment to go. Moreover, Allison does not pay due attention to the fact that the disciples fall down and worship Jesus (28.17; see further below on pp. 96-98). This theme is a Matthean element that goes beyond comparable Moses traditions. While Matthew makes liberal use of such traditions, his picture of Jesus is not really modeled upon them. Matthew goes much further. While the Matthean Jesus often reminds one of Moses, he also dwarfs Moses.

There are also notable similarities between Mt. 28.18-20 and 2 Chron. 36.23: "Thus says King Cyrus of Persia: The Lord, the God of heaven, has given me all the kingdoms of the earth, and he has charged me to build him a house at Jerusalem, which is in Judah. Whoever is among you of all his people, may the Lord his God be with him! Let him go up." In the Hebrew canon, the scriptures follow the prophets, so that 2 Chron. 36.23 is the last verse in the Hebrew Bible. These words of Cyrus also contain an announcement regarding conferment of universal authority ("The Lord, the God of heaven, has given me all the kingdoms of the earth"), an exhortation to go ("Let him go up") and a statement regarding divine presence ("may the Lord his God be with him!"). The sequence is different, however, as Cyrus concludes with the exhortation to go, and the theme of divine presence functions very differently. Whereas Cyrus merely expresses a wish for God's presence (cf. Ezra 1.3), Jesus promises his own presence. Jesus also makes commandments on his own, whereas Cyrus was first commanded by God. While Matthew's Great Commission draws heavily on biblical motifs, he uses them freely, and the effect is a highly exalted picture of Jesus. The leading Matthean scholar Ulrich Luz's conclusion is worth repeating: "Although Mt. 28.18b-20 is in many ways rooted in biblical traditions, I would like to regard the form here as a unique Matthean creation and to forgo the attempt to define a genre."[13]

By claiming to have received all authority in heaven and on earth, Matthew's Jesus brings a climactic conclusion to the previous statements about his authority (7.29; 9.6; 21.23-27). Whereas the earthly Jesus had authority on earth, the resurrected Jesus has authority both in heaven and on earth. The pairing of references to heaven and earth emphasizes the contrast between earth as the realm of human beings and heaven as the realm of God (cf. 6.19-20; 18.18; 23.9). Having authority in heaven, Jesus is seen with an authority that places him on a par with God over against human beings.

The commandment to baptize in the name of the Father, the Son, and the Holy Spirit contributes to the exalted picture of Jesus as well. Even though Matthew demonstrates no developed Trinitarian theology, Jesus is here placed on the same level as the Father and his Spirit.

The point may even be made that he shares the same name as they, depending on how we understand the formula "in the name of the Father and of the Son and of the Holy Spirit." Two interpretations are possible. The meaning may be that the same name belongs to the Father, Son and the Holy Spirit ("in the name [note the singular form] that belongs to the Father, and the Son, and the Holy Spirit"). The other possibility is that the formula is simply an abbreviated way of saying "the name of the Father, the name of the Son, and the name of Holy Spirit." The grammar would allow for both possibilities, but if Matthew wanted to refer to baptism in the name of the Father, the name of the Son, and the name of the Holy Spirit, we would have expected him to repeat the word "name."[14] The idea that Jesus shares God's name is attested as early as in Phil. 2.9-11 (Philippians is variously dated between the mid 50s and the early 60s CE, but many scholars believe that the hymn in Phil. 2.5-11 is even older). There are good reasons to understand Mark's Gospel to be hinting at the same idea (cf. pp. 51-52). This idea would be appropriate in the context of Matthew's Gospel as well. The most likely reading of the phrase is therefore that the Father, the Son, and the Holy Spirit share the same name.

The Great Commission is thus a powerful conclusion to Matthew's Gospel. As God commissioned his servants in the Scriptures of Israel, so does Jesus commission his disciples. Joshua's function would be to consolidate God's people in the land. Solomon was to build the house for God's presence. Jeremiah was sent to build the kingdom of Israel after he had destroyed it (Jer. 1.10; 31.4 etc.). Jesus sends his disciples to build the new community. As God commanded his servants in the Old Testament to observe everything he had commanded, so does Jesus give the command that everything he has taught should be observed. As God's presence on earth, Jesus promises his disciples his eternal, personal presence.

Jesus as God's Presence in the Community

Matthew's conviction that Jesus represents God's presence with his people has influenced his biography of Jesus in a number of ways. Since Jesus' presence replaces God's presence, Jesus interacts with the people in a way that echoes God's interaction with Israel in the Scriptures. When his disciples fail at an exorcism he complains: "you faithless and perverse generation, how much longer must I be with you? How much longer must I put up with you?" (Mt. 17.17). The addressees may be both the disciples and the people at-large. Jesus' characterization of them (Gr.: *genea apistos kai diestrammene*) resembles God's verdict on Israel's wilderness generation (Gr.: *genea skolia kai diestrammene* [Deut. 32.5 **LXX**]). His reluctance to be with the people also mirrors God's rebuke when he had to withhold his presence from Israel (Exod. 33.3; cf. Deut. 32.20) and lamented "how long?" (Num. 14.27).[15]

As Jesus is the earthly presence of God, coming to establish a new community, it comes as no surprise that he has taken God's place *vis à vis* this community. This role is clearest in the response he gives to Peter's confession in Mt. 16.17-19: "Blessed are you, Simon son of Jonah! For flesh and blood has not revealed this to you, but my Father in heaven. And I tell you, you are Peter, and on this rock I will build my church, and the gates of Hades will not prevail against it. I will give you the keys of the kingdom of heaven, and whatever you bind on earth will be bound in heaven, and whatever you loose on earth will be loosed in heaven."

Jesus here presupposes that he has all authority on earth and in heaven (cf. Mt. 28.18b) so that he can give Peter the authority to bind and loose. He now uses this authority to promise that he will build his church (Gr.: *ekklesia*). The conceptual background is found in the congregation of Israel centered around the tabernacle. This congregation is known as the congregation of the Lord (Hebr.: *qahal Yahweh*; Num. 16.3; 20.4; Deut. 23.1, 2, 3, 8; 1 Chron. 28.8; Mic. 2.5; cf. **1QM** 4.10) or the congregation of God (Hebr.: *qahal elohim*; Neh. 13.1), a natural consequence of the fact that God brought Israel into existence as a nation and created her (Gen. 12.2; Exod. 19.4-6; Isa. 43.1). **Post-exilic** writings attest to the expectation that God would re-establish his community around the temple and let his glory return (**Tobit** 14.5; **2 Maccabees** 2.7-8; **Jubilees** 1.17, 29; **2 Baruch** 6.8-9). In Matthew's Gospel, this expectation is fulfilled by Jesus, who takes God's place as the builder of his own congregation.

Davies and Allison correctly observe that the background of the Greek term *ekklesia* in Mt. 16.18 is the concept of Israel as the congregation of God.

They also note that Jesus does not speak of God's church, but rather "my church." They add: "For Matthew the community belongs to God *through Jesus*."[16] This conclusion is unwarranted. Matthew does not describe Jesus as such a liaison and the church is never said to be God's church. Rather, Jesus is seen to take God's place. An illustrative comparison is found in **Qumran's Teacher of Righteousness**, who also builds a congregation, but who builds it for God (**4Q171** 3.16).

Since the community is Jesus' community, the activities of the disciples are no longer performed in God's name but in Jesus' name. In his name, they suffer persecution (10.22; 24.9), welcome a child (18.5), leave family and possessions (19.29), and come together as community (Mt. 18.20). Even false disciples cast out demons, perform powerful deeds, and prophesy in his name (Mt. 7.22), and in his name false messiahs will come (24.5).

Jesus in the Role of God

Like Mark, Matthew has included ample references to Jesus' ministry as the fulfillment of the prophecies regarding God's eschatological presence. As in Mark, John the Baptist is presented both as the messenger of the Lord (Mt. 3.3) and the forerunner of Jesus (Mt. 3.11-13). In Matthew, he is explicitly identified as Elijah (11.14), who would prepare the people for the coming of God to earth (cf. p. 38). Whereas Mark implicitly said that Jesus fulfilled the prophecies regarding eschatological salvation, such as the one in Isa. 35.5-6, Matthew makes the point explicit. When John the Baptist sent messengers to ask Jesus if he was the one who was to come, "Jesus answered them, 'Go and tell John what you hear and see: the blind receive their sight, the lame walk, the lepers are cleansed, the deaf hear, the dead are raised, and the poor have good news brought to them'" (Mt. 11.4-5).

Matthew is less interested than Mark in presenting Jesus as the divine warrior who casts out the demons, but his **realized eschatology** is more explicit than Mark's. Jesus' clearest saying regarding the presence of the kingdom of God is Mt. 12.28: "But if it is by the Spirit of God that I cast out demons, then the kingdom of God has come to you." Luke includes a variant of the same saying, but Mark has omitted it altogether, even though he also tells the story of the controversy over Jesus' casting out the demons (Mk 3.22-32). Matthew thus leaves no doubt that the kingdom of God is already present, even though it is in some sense also future (cf. Mt. 6.10; 26.29). That this kingdom is present means that God himself is present to rule without opposition (cf. pp. 38-40). Accordingly, Jesus also anticipates his divine role as the one who sends out angels and gathers the elect (Mt. 24.31), as he also does in Mark's Gospel.

Compared to Mark, Matthew gives considerably more attention to Jesus as the eschatological judge, and he finds the blueprint for his description in the Scriptural prophecies regarding the day of the Lord. In Mt. 13.41-42 Jesus proclaims that "the Son of Man will send his angels, and they will collect out of his kingdom all causes of sin and all evildoers, and they will throw them into the furnace of fire, where there will be weeping and gnashing of teeth." The work of the angels will be to "collect out of his kingdom all causes of sin and all evildoers." This phrase is probably an echo of Zeph. 1.3, where the prophet foretells God's sweeping away of the stumbling-blocks with the wicked. The picture is that of judgment on the day of the Lord. By applying this prophecy to Jesus, Matthew portrays him as the one who will fulfill the prophecies regarding God's own eschatological judgment.

Jesus' function as judge is highlighted in Matthew's version of the saying about cross-bearing as well. Mark and Luke refer to the Son of Man being ashamed of those who are ashamed of him (Mk 8.38; Lk. 9.26), and their statement is compatible both with an understanding of Jesus as judge and of Jesus as merely a prosecutor or advocate in court. In the Gospel of Matthew, however, the Son of Man appears more clearly in the role of the judge. He will not only be ashamed of those who have been ashamed of him, but "he will repay everyone for what has been done" (Mt. 16.27; cf. 7.23).

The most elaborate picture of Jesus as the eschatological judge is found in Mt. 25.31-46. In Matthew's retelling, the scene is evocative of several Scriptural texts that portray Yahweh as the judge. Matthew's picture is of the Son of Man coming in his glory (v. 31a), and he holds nothing back. Applying the prophecy of the day of the Lord from Zech. 14.5, Matthew sees all the angels coming with him (v. 31b). The image of the Son of Man in glory recalls Dan. 7.13-14, but, in Matthew's vision, the Son of Man has replaced even the Ancient of Days, as he is the one sitting on the throne (v. 31c). As if to make plain that the throne truly belongs to him, the throne is described as the throne of his glory (v. 31c). Switching to a scene from Joel 3.1-12, Matthew adds that "all the nations will be gathered before him" (v. 32a). Joel 3.2 describes how God gathers all the nations for judgment, but in Matthew judgment belongs to the Son of Man. It is striking that it is specifically as the Son of Man that Jesus appears in all this glory. Matthew's Gospel expands on the picture of the Son of Man as we know it from Mark and puts a stronger emphasis on the divine splendor of the Son of Man.

Interpreters debate whether "all the nations" (v. 32) gathered before the Son of Man refers to all the Gentiles or if it is also meant to include the Jews. In any case, it is clear that Matthew envisions Jesus as the eschatological judge who pronounces the final judgment. His authority is formidable. There is no regular procedure, but Jesus appears as an omniscient judge who presents the evidence in each case and also pronounces an unappealable verdict. This verdict concerns the entire life of the respective groups and determines whether they will participate in the eschatological reward or suffer eschatological punishment (vv. 34, 41, 46). It is not stated explicitly, but the scene most likely presupposes a general resurrection and the gathering of some or all of the resurrected for the final verdict. If so, then Jesus emerges as the judge that on his own authority passes a verdict that determines people's destiny in the afterlife.

Although the literature from Second Temple Judaism describes human and angelic figures that serve as eschatological judges, none of them compare to this picture of Jesus.[17] The Messiah may be envisioned as a judge (*Psalms of Solomon* 17.26; *4Q246* 2.5-6), but his role is more comparable to that of the Old Testament judges. His function is to rule justly and to punish the enemies of God's people.

The most exalted of the judges that are described in these sources is the Son of Man as he emerges in *1 Enoch* 37–71 (cf. pp. 24-27). Even though this Son of Man is seated on God's throne (*1 Enoch* 45.3; 51.3; 55.4; 61.8; 62.5; 69.29), however, the Son of Man is nothing more than one of God's deputy judges. God is the one who will finally reward the righteous and punish the sinners (*1 Enoch* 45.6). The judgment of the Son of Man is not his own, but according to the righteous judgment of the Lord of Spirits (*1 Enoch* 61.9).

Jesus claims God's role in judgment, a conviction that is also reflected in Mt. 21.44: "The one who falls on this stone will be broken to pieces; and it will crush anyone on whom it falls." **Textual critics** discuss whether or not this verse belonged to the original text of Matthew's Gospel. All in all, the arguments in favor of including this verse are stronger.[18] When Jesus announces that "the one who falls on this stone will be broken to pieces," the imagery recalls that of Isa. 8.14-15. In this passage, Yahweh is the stone upon which people will fall and be broken, but in Mt. 21.44 Jesus is the stone that has this function.

In addition to the texts about eschatological fulfillment, Matthew also applies to Jesus other Scripture passages that originally referred to God. In 21.14-16, Jesus is seen ministering in the temple, and the children are cheering "Hosanna to the Son of David" (v. 15). When the chief priests and the scribes complain, Jesus quotes from Ps. 8.3 **LXX** (ET: 8.2): "Out of the mouths of infants and nursing babies you have prepared praise for yourself" (21.16). In its original context, Ps. 8.3 LXX speaks of praise given to God, but Jesus applies it to the children who were giving praise to him. Jesus may thus be seen to claim for himself the praise that is offered to God.

However, this verse is frequently understood to imply simply that the children, like their predecessors in Ps. 8.3 **LXX**, are more justified in their actions than the scribes.[19] On this interpretation, the verse does not contain any implicit claim on Jesus' part. But Ps. 8.3 LXX can hardly be used to justify children shouting in the temple. Jesus' argument makes better sense if Ps. 8.3 LXX is quoted to show that the shouts of the children are indeed appropriate when they give praise to God and if the unspoken premise is that Jesus takes the place of God. Moreover, as France correctly points out, Jesus' appearing in the temple may be read as the fulfillment of Malachi's promise that the Lord will come to his temple (Mal. 3.1; cf. Mt. 11.10).[20]

In a rabbinic tradition that appears to have its origin at least as early as the **Wisdom of Solomon** (10.21), the praise of Ps. 8.3 LXX is connected with the exodus and the crossing of the Red Sea. In Wisdom of Solomon 10.21, personified Wisdom is credited with making the infants speak clearly to praise God at the exodus. On this basis, Davies and Allison find in Mt. 21.16 a typical Matthean tendency of linking Jesus and Moses.[21] But if there is a link to the exodus, Jesus is not portrayed as the counterpart to Moses (who is not even mentioned in the relevant passage in the Wisdom of Solomon). Rather, Jesus takes the place of God, as the object of the worship presented to him.

Like Mark, Matthew has included several stories where Jesus appears in a role that Jewish tradition reserved for God. He controls the sea (Mt. 8.23-27; 14.22-33) and exercises the exclusive divine prerogative of forgiving sins (Mt. 9.1-7). The scribes understood Jesus to be blaspheming (9.3), but Matthew also mentions the crowds' reaction: "they were filled with awe, and they glorified God, who had given such authority to human beings" (9.8). If we take this information as indicative of Matthew's own interpretation of the event, it would appear that he does not see Jesus' action as a claim to equality with God. Many scholars interpret the "authority" given to human beings as the church's authority to forgive sins. On this interpretation, the statement does not provide an explanation of Jesus' actions in their historical context, but reflects the evangelist's own situation.[22]

This interpretation runs into considerable difficulties. Matthew's Gospel does not place Jesus and the disciples on the same level with regard to the authority to forgive sins. As Mt. 18.18 shows, the disciples' authority stems from the authorization given by Jesus. What is more, if Matthew's point were to allude to the church's practice of forgiving sins, he was not very precise. As it stands, the statement concerns human beings in general, not specifically disciples or church members. It is therefore better to read the comment as an expression of the crowds' failure to understand the significance of Jesus' acts. In Matthew's Gospel, the crowds are bewildered by the mighty acts of Jesus and puzzled as to his true identity (7.28; 8.27; 9.33; 12.23; 15.31). Matthew does not portray them as reliable witnesses of Jesus' identity. He reports Jesus' judgment that the crowds lack direction (9.36) and are reluctant to accept his message (11.7-19). As they are deemed to be outsiders, Jesus even withholds from them the teaching that explains his message (13.10-15, 34-35).[23]

Further indications of Jesus' equality with God are found in the fact that he appears to share God's name. Jesus is frequently called "Lord." Like Mark, Matthew indicates that this title occasionally may be intended as more than a polite address (cf. pp. 51-52). With a quotation from Isa. 40.3, John the Baptist is said to prepare the way of the Lord (Mt. 3.3). In the context of the book of Isaiah, this Lord is God, but in Matthew's story John prepares the way for Jesus. Matthew goes further than Mark, however, in using "Lord" as a title for Jesus as the eschatological judge (7.21-22; 24.42). While Matthew does not exploit the possibilities of this title as much as Luke does (cf. pp.118-121), he intimates that associations with the divine name are not entirely unjustified.

More than the other evangelists, however, Matthew shows that Jesus relates to his disciples in a way that only compares to the way that God relates to his people. In Matthew's Gospel, Jesus speaks with an authority that only has one true parallel: the way that God speaks. The most astonishing example of this way of speaking is found in the so-called antitheses (Mt. 5.21-48). In these sayings, Jesus quotes Israel's Scriptures with the introductory formula "you have heard that it was said to those of ancient times" (5.21, 27, 31, 33, 38, 43) and contrasts it with the emphatic "but I tell you" (5.22, 28, 32, 34, 39, 44). The implied subject of the passive verbs "it was said" must be God; God was the one who spoke to those in ancient times. Not only is Jesus here comparing his own words to those of God, but he implies that the authority of his own words is superior to that of the words that God spoke in the Old Testament.

Jesus' authority, then, goes beyond even that of the Old Testament prophets. With the formula "thus says the Lord," the prophets always referred to the authority of God. Jesus, by contrast, refers no further than to the authoritative "I": "but I tell you." Once again, he stands in God's place.[24]

Not all scholars agree with this interpretation. Many interpreters observe that Jesus' words in the antitheses concern the interpretation of the Old Testament law. He never actually contradicts anything that was written in the Pentateuch, but speaks authoritatively regarding its interpretation. Even on this understanding, Jesus is making exceptional claims. As far as we know, no scribe in **Second Temple Judaism** referred to his own authority when interpreting Scripture. They were careful to appeal to the accumulated wisdom of the community, and always referred to other scribes when they weighed in on the interpretation of the law.

It must be insisted, however, that the formula "but I tell you" is not intended to provide an interpretation of the previously quoted statements. Rather, the formula is intended to challenge the authority of other statements. This much becomes clear in the sixth antithesis: "You have heard that it was said, 'You shall love your neighbor and hate your enemy.' But I say to you, Love your enemies and pray for those who persecute you" (Mt. 5.43-44). Here, Jesus is contradicting the quoted saying. In this case, Jesus is not contradicting Scripture, because the commandment to hate one's enemies is not from the Bible. The closest parallel is found in Qumran (**1QS** 1.9-11; cf. **Josephus**, *Jewish War* 2.139). The point, however, is that this example shows that Jesus' "but I tell you" introduces an authority that is superior to the quoted saying. In the first five antitheses, he used this superior authority to make demands that were more far-reaching than God had done in the Old Testament. In the sixth antithesis, he used his superior authority to contradict a popular interpretation of God's commandments. When the antitheses are seen together, the implication is that Jesus speaks with an authority that is superior to the authority of the Old Testament.

However, the antitheses do not contain Jesus' most radical statements regarding the law. He goes even further in his answer to the would-be disciple that asked permission to bury his father before accompanying Jesus. In this saying, which is preserved in Matthew and Luke, but not in Mark, Jesus answers the man: "Follow me, and let the dead bury their own dead" (Mt. 8.22). In a magisterial treatment of this saying, Martin Hengel has shown that Jesus transcends all known categories for teacher-pupil relationships.[25] Within Judaism, the responsibility to provide a funeral for one's parents ranked highest among the law's requirements, as it was derived from the commandment to honor one's father and mother (cf. Gen. 50.5; **Tobit** 4.3; 6.13-15; **Sirach** 38.16; *Mishnah Berakot* 3.1; *Babylonian Talmud Soṭah* 14a).[26] This requirement was so important that it trumped other requirements of the Mosaic law. As a general rule, the *Mishnah* states: "[o]ne whose dead is lying before him [awaiting burial] is exempt from the recitation of the *Shema*, and from [wearing] phylacteries" (*Mishnah Berakot* 3.1).

According to Hengel, Jesus' refusal of the would-be disciple to bury his father is the clearest example of him setting aside the requirements of the Mosaic law. The explanation for this radical break with conventional piety cannot be found in any overruling ethical principle, but only in Jesus' absolute demand for loyalty to his person, a demand that only compares to God's own call of the prophets of Israel.

Accordingly, Matthew's Jesus also compares the fate of his disciples to that of the prophets. As the prophets were persecuted for God's sake, so will the disciples be persecuted for Jesus' name's sake (Mt. 5.11-12; 10.16-25; 24.9; see also p. 49).

If Jesus appears in the role of God, the appropriate response to him is worship. In a Jewish context, worship effectively marked the dividing line between God and created beings. Created beings such as angels, no matter how exalted, were not to be worshiped. Sometimes this distinction is emphasized by telling stories of angels who refuse to be worshiped (**Tobit** 12.16-22; *Apocalypse of Zephaniah* 6.11-15; cf. Rev. 19.10; 22.8-9).

Unlike the other evangelists, Matthew devotes considerable attention to people that fall down in reverence before Jesus. Whereas the Greek word *proskuneo* only occurs twice in Mark (5.6; 15.19) and three times in Luke (4.7, 8; 24.52), Matthew uses the word ten times with Jesus as the object (2.2, 8, 11; 8.2; 9.18; 14.33; 15.25; 20.20; 28.9, 17). However, the question on which commentators and translators differ is whether *proskuneo* should be translated "worship" or merely "pay homage." The basic meaning of the word is to prostrate oneself and kiss the ground, someone's feet, or the hem of the person's garment. In the **Septuagint**, the word frequently refers to worship, but it may also be used for the homage paid by a submissive to a king or a dignitary.[27] It does not necessarily imply worship, therefore, which is only due God (Deut. 10.20; 2 Kgs 17.35-36). In the context of Matthew's Gospel, however, Jesus refuses to fall down and worship (Gr.: *peson proskuneses*) Satan. The reason is that Scripture says to worship (Gr.: *proskuneseis*) God alone (Mt.

4.9-10). It appears that Matthew reserves the term for a worshiping act that is appropriately rendered only to God.

With a few exceptions, Jesus is always the object of the verb *proskuneo* in Matthew. The exceptions include Satan's request for worship (4.9), Jesus' response that only God is to be worshiped (4.10), and the unforgiving slave falling down before the king in Jesus' parable (18.26). The king represents God, so overtones of worship are appropriate (note that the word *proskuneo* is not used when the one slave falls down before the other in 18.29), as they are every time Matthew uses the word. The restricted semantic range of the term in Matthew's Gospel can perhaps also be seen by a comparison with Mark's Gospel. Mark uses the word twice, when the Gerasene demoniac expresses submission (5.6) and when the solders pay their mock homage to Jesus on the cross (15.19). Matthew uses a different wording in both these instances, perhaps because he wants to avoid all ambiguity with respect to the meaning of *proskuneo*.

The first occurrence of *proskuneo* in Matthew comes in the story of the magi (2.1-12), who ask King Herod how to find the one who has been born king of the Jews, as they "have come to pay him homage" (2.2 NRSV; cf. 2.11). As the immediate context refers to the king of the Jews, the idea of submission to a king, rather than worship, is perhaps all that is intended. But the supernatural nature of the magi's knowledge of his birth and their international travel in order to fall down before an infant indicate that something more than a king may be in view. The larger context confirms such an interpretation. The story follows immediately after the account of Jesus' birth, which highlights his virginal conception and the two names that identify him as God's saving presence on earth. It is only fitting that a story of worship should follow.

Conservative scholars who maintain the historicity of the magi's visit often argue against the view that they actually worshiped Jesus. David Peterson maintains that the magi could not have recognized the divinity of Jesus at this stage.[28] We cannot know, however, what the magi were thinking. We can only know how Matthew has portrayed them. In Matthew's story, they are portrayed as exclusively good characters. All their actions are based on divine revelation. Their source of knowledge of Jesus is shrouded in mystery; the nature and extent of it are never fully explained. They are not among the disciples whose realization of Jesus' identity is described as gradual.

Even if one hesitates to read the full connotations of worship into the early occurrences of *proskuneo* in the Gospel of Matthew, however, most scholars agree that the term takes on such profound significance later in the Gospel, at least in 14.33 and 28.9, 17. The first individual who receives a miracle in Matthew's Gospel does so after worshiping Jesus (8.2; cf. 9.18; 15.25; 20.20). For the supplicants coming to Jesus, such worship is characterized by unconditional dependence upon Jesus and trust in him. Matthew also describes the disciples' worship in connection with the **epiphanic** revelations of Jesus. When Jesus walks on water, the disciples' response is to worship him and recognize him as the Son of God (14.33).

The climax of the disciples' worship comes after the resurrection. When they meet the resurrected Jesus, Mary Magdalene and the other Mary fall at his feet and worship him (28.9). In the Gospel's concluding passage, the eleven disciples meet Jesus at the mountain in Galilee where they worship him (28.17). As Jesus' very first worshipers were Gentiles (2.11), so are the disciples now called to make disciples of all nations (28.19). Worship is now associated with Jesus' death-defying power, universal authority, and eternal presence.

Jesus as God's servant

Over against these exalted pictures of Jesus, Matthew has placed several images of Jesus as God's servant who is subordinate and obedient to him.

The Messiah

Among the Gospels, Matthew stands out with its heightened interest in the fulfillment of Scripture. It is only natural, therefore, that Matthew has a strong focus on Jesus as the Messiah, Israel's promised savior king. In Matthew, Jesus is called the Messiah thirteen times, five times in the infancy narrative alone.[29] The messianic title "son of David" is also a favorite of Matthew's and occurs eight times.[30]

The very first line of Matthew's Gospel directs attention to Jesus' messiahship: "An account of the genealogy of Jesus the Messiah, the son of David, the son of Abraham" (Mt. 1.1). Matthew not only identifies Jesus as the Messiah, but stresses the point by adding the synonymous title "son of David." Capitalizing on the theme of God's promises, he further adds that Jesus is the son of Abraham. Matthew then provides a stylized genealogy with the fourteen generations from Abraham to David, from David to Babylon, and from Babylon to Jesus (1.2-17). This genealogy serves to evoke quickly all the high points of Israel's history, establish that Jesus is the climax of this history, and legitimize his messiahship as a descendant of David.

The infancy narrative maintains this interest in messianic imagery. Jesus is announced as the fulfillment of the messianic prophecy from Isa. 7.14 (Mt. 1.23). He is born in Bethlehem, in fulfillment of the prophecy from Mic. 5.2 (Mt. 2.6). The magi from the east come to see the king that is born (Mt. 2.1-12).

Unlike Mark, Matthew refers to Jesus as the Christ in his redactional remarks (Mt. 11.2). Compared to Mark, Matthew has also toned down the theme of secrecy regarding Jesus' identity. Most strikingly, he shows that people approaching Jesus freely address him as "son of David," a title with clear messianic overtones. In his use of this title, Matthew also develops an unconventional picture of the Messiah. The Messiah was not expected to be a healer, but Matthew associates the son of David title specifically with Jesus' healing miracles (cf. Mt. 9.27; 12.23; 15.22; 20.30, 31). As the son of David, Jesus emerges as powerful, but also as merciful and compassionate. The theme is closely related to that of the eschatological shepherd (see further below on pp. 101-102).

As we have seen above (pp. 81-85), Matthew has from the beginning portrayed Jesus as something much more than a conventional Messiah. As Emmanuel (Mt. 1.23), he represents the presence of God among his people and is appropriately the object of worship (Mt. 2.11; 14.33; 28.9, 17).

In Mt. 22.41-46, Jesus challenges common ideas about the Messiah explicitly. People consider the Messiah to be the son of David, but Jesus quotes Ps. 110.1, where David calls the Messiah "Lord." He asks: "If David thus calls him Lord, how can he be his son?" (22.45). Jesus does not answer his own question, but the audience of Matthew's Gospel has been prepared to supply the answer on their own.

The Embodiment of Israel

Matthew's introductory genealogy connects evocatively with Israel's history, a connection that Matthew maintains through his infancy narrative. He includes many echoes of the story of Israel, especially of her formative events. The frequent communication by God in dreams (1.20; 2.12, 13, 19, 22) recalls the patriarchal narratives (Gen. 20.1-7; 28.10–22; 31.10-16, 24). Most obviously, this theme brings to mind the character of Joseph (Gen. 37.5-11; 40.1–41.36; 46.2-4), through whom God saved his fledgling people. When the time comes for Jesus to be born, the circumstances recall those of Moses. A royal decree to kill all newborn children is issued (Mt 2.16; cf. Exod. 1.15-22), but the child is providentially saved (Mt. 2.13-15; cf. Exod. 2.1-10). An allusion to Exod. 4.19 makes it likely that Matthew intended the correspondence to be noted (Mt. 2.20).

In connection with Jesus' sojourn in Egypt, Matthew quotes from Hos. 11.1: "Out of Egypt I have called my son" (Mt. 2.15). In its original context, Hosea's oracle concerned the people of Israel, but Matthew has applied it to Jesus. Jesus is thus identified as God's Son, and sonship is also connected with Israel as God's people. As God's Son, Jesus is the embodiment of God's people. With this quotation, Matthew also recalls the exodus event, the event that brought Israel into existence as a nation. Matthew's next explicit quotation comes in 2.18 and develops the same idea one step further. The quotation is taken from Jer. 31.15: "a voice was heard in Ramah, wailing and loud lamentation, Rachel weeping for her children; she refused to be consoled, because they are no more." This lament invokes the image of Babylonian captivity and a second exodus, through which the people were reborn. When John the Baptist soon afterwards appears on stage, he is also associated with the return from Babylon, as he is the messenger spoken of in Isa. 40.3 (Mt. 3.3). As Matthew will continue to emphasize, in the ministry of Jesus, God's people find a new beginning. Jesus' life is hereby identified as the salvific event to which this people owe its existence. When Jesus embarks on his public ministry after the baptism and temptation, he proclaims that the kingdom of heaven has come near (4.17) and begins to form a community around himself (4.18-22).

The New Moses

As the fountainhead and embodiment of the people of God, Jesus is naturally compared to Moses, the founder of Israel as a nation. The comparison is important to Matthew, who includes several echoes of the Moses tradition in his story. Perhaps the most obvious parallel is found in the Sermon on the Mount, which Matthew introduces with a note that Jesus goes up to a mountain and sits down (Mt. 5.1). The **Septuagint** frequently uses similar terminology (*anabaino* + *eis to oros*) for Moses' ascent to Sinai. Jesus' teaching in the Sermon on the Mount has also frequently been seen as the counterpart to Moses' giving of the Torah from Mount Sinai. The content of the teaching lends itself to such an understanding, as Jesus may be seen as giving a new or renewed law.

However, Jesus must be understood in a different category than Moses, as he gives his instructions on his own authority (cf. pp. 94-95). Whereas Moses spoke the words of God, the Matthean Jesus refers to his own words. Whereas Moses functioned as the mediator between God and the people, Jesus refers to himself and his own authority (7.28-29).

Matthew's use of Moses traditions occurs in the transfiguration account as well (Mt. 17.1-8). Matthew here clearly goes beyond Mark in emphasizing the parallels with Moses. In contrast to Mark, Matthew includes a reference to the shining face of Jesus, a well-known aspect of the Moses traditions (Exod. 34.29-30; **Philo**, *On the Life of Moses* 2.70; ***Liber Antiquitate Biblicarum*** 12.1; 2 Cor. 3.7). Like Mark, however, Matthew also shows that Jesus' role transcends that of Moses. Jesus brings divine revelation, not as its messenger, but as its source.

There are also some obvious connections between Jesus and Moses in the Last Supper, which, according to Matthew's Gospel, was celebrated as a Passover meal (26.17-19). The interpretation of the cup as the blood of the covenant (26.28) is a clear allusion to the covenant sacrifice at Sinai (Exod. 24.8). There is also a verbal as well as conceptual similarity between Exod. 12.28 and Mt. 26.19, which states that the disciples did as they were told. If this last correspondence is considered an allusion or an echo, Matthew also makes a significant distinction. Whereas the people of Israel did as the Lord had told Moses and Aaron, the disciples did what Jesus had told them. As in the Sermon on the Mount, Jesus is not the intermediary; he gives the instructions.

As teacher, therefore, Jesus' role goes beyond that of Moses and compares to that of God himself. This view of Jesus also comes to expression in his exclusive claim to the titles "rabbi" and "teacher" (Mt. 23.8-10). Jesus' insistence that his disciples only have one teacher (23.8) and one instructor (23.10) parallels his point that they only have one father, their father in heaven (23.9). The repeated, emphatic "one" (*heis*) may be an allusion to Israel's creed, the Shema: "Hear, O Israel: The Lord is our God, the Lord alone. You shall love the Lord your God with all your heart, and with all your soul, and with all your might" (Deut. 6.4). If so, Jesus makes himself the object of the disciples' confession to the one God. In any case, Jesus claims a unique role as teacher, a role that compares to the uniqueness of God.

The Eschatological Shepherd

Another theme that shows Jesus as a servant of God, but also goes beyond the categories of agency, is that of Jesus as the eschatological shepherd.[31] Several of the prophets contain promises to Israel regarding an eschatological shepherd, but there is some ambivalence as to the identity of the shepherd. In Micah and Ezekiel, God promises that he will come to shepherd his people (Mic. 2.12-13; Ezek. 34.12). The same prophets also announce that a messianic figure will come as Israel's shepherd (Mic. 5.4; Ezek. 34.23). Jeremiah also announces the promise of the Lord's shepherding (23.3), but immediately goes on to predict the raising up of many shepherds (23.4). Zechariah also foresees the Lord as the shepherd of his people (9.16). In addition, the prophet himself performs a symbolic role as shepherd (11.4-17). A third shepherd is identified as the Lord's associate, who will be stricken by the sword (13.7).

Matthew's clearest reference to the eschatological shepherd comes in two direct quotations. The first is found in the infancy narrative, where Herod asks the Jewish scribes where the Messiah will be born and they answer with a quotation from Mic. 5.2: "And you, Bethlehem, in the land of Judah, are by no means least among the rulers of Judah; for from you shall come a ruler who is to shepherd my people Israel" (Mt. 2.6). The second quotation occurs in the passion narrative, where Jesus predicts Peter's denial by quoting Zech. 13.7: "You will all become deserters because of me this night; for it is written, 'I will strike the shepherd, and the sheep of the flock will be scattered'" (Mt. 26.31). Both of these quotations identify Jesus as God's eschatological agent.

In Mt. 9.36, Jesus observes that the crowds "were harassed and helpless, like sheep without a shepherd." Jesus is thus implicitly identified as the people's true shepherd who genuinely cares for them. The expression "sheep without a shepherd" is relatively common in the Septuagint (Num. 27.17, Ezek. 34.5; 3 Kgdms 22.17 [ET 1 Kgs 22.17]; 2 Chron. 18.16; **Judith** 11.19), although the wording differs somewhat from what is found here. Conceptually, however, the closest parallel is Ezek. 34.5, which describes God's compassion for his people, leading up to the portrayal of God as Israel's shepherd (Ezek. 34.11-16). Messianic expectations are not primarily in view here, therefore. Matthew has instead tacitly placed Jesus in the role of God as Israel's shepherd.

Jesus also compares himself to a shepherd in Mt. 25.32, where he announces that he "will separate people one from another as a shepherd separates the sheep from the goats." This picture of the shepherd also has connections with God as shepherd in Ezekiel 34. As God empathizes with the marginalized (Ezek. 34.4-8), so does Jesus identify with the plight of the least (Mt. 25.35-36, 40, 42-43, 45). As God will judge between the good and the bad among the herd (Ezek. 34.17-22), so will Jesus separate and judge the sheep and the goats (Mt. 25.32-33).

The Servant of the Lord

Matthew has also capitalized on the theme of Jesus as the Servant of the Lord, as described in the Servant songs in Isaiah (Isa. 42.1-9; 49.1-7; 50.4-9; 52.13–53.12). In contrast to Mark, who usually leaves the identification implicit, Matthew makes it very explicit. In fact, the lengthiest of Matthew's many quotations from the Old Testament is from Isa. 42.1-4 (Mt. 12.18-21). Matthew understands the first Servant song as a prophecy that was fulfilled in Jesus' healing ministry. He reads Isa. 53.4 in the same light. When Jesus cast out demons and cured the sick, he fulfilled "what had been spoken through the prophet Isaiah 'He took our infirmities and bore our diseases'" (Mt. 8.17).

The latter of these quotations occurs in a summary statement regarding Jesus' activities. That is important, because it shows that Matthew is not only more explicit than Mark; he also understands Isaiah's servant as providing the paradigm for Jesus' entire ministry. Mark alluded to Isaiah's Servant songs in order to explain Jesus' suffering and death, but Matthew does not limit his application of these themes to Jesus' suffering. He sees Jesus' public ministry, specifically his healing activity, as the fulfillment of Isa. 53.4 (Mt. 8.17).

In Mt. 12.18-21, Matthew uses Isa. 42.1-4 to explain why Jesus did not seek fame and public adulation. Isaiah's song describes a humble servant, and this servant provides the model for Jesus' character.

Perhaps somewhat surprisingly, Matthew does not quote from the Servant songs in connection with Jesus' death. Mark's allusions to the Servant songs are toned down in Matthew (compare Mk 10.33-34 and Mt. 20.18-19). Like Mark, Matthew has included the saying about Jesus giving "his life as a ransom for many" (Mt. 20.28), which appears to be inspired by the prophecy about the servant's vicarious suffering in Isa. 53.10-11. This prophecy may also lie behind Jesus' words at the Last Supper, that his blood "is poured out for many" (Mt. 26.28; cf. pp. 59-60).

In Mark, the clearest identification of Jesus as Isaiah's servant occurs at his baptism, when the heavenly voice declares that with Jesus he is "well pleased" (Mk 1.11; cf. Isa. 42.1). According to Matthew, the heavenly voice makes this allusion not only at Jesus' baptism (Mt. 3.17), but at his transfiguration as well (Mt. 17.5). Finally, some scholars have suggested that Jesus alludes to Isa. 53.11 when he prepares to be baptized by John and insists that they must "fulfill all righteousness" (Mt. 3.15). According to Isa. 53.11, "the righteous one, my servant, shall make many righteous."

Son of God

The upshot of all of this is that there is a certain ambiguity in Matthew's descriptions of Jesus as God's servant. Jesus is seen as a human agent of God, but at the same time this category does not do him full justice. Jesus is also God's equal. Nowhere is this ambiguity more pronounced than in Matthew's picture of Jesus as God's Son.

Unlike Luke, Matthew does not tie Jesus' divine sonship to his miraculous conception. Matthew's mention of this element rather serves to show that Jesus' birth was in fulfillment of Scripture (Isa. 7.14) and according to the plan of God (Mt. 1.22-23).

As we have seen above (p. 100), Matthew introduces the idea of Jesus as God's Son with a quotation from Hos. 11.1, a text which in its original context referred to Israel as God's son. Matthew then develops the sonship theme in the baptism and temptation stories. At Jesus' baptism, the heavenly voice alludes to Ps. 2.7, Gen. 22.2, 12, 16 and Isa. 42.1 (Mt. 3.17). Jesus is again associated with God's chosen servants within Israel (cf. the discussion of Mark's baptism account in Chapter 2 on pp. 61-64). Compared to Mark, Matthew has changed the second person address to a statement in the third person, clarifying that the saying is a declaration, not an installation.

The subsequent satanic temptations centre around the meaning of the Son of God title (Mt. 4.1-11).[32] Satan presupposes an understanding of the Son of God as a character who may wield divine powers at his whim, and he dares Jesus to demonstrate them. In resisting the temptations, Jesus applies three sayings from Scripture, all taken from Deuteronomy 6–8. In this section of Scripture, Moses recapitulates Israel's wilderness experience. During this time, God had tested them to see what was in their heart, a test Israel sorely failed. Jesus' test corresponds to that of Israel. As the people were 40 years in the wilderness, so does Jesus spend 40 days. But where Israel failed the test, Jesus passes. He is content to live by the word of God and does not complain like Israel did (4.4; cf. Deut. 8.3), he does not put God to the test as Israel did at Massah (4.7; cf. Deut. 6.16), and he refuses to engage in misplaced worship like Israel did (4.10; cf. Deut. 6.13). Sonship is here demonstrated in humble obedience and willingness to accept suffering, which Jesus does as the ideal Israelite. In an acknowledgement of his fortitude, Jesus receives the reward of the righteous: the devil leaves and the angels serve him (4.11; cf. *Testament of Naphtali* 8.4; *Testament of Issachar* 7.7; *Testament of Benjamin* 5.2; 6.1).

Since the Son of God title refers to Jesus as the representative of Israel, and since Jesus through his ministry forms a new community, it is not surprising that the members of this community should also be known as sons of God. In the Sermon on the Mount, Jesus twice refers to those who internalize his teaching as sons of God (5.9, 45; cf. 12.50; 17.26; 18.21, 35; 23.8, 9; 28.10). For Matthew, the connotations of the Son of God title are those of the ideal representative of the people of God.

The reader of Matthew's Gospel already knows, however, that Jesus is more than an Israelite, even an ideal one. But it is not until after the Sermon on the Mount that Matthew begins to associate the Son of God title with Jesus as God's presence on earth. The first hint comes when he is addressed by the Gadarene demoniacs as Son of God (8.29). This encounter follows Jesus' demonstration of his ability to still the storm (8.23-27), a demonstration evocative of the mighty power of God himself (Exod. 14.21; Nah. 1.4; Pss. 104.3; 106.9; 107.23-30; Job 26.12). Although Matthew is not as interested as Mark in the divine warrior theme, the encounter with the Gadarenes has overtones of the great eschatological showdown ("Have you come here to torment us before the time?" [8.29]).

The first time any human characters in Matthew's Gospel confess Jesus as the Son of God occurs when the disciples have been rescued at sea (14.22-32). Jesus demonstrates that he has the same power over the sea that God has, and he appears to the disciples in a way that duplicates the great **theophanies** in Israel's past (cf. the discussion of Mark's account of Jesus' walking on the sea on pp. 47-48). In Matthew's account, the disciples respond with worship (cf. pp. 96-98) and the exclamation "truly you are the Son of God" (14.33). The context gives content to the title and explains sonship as a sharing of divine powers. Many scholars explain this use of the title as a result of influence from Greek myths about demigods. However, it is the role of Israel's Yahweh, not **Hellenistic** sons of God, that serves as the model for ascribing divinity to Jesus.

Peter's confession of Jesus as the Messiah is in Matthew also a confession of him as the Son of God: "You are the Messiah, the Son of the living God" (16.16). In Matthew's story, Peter's confession is more climactic than it is in Mark. Only Matthew includes Jesus' commendatory words: "Blessed are you, Simon son of Jonah! For flesh and blood has not revealed this to you, but my Father in heaven. And I tell you, you are Peter, and on this rock I will build my church, and the gates of Hades will not prevail against it. I will give you the keys of the kingdom of heaven, and whatever you bind on earth will be bound in heaven, and whatever you loose on earth will be loosed in heaven" (16.17-19). Perhaps it is because Matthew invests the confession with such significance that he is not content with the mere confession of Jesus as the Messiah, but includes "Son of the living God" as well. According to Matthew, Peter's confession is so significant that it could not have been the result of mere human insight. Spiritual beings know Jesus as God's Son (8.29), but for humans a divine revelation was necessary, another hint that the character of Jesus' sonship is not of this world. This indication is further confirmed at the transfiguration, where Jesus' divine sonship is revealed through a **theophany**. Birger Gerhardsson correctly observes that the Son of God title is the preeminent insider title in the Gospel of Matthew. It belongs in the context of non-therapeutic, **epiphanic** miracles. Whereas the outsiders who seek healing miracles may address Jesus as the son of David (9.27; 12.23; 15.22; 20.30, 31; 21.9, 15), the Son of God title is reserved for those with special insight. The demons use it (8.29), and the disciples realize its appropriateness on the basis of the **theophany** they are given.[33]

Like Mark, Matthew also connects the Son of God title to the passion and the cross. The title is at the center of the accusations and taunts made against Jesus (26.63; 27.40, 43). As Jesus expired, not only the centurion but also those present with him recognized Jesus for who he was: the Son of God (27.54). The earthquake and the accompanying events prompted the recognition; again an indication that divine sonship has associations with divine powers. With a characteristic Matthean expression elsewhere used in connection with a **theophany** (17.6), the evangelist reports their reaction as one of great fear (27.54).

The connection between the Son of God title and the cross also has connotations of obedience. Jesus is the obedient Son who does the will of his heavenly father, even when it conflicts with his own will and entails gruesome suffering (26.39, 42). Matthew has enhanced this emphasis on Jesus' deferral to his father and has included more frequent references to Jesus' addressing God as "father."

The Unique Son (Mt. 11.25-30)

Whereas the reader of Mark's Gospel has to make inferences from the narrative regarding the nature of Jesus' divine sonship, Matthew's Jesus offers at least some reflection about his relationship to the Father. In Mt. 11.25-30, Jesus says:

"I thank you, Father, Lord of heaven and earth, because you have hidden these things from the wise and the intelligent and have revealed them to infants; yes, Father, for such was your gracious will. All things have been handed over to me by my Father; and no one knows the Son except the Father, and no one knows the Father except the Son and anyone to whom the Son chooses to reveal him. Come to me, all you that are weary and are carrying heavy burdens, and I will give you rest. Take my yoke upon you, and learn from me; for I am gentle and humble in heart, and you will find rest for your souls. For my yoke is easy, and my burden is light."[34]

This saying is influenced by Jewish traditions regarding God's wisdom. When Jesus praises God for granting his revelation to the simple-minded he connects with common ideas (Prov. 8.5; 9.4; **11Q5** 18.3-5). But he goes beyond these traditions when he claims that God's revelation is withheld from the wise. This claim appears to be a radical dismissal of the existing wisdom tradition, and Jesus thus implicitly claims to be more intimately related to God's wisdom than previous sages.

In v. 27, Jesus explains why he can make this startling claim: "All things have been handed over to me by my Father; and no one knows the Son except the Father, and no one knows the Father except the Son and anyone to whom the Son chooses to reveal him." When he discusses this saying, Allison compares Jesus to Moses. Moses' humility (cf. Mt. 11.29) was exceptional, and he enjoyed a closer relationship to God than anyone else (Exod. 33.11-23; Num. 12.1-8; Deut. 34.9-12; cf. **Sirach** 45.3-5; **Philo**, *Allegorical Interpretation* 3.100–103; *Who Is the Heir?* 262). Just as Moses received a revelation and handed it over to Israel, so did Jesus receive the revelation of all things from the Father and passed it on to his disciples. The Greek verb *paradidomi* in v. 27 is a technical term for the handing over of tradition, and Allison points out that Moses received the Torah from God and started the chain of tradition (Deut. 10.4 **LXX**; Sirach 45.5; *Liber Antiquitate Biblicarum* 11.2; *Mishnah Avot* 1.1).[35]

But once again, the comparison demonstrates that Moses was no Jesus. The Greek word that is used for God's giving of the Torah to Moses is *didomi*, not *paradidomi*, which is found in Mt. 11.27. Whereas *paradidomi* denotes a horizontal relationship, and therefore is aptly used for the chains of tradition, *didomi* is a broader term. In the story of Moses, the verb *didomi* is not used to denote the handing over of tradition from God to Moses, but to describe God's act of revelation to Moses. The revelatory link in the chain is the act of God, who sovereignly chooses to break through the divine–human barrier and give his law to Moses. The revelatory link in Mt. 11.27 that is comparable to the one between God and Moses is the link between Jesus and his disciples. Jesus is the one who breaks through the divine–human barrier and gives his revelation to his disciples. Accordingly, there is a terminological distinction between Jesus' and the Father's relationship on the one hand and Jesus' and the disciples' relationship on the other. Everything has been handed over (Gr.: *paredothe*) to Jesus from the Father, but Jesus reveals (Gr.: *apokalupsai*) knowledge to those whom he chooses.

What is striking in Jesus' words is the reciprocity between himself and the Father. God's relationship to Moses is described as a one-way street: God grants Moses knowledge of him. But in Jesus' words, not only does the Son know the Father, the Father is also privy to exclusive knowledge of the Son. Again, this is where the parallel with Moses breaks down. When Moses is granted exclusive knowledge of God, the exclusiveness of the knowledge has to do with the fact that no one can know God (Exod. 33.20). In Jesus' words, the Father has been granted an equally exclusive knowledge of the Son. If the parallel with Moses be maintained, the logic requires that God also is given exclusive knowledge of Moses, as no one else can know him. But there is no such reciprocity in the relationship between God and Moses, and the comparison between Jesus and Moses merely shows that Jesus must be seen in a different category. Jesus' saying places the Father and the Son on the same level. Ulrich Luz captures it well: "The knowledge here spoken of is knowledge of like by like."[36]

This observation militates against the argument of James Dunn as well. Dunn thinks Jesus in Mt. 11.25-30 emerges as the quintessential, righteous Israelite, "the one who represents Israel in the last days." He should be understood against the background of what the Old Testament has to say about God's election of Israel and about the Son of Man. According to Dunn, the handing over of all things to Jesus corresponds to the giving of all authority to the Son of Man and the holy ones of the Most High in Dan. 7.13-14, 27. He also points out that knowledge language may frequently have overtones of election (Gen. 18.19; Exod. 33.12; Num. 16.5 **LXX**; Jer. 1.5; Hos. 13.5; Amos 3.2) and that Israel's relationship to God can be described as that of a son to a father (Exod. 4.22; Jer. 31.9; Hos. 11.1). Israel's knowledge of the Lord is also expected to be shared more broadly (Isa. 11.9; 19.21; Hab. 2.14).[37]

Dunn's view is based on the interpretation of "all things" (*panta*) as referring to authority, a view he shares with many scholars. In favor of this view, one may point to the parallels with Dan. 7.13-14 and Mt. 28.18, where the Son of Man and Jesus respectively are given authority. It is also argued that "all things" refers back to "these things" (*tauta*) in Mt. 11.25 par., and that the Son's knowledge of the Father can hardly be the referent of "these things." Instead, "these things" must refer to Jesus' authority.

However, the connection between this saying and the Danielic Son of Man is not very close. The concept of the Son of Man is not mentioned here; it must be inferred on the basis of the "handing over." But the mere occurrence of this idea is insufficient ground to posit a connection to Dan. 7.14. In the forms that Dan. 7.13-14 and Mt. 11.27 par. have survived, there are no verbal links between the two texts. Mt. 11.27 uses the word *paradidomi*, whereas the word *didomi* is used in the Greek versions of Dan. 7.14. The father/son metaphor is also missing from Dan. 7.13-14.

Mt. 11.27 consists of four lines: 1) "All things have been handed over to me by my Father;" 2) "and no one knows the Son except the Father;" 3) "and no one knows the Father except the Son;" 4) "and anyone to whom the Son chooses to reveal him." The second and third of these lines refer to knowledge ("no one knows"), not authority. It is most likely, therefore, that "all things" refers primarily to knowledge. But in light of the broader context, perhaps "all things" should be understood comprehensively, to include both knowledge and authority.

The Son of Man traditions do not offer a parallel to the exclusive knowledge that the Son has been granted by the Father. This saying cannot be explained on the basis of Son of Man Christology, therefore.

As for the appeal to election language, it is clear that election may be expressed in terms of knowledge and fatherhood, and that exclusivity is a characteristic of election. But these concepts do not explain the focus on reciprocity that is so striking in Mt. 11.27. Because of the reciprocal nature of the saying, the verb "know" must have the same meaning throughout. If the verb refers to election, does the Son choose the Father? And why is the verb in the present tense? Is the verse describing a continuous choosing?

Dunn also compares Jesus' revelatory function to that of Israel, who in prophetic texts is said to spread knowledge of God. But again it must be insisted that Israel does not "reveal" God's nature. In the prophetic texts, God is the one who grants knowledge to the Gentiles (Isa. 11.9; 19.21; Hab. 2.14). In Mt. 11.27, however, Jesus has taken God's place. He is the one who dispenses revelation and he is the one who elects.

According to the majority of scholars, the lofty self-claims that Jesus makes in Mt. 11.27 can only be explained against the background of Jewish ideas regarding God's wisdom (cf. pp. 29-31). Jesus' assurance that no one knows the Son except the Father is paralleled by the conviction that no one but the Lord knows his wisdom (Job 28.20-28; **Sirach** 1.6-8; **Baruch** 3.15-35; cf. *1 Enoch* 63.2-3; 84.3). The corresponding claim that no one knows the Father except the Son mirrors the idea of wisdom's perfect knowledge of God (**Wisdom of Solomon** 8.4, 8; 9.4, 9, 11). Also, Jesus' claim to be the exclusive revealer of the Father can be compared to the theme of wisdom granting knowledge of God (Wisdom of Solomon 7.27; cf. 9.17-18; 10.10; Sirach 4.11-14). Several scholars therefore conclude that, for Matthew, Jesus has taken the place of God's wisdom and even may be identified with the wisdom of God.[38]

However, there are also problems with the view that Jesus has made use of wisdom traditions. Dunn notes that the Father-Son imagery does not fit wisdom ideas very well. He observes that it is only the locus of wisdom – not wisdom itself – that is hidden from all except God, according to Job 28.20, 23; **Sirach** 1.6; **Baruch** 3.27, 29-31, 36. Finally, he argues that wisdom traditions do not provide a good parallel to the idea of the Son as the exclusive revealer of wisdom.[39] These arguments show that Jesus has not merely repeated wisdom ideas and applied them to himself. His thoughts about his own relationship to his Father cannot be neatly matched to a known category.

The parallels are not close enough, therefore, to conclude that Jesus here identifies himself with wisdom. But the closest parallel to the idea of exclusive mutual knowledge remains the traditions regarding God and his wisdom. It seems plausible, then, that Jesus has made use of wisdom motifs and reshaped them to express the nature of his relationship to the Father. If so, the implication is that he is equally inextricably linked to the Father as God's own wisdom is linked to God. But Jesus takes the tendencies regarding the personification of wisdom to a new level when he combines the wisdom motif with the theme of father and son. Jesus clearly distinguishes his own identity from the identity of the Father. His appearance in the role of God can therefore not mean that he thinks he is the Father or that he is the earthly manifestation of the Father. Jesus is the Father's son. He understands this sonship to mean that he has a relationship to the Father that is qualitatively different from that of all other human beings. The fundamental distinction between God and human beings is not found in the distinction between Jesus and God – it is found in the distinction between Jesus and other human beings. As a result, Jesus is able to take the Father's place on earth.

If one asks about Jesus' identity, the answer is not that he is God's wisdom. He is God's Son, but sonship is redefined through the use of wisdom ideas.

"God's Son" is no longer merely an honorary title; it describes the intimate relationship between Father and Son, a relationship between equals, yet with a clear hierarchy.

Matthew's development of the Son of God theme has combined the picture of Jesus as the obedient representative Israelite with the picture of the Son who stands in a unique relationship to the Father, a relationship so close that Jesus can be seen as God's equal and as his presence on earth. Consequently, he can be worshiped as the Son of God.

Jesus and wisdom

Matthew continues his play on wisdom themes in the verses immediately following, where Jesus invites the weary to come to him and find rest (Mt. 11.28-30). They are urged to take his yoke upon them, as his yoke is easy. Similarly, **Sirach** knows that wisdom invites those who so desire and those who are uneducated to come to her (Sirach 24.19; 51.23), and that those who do will find rest (Sirach 6.28; cf. 22.13; 51.27). Moreover, Sirach also likens wisdom to a yoke (Sirach 51.26). These verbal parallels are not sufficient to assume any kind of dependency, however. Rather than invite his hearers to accept the yoke of wisdom, Jesus presents his own yoke. With the emphasis on humility and weakness (11.29), Jesus' character also differs from Sirach's description of wisdom. Matthew's portrait of Jesus owes at least as much to the humble, donkey-riding king of Zech. 9.9 as to wisdom. In Mt. 11.28, Jesus also claims more for himself than what Sirach attributes to God's wisdom. Jesus promises that he will be the one to give rest, whereas Sirach is content to note that those who take hold of wisdom will find "her rest" (6.28). With this promise, Jesus' role is more similar to that of God than to that of wisdom. God is the one who gives rest to his people (Sirach 38.14 **LXX**). In Exod. 33.14 the rest God gives is also connected with his presence.

The saying in Mt. 11.25-30 is not the only one where Matthew's Jesus makes use of wisdom ideas. In Mt. 11.19, he refers to God's wisdom directly. Jesus first notes the opposition with which he and the Baptist are met, but counters that "wisdom is vindicated by her deeds." The Lukan parallel reads: "wisdom is vindicated by all her children" (7.35). Most scholars believe that the Lukan version is the original and that Matthew has changed "children" to "works" in order to forge a more direct identification between Jesus and wisdom. Luke's version may be ambiguous as to whether "children" refers to Jesus and the Baptist or to their followers. If Jesus and the Baptist are understood as wisdom's children, they cannot be identified with wisdom. In Matthew's version, however, wisdom's "works" can only refer to Jesus' and the Baptist's works. The conclusion that Matthew identifies Jesus with wisdom thus lies close at hand. But the implication would then be that John the Baptist is also so identified, as Jesus' words in Mt. 11.7-19 concern the Baptist more than they concern himself. It is unlikely, however, that the Baptist could be identified with God's wisdom. Therefore, the "works" through which wisdom is justified must be the works that God's wisdom does through Jesus and the Baptist.

Such a loose association between Jesus and wisdom accounts for the saying in Mt. 12.42 as well. Jesus maintains that "something greater than Solomon is here!" The implication is that Jesus exceeds Solomon's wisdom. In other words, the climactic revelation of God's wisdom is found in him.

The closest connection between Jesus and wisdom is found in Mt. 23.37-39: "Jerusalem, Jerusalem, the city that kills the prophets and stones those who are sent to it! How often have I desired to gather your children together as a hen gathers her brood under her wings, and you were not willing! See, your house is left to you, desolate. For I tell you, you will not see me again until you say, 'Blessed is the one who comes in the name of the Lord.'"

The image of the mother bird that Jesus used has a rich background in the Scriptures of Israel. The Lord, Israel's God, sustained his people in the wilderness, like an eagle that spreads its wings over its young (Deut. 32.11-12). His continued protection means that Jerusalem need not seek political alliances. God protects Jerusalem "like birds hovering overhead" (Isa. 31.5). Consequently, "the shadow of your wings" becomes a favorite metaphor for taking one's refuge in God (Pss. 17.8; 36.7; 57.1; 63.7; cf. Pss. 61.4; 91.4; Ruth 2.12; *2 Baruch* 41.4; **2 Esdras** 1.30).

When Jesus refers to himself as a protective mother bird, he is applying to himself a well-established metaphor for God and his care for his people. A very similar application of the metaphor is found in **2 Esdras**, where it refers to the Lord Almighty's care for Israel: "I gathered you as a hen gathers her chicks under her wings" (1.30). More broadly, the image of the mother bird could also be applied to God's wisdom, building her nest among human beings (**Sirach** 1.15 **LXX**; Prov. 16.16 LXX).

The way that Jesus speaks in Mt. 23.37-39 makes one wonder if he is an eternal or at least a pre-existent being. In Matthew's Gospel, Jesus has not appeared in Jerusalem until his triumphant entry in Mt. 21.1-10 (excepting the devil's temptation in Mt. 4.5). It is therefore more than odd that he should lament the fact that so "often" he had desired to gather together the children of Jerusalem (Mt. 23.37b). The implication seems to be that Jesus sees himself as the one who had sent the prophets to the city (Mt. 23.37a). Matthew does not develop the point, but the best explanation for his language may well be that pre-existence is presupposed here.[40]

Jesus' role in sending the prophets is stated more directly a couple of verses earlier, where Jesus says: "therefore I send you prophets, sages, and scribes, some of whom you will kill and crucify, and some you will flog in your synagogues and pursue from town to town" (23.34). It is not perfectly clear if Matthew here understands Jesus as the sender of the prophets of old or if he only means to announce the sending of his messengers to Israel from now on. The verb "send" occurs in the present tense (*apostello*), which seems to indicate that Jesus does not refer to the prophets of the past. On the other hand, the threefold "prophets, sages and scribes" may be intended as a more comprehensive category than only Christian witnesses. In any case, Jesus' role is that of the sender of prophets, not that of the prophet who is sent. If v. 37 is read in this light, Jesus appears as the one who sends the prophets that have been killed in the past. There is still no explicit identification of Jesus and wisdom, but Matthew also goes beyond a portrayal of Jesus as a spokesperson for wisdom. Jesus takes wisdom's place as the originator of the divine address to Israel.

It is unwarranted, therefore, to conclude that Jesus is outright identified with wisdom. But it would also be unwarranted to rule out wisdom influence altogether. It appears that Matthew has found wisdom ideas as one motif among several others that were useful in painting his picture of Jesus.

Conclusion

In accordance with his focus on fulfillment, Matthew has tied together a number of Scriptural themes in his picture of Jesus. The tone is set in the infancy narrative, where Jesus is given the name Emmanuel and appears as the one who brings the presence of God. This theme is reinforced throughout Matthew's narrative (10.40; 18.20; 25.31-46; 28.20) and reaches its climax in the Great Commission (28.18-20), where Jesus emerges with full divine power and authority, promising his eternal presence to his disciples. With a broader repertoire than Mark, Matthew shows Jesus to be the one who acts as God on earth and fulfills the prophecies regarding God's own eschatological acts. Jesus issues a call analogous to God's call of the prophets, forgives sins, exercises

God's power over nature and promises to come as the eschatological judge. Accordingly, he receives the worship of human beings.

Matthew's Jesus is also Israel's Messiah and the ultimate eschatological agent of God. As such, he can be compared to Moses, conforms to the ministerial pattern of the humble Servant of the Lord, fulfills the promises regarding the eschatological shepherd and emerges as the ideal obedient Israelite. But Matthew also shows that Jesus transcends these categories. He differs from Moses when he speaks on his own authority and calls his disciples to absolute obedience to himself. He is the fulfillment not only of the prophecies regarding the human eschatological shepherd, but also of those regarding God as the shepherd of his people.

Most significantly, as God's servant, Jesus is God's Son. His sonship means that he is an obedient and suffering righteous human being, but also that he stands on the divine side of the divine–human divide and that he is the recipient of worship that is due only God. As God's Son, Jesus is also God's equal.

Matthew has also found wisdom ideas a useful tool in painting his picture of Jesus. He stands in the closest proximity to God, while he is at the same time distinct from him. As God's intimate, Jesus carries out functions known to be the functions of divine wisdom in Jewish tradition. Like God's wisdom, he transcends history, reveals God's will, and communicates with God's people.

Notes

1   E.g. Gen. 49.18; Exod. 14.13, 30; 15.2; Deut. 20.4; Judg. 6.36, 37; 7.7; 1 Sam. 2.1; 11.13; 1 Chron. 16.23; 2 Chron. 20.17; Pss. 106.8, 10; 107.13, 19; 118.14; 149.4; Prov. 20.22; Isa. 25.9; 30.15; 35.4; 37.35; 43.3, 11, 12; 45.17; 46.13; 49.25, 26; 52.10; 60.16; Jer. 3.23; 30.11; 31.7; 42.11; Ezek. 34.22; 36.29; Hos. 1.7; 13.4; Zeph. 3.17; Zech. 8.7, 13.

2   Quotations from the **Septuagint** are taken from *English Translation of the Septuagint*, ed. Albert Pietersma and Benjamin G. Wright.

3   John Nolland, "No Son-of-God Christology in Matthew 1.18–25," *JSNT* 62 (1996): 9–10.

4   If the prepositional phrase "with us" were to be taken as an adjective, it would normally require that the Greek phrase included the article (such as: *ho meth hemon ho theos*). When the prepositional phrase lacks the article and precedes the noun the meaning is almost always adverbial. This is a weighty argument for the reading "God is with us." However, Matthew's wording may not be dictated by conventional grammar. It should also be noted that the rule requiring the adjectival phrase to be articular is not followed slavishly by New Testament authors. In Rom. 11.25, Paul makes a similarly ambiguous statement. The Greek phrase *porosis apo merous to Israel gegonen*

may be translated either "Israel has been partially hardened" (possibly "a partial hardening has come upon Israel") or "a hardening has come upon part of Israel." The prepositional phrase *apo merous* lacks the article and precedes the articular *to Israel*. According to the rules of grammar, the phrase *apo merous* should therefore not be adjectival and should not modify "Israel." But the argument of Romans 9–11 requires precisely that: a part of Israel has been hardened. Despite the rules of grammar, the **anarthrous** prepositional phrase *apo merous* must be understood as an adjective, modifying *to Israel*.

5   A comparable reapplication of Scripture may be found in Paul's use of Hab. 2.4 in Gal. 3.11 and Rom. 1.17, provided that one accepts the translation "the one who is righteous by faith shall live." In Hab. 2.4, the prepositional phrase is adverbial, but Paul may have given it an adjectival meaning.

6   W. D. Davies and Dale C. Allison, Jr., *A Critical and Exegetical Commentary on the Gospel According to Saint Matthew*, vol. 1, ICC (Edinburgh: T & T Clark, 1988), 217.

7   For the following interpretation of "Emmanuel" I am dependent on several scholars, first and foremost Hubert Frankemölle, *Jahwebund und Kirche Christi: Studien zur Form- und Traditionsgeschichte des Evangeliums nach Matthäus*, NTAbh 10 (Münster: Aschendorff, 1974); J. C. Fenton, "Matthew and the Divinity of Jesus: Three Questions Concerning Matthew 1:20–23," in *Papers on the Gospels*, vol. 2 of *Studia Biblica 1978*, ed. Elizabeth Anne Livingstone, JSNTSup 2 (Sheffield: JSOT Press, 1980), 79–82; J. A. Ziesler, "Matthew and the Presence of Jesus (1)," *Epworth Review* 11, no. 1 (1984): 55–63; David D. Kupp, *Matthew's Emmanuel: Divine Presence and God's People in the First Gospel*, SNTSMS 90 (Cambridge: Cambridge University Press, 1996).

8   It is not technically correct to call this an *inclusio* as Mt. 1.23 does not begin a unit that is concluded in Mt. 28.20. But the prominence of the presence theme both in the beginning and the conclusion of Matthew's Gospel is nevertheless striking.

9   See Mt. 2.11; 4.21; 5.25, 41; 8.11; 9.11, 15; 12.3, 4, 41, 42, 45; 15.30; 16.27; 17.17; 18.16; 20.20; 21.2; 22.16; 24.49, 51; 25.10; 25.31; 26.11, 18, 20, 23, 29, 36, 38, 40, 47, 51, 58, 69, 71; 27.41, 54; 28.12.

10   "Dominus Vobiscum: The Backgound of a Liturgical Formula," in *New Testament Essays: Studies in Memory of Thomas Walter Manson, 1893–1958*, ed. A. J. B. Higgins (Manchester: Manchester University Press, 1959), 276–86.

11   Translation taken from Jacob Neusner, tr., *The Mishnah: A New Translation* (New Haven, CT: Yale University Press, 1988). Cf. also **Mishnah Avot** 3.6; **Mekilta** Exod. 20.24; **Babylonian Talmud Sanhedrin** 39a; **Midrash Psalms** 90.10.

12   Dale C. Allison, Jr., *The New Moses: A Matthean Typology* (Minneapolis: Fortress, 1993), 263–4.

13   Ulrich Luz, *Matthew 21–28*, tr. James E. Crouch, Hermeneia (Minneapolis: Fortress, 2005), 619.

14   In favor of the interpretation "in the name that belongs to the Father, and the Son, and the Holy Spirit," we note that when a singular noun is followed by more than one genitive, the meaning is frequently that the genitives modify the same noun (cf. Mt. 11.25 par.; 16.6 par., 11, 12; Mark 1.29; 6.3; 15.21; Lk. 3.2; Jn 1.44; 11.1; Acts 1.25; 23.7; Rom. 2.5, 20; 8.2; 15.5, 19; 1 Cor. 2.4; 5.8; 2 Cor. 8.24; 13.11; Gal. 1.4; Eph. 1.17; 2.20; 4.13; 5.5; Phil. 4.15; 1 Thess. 5.8; 2 Thess. 1.12; 1 Tim. 1.1; 2 Tim. 1.7; Tit. 3.5; Heb. 10.24, 27; Jas. 1.1; 2 Pet. 1.1, 2, 11; 3.7, 18; Rev. 11.15; 17.5; 20.10; 22.1, 3). The repetition of the noun may be implied, but that is usually the case only when there is no

potential for misunderstanding (cf. Mt. 10.15; Lk. 12.56; Acts 13.15; 1 Cor. 16.17; Heb. 9.12, 13, 19; 10.4; Rev. 18.12, 22, 23; but see Rev. 17.7).

15 For Matthew's appropriation of Old Testament language, see especially Robert H. Gundry, *The Use of the Old Testament in St Matthew's Gospel with Special Reference to the Messianic Hope*, NovTSup 18 (Leiden: Brill, 1967); R. T. France, *Jesus and the Old Testament: His Application of Old Testament Passages to Himself and His Mission* (London: Tyndale, 1971).

16 W. D. Davies and Dale C. Allison, Jr., *A Critical and Exegetical Commentary on the Gospel According to Saint Matthew*, vol. 2, ICC (Edinburgh: T & T Clark, 1991), 629–30, their emphasis.

17 See further Grindheim, *God's Equal*, 93–7.

18 External evidence favors authenticity, as it is included in Sinaiticus, Vaticanus, Ephraemi and the majority text, as well as in the old Latin, the Vulgate, Coptic and Syriac versions. In other words, it occurs in the earliest witnesses, and it has the broadest attestation in all text-types. However, there is also strong evidence for omission, as the verse is one of the so-called Western non-**interpolations**. Important witnesses that omit the verse include Bezae Cantabrigiensis, the Sinaitic Syriac and most Latin versions. Origen and Eusebius also attest to the omission. Many critics therefore conclude that the shorter reading is likely original. The reason is that it is difficult to explain why a scribe would have skipped the verse. On the other hand, the addition can be explained as a result of assimilation to Lk. 20.18. There is also a source-critical argument. Since the Markan version of the parable does not include the verse, it is argued that the verse can only be original in both Matthew and Luke if one assumes that Luke is literary dependent upon Matthew or vice versa (Bruce M. Metzger, *A Textual Commentary on the Greek New Testament*, 4th revised ed. [New York: United Bible Societies, 1994], 47; W. D. Davies and Dale C. Allison, Jr., *A Critical and Exegetical Commentary on the Gospel According to Saint Matthew*, vol. 3, ICC [Edinburgh: T & T Clark, 1997], 186). These arguments fail to convince. The hypothesis of an assimilation to Lk. 20.18 explains nothing. If that were the case, why did the scribe not include this verse immediately after the quotation from Ps. 118.22-23, where it belongs in Luke? And why did the scribe delete the words *pas* and *ekeinon*? On the other hand, both verse 44 and 45 begin with the word *kai*, which may explain the omission. The copyist may have read *kai* in v. 44 and skipped to the text following *kai* in v. 45. As for the source-critical argument, it is not unlikely that a similar form of the parable was known by both Matthew and Luke. Even if it was not, the combination of the related Scriptural themes from Ps. 118.22-23 and Isa. 8.14-15; Dan. 2.34-35, 44-45 may well have been part of early Christian Scripture interpretation. All in all, external arguments tip the balance in favor of authenticity. Cf. also Snodgrass, *Parable of the Wicked Tenants*, 66–68; R. T. France, *The Gospel of Matthew*, NICNT (Grand Rapids: Eerdmans, 2007), 807–8.

19 Joachim Gnilka, *Das Matthäusevangelium*, vol. 2, HTKNT I/2 (Freiburg: Herder, 1988), 209.

20 France, *Gospel of Matthew*, 789–90.

21 Davies and Allison, *Matthew*, vol. 3, 142.

22 Davies and Allison, *Matthew*, vol. 2, 96; Ulrich Luz, *Matthew 8–20*, tr. Wilhelm C. Linss, Hermeneia (Minneapolis: Fortress, 2001), 28; John Nolland, *The Gospel of Matthew*, NIGTC (Grand Rapids: Eerdmans, 2005), 383.

23 Cf. Jack Dean Kingsbury, *Matthew as Story*, 2nd ed. (Philadelphia: Fortress, 1988), 74–5.

24 See further Grindhcim, *God's Equal*, 101–16.

25 Martin Hengel, *The Charismatic Leader and His Followers*, ed. John Riches, tr. James C. G. Greig, reprint, 1981 (New York: Crossroad, 1996).

26 Quoted from Neusner, *The Mishnah*, 6.

27 For the former, see, e.g., Gen. 22.5; 24.26; Pss. 21.28 (ET: 21.27); 28.2; 1 Kgdms 1.3 [ET: 1 Sam. 1.3]; 4 Kgdms 17.35-36 [ET: 2 Kgs 17.35-36]. For the latter, see, e.g., Gen. 23.7; 27.29; 37.9; 1 Kgdms 25.23; 2 Kgdms 18.28; 24.20; 3 Kgdms 1.16, 53; 4 Kgdms 2.15; 4.37.

28 David Peterson, *Engaging With God: A Biblical Theology of Worship* (Downers Grove: IVP, 2002), 85.

29 Mt. 1.1, 16, 17, 18; 2.4; 11.2; 16.16, 20; 23.10; 26.63, 68; 27.17, 22.

30 Mt. 1.1; 9.27; 12.23; 15.22; 20.30, 31; 21.9, 15.

31 See further Young S. Chae, *Jesus as the Eschatological Davidic Shepherd: Studies in the Old Testament, Second Temple Judaism, and in the Gospel of Matthew*, WUNT II/216 (Tübingen: Mohr Siebeck, 2006).

32 For the temptation account, see especially Birger Gerhardsson, *The Testing of God's Son (Matt. 4: 1–11 & par.): An Analysis of an Early Christian Midrash*, ConBNT 2 (Lund: Gleerup, 1966).

33 Birger Gerhardsson, *The Mighty Acts of Jesus According to Matthew*, Scripta Minora Regiae Societatis Humaniorum Litterarum Lundensis (Lund: Gleerup, 1979), 89–90.

34 For a detailed discussion of this saying, see Grindheim, *God's Equal*, 174–88.

35 Allison, *The New Moses*, 218–33.

36 Luz, *Matthew 8–20*, 168.

37 James D. G. Dunn, *Christology in the Making: A New Testament Inquiry into the Origins of the Doctrine of the Incarnation*, 2nd ed. (Grand Rapids: Eerdmans, 1989), 199–200.

38 See especially Felix Christ, *Jesus Sophia: Die Sophia-Christologie bei den Synoptikern*, ATANT 57 (Zurich: Zwingli, 1970); M. Jack Suggs, *Wisdom, Christology, and Law in Matthew's Gospel* (Cambridge, MA: Harvard University Press, 1970); and, more cautiously, Martin Hengel, *Studies in Early Christology*, reprint, 1995 (London: T & T Clark, 2004), 73–108.

39 Dunn, *Christology in the Making*, 199.

40 Cf. Simon J. Gathercole, *The Preexistent Son: Recovering the Christologies of Matthew, Mark, and Luke* (Grand Rapids: Eerdmans, 2006), 214–21.

4

God's Name: Christology in Luke's Gospel

Compared to Matthew and Mark, Luke displays a heightened interest in the titles of Jesus. The most important title in Luke's Gospel is the title "Lord," which Luke uses with considerable ingenuity to show that Jesus shares God's name. The Son of God title is also important to Luke and he uses the infancy narrative to show its profound meaning. Luke's infancy narrative also sets the stage for showing that Jesus is the one who carries out God's visitation on earth.

Luke has included many images of Jesus as God's servant as well. Jesus fills the role of prophet, Messiah, the coming one, and Isaiah's Servant of the Lord. But Luke's Jesus also transcends these categories. Luke is therefore capable of using language that ties Jesus very closely to God. Like Matthew, he sees Jesus as the one who takes the place of God's wisdom.

Lord

Luke stands out among the Synoptic Gospels in his use the title of "Lord" for Jesus. Mark and Matthew report that Jesus is called "Lord" by those who approach him, but that is not likely to be more than a polite address. They also include some Scripture quotations where the referent of "Lord" is ambiguous. In the Old Testament context "Lord" refers to God, but in the gospel narrative the referent may be understood as Jesus. All the Synoptic Gospels also report Jesus' discussion of David's Lord on the basis of Ps. 110.1. We are not told who this Lord is, but the gospel narrative leads us to the conclusion that it is Jesus (cf. pp. 51-52).

When reporting the words of the characters in the gospel story, Luke's use of the title "Lord" does not differ much from the other Synoptists. But where Luke is free to use his own voice as a narrator, his special interest in the title "Lord" is played out. Whereas Matthew and Mark never refer to Jesus as the Lord, this title is a favorite of Luke's. The first clear example of this practice occurs in 7.13, where Luke observes that "the Lord saw" the widow at Nain and "had compassion for her" (cf. 7.19; 10.1, 39, 41; 11.39; 12.42; 13.15; 17.5, 6; 18.6; 19.8; 22.61).

Luke has thus applied the same name to the earthly Jesus as that with which the post-Easter community referred to the exalted Christ. Inspired by Ps. 110.1, the early church hailed the resurrected Christ as Lord (Acts 2.35-36; Rom. 8.34; Heb. 1.3, 13). By so doing, they attributed to him what was known as God's name par excellence in the Greek Bible (cf. Phil. 2.9-11). God's name YHWH is there translated *kurios* ("Lord").[1]

When Luke's use of the term "Lord" is analyzed in its narrative context, we see that it takes on the full connotations of the divine name. As Kavin Rowe has aptly demonstrated, Luke plays on a clever ambiguity in his use of this title, and the development begins in the infancy narrative.[2] Initially, the title serves as an unambiguous reference to God. In 1.6, Zechariah and Elizabeth are said to observe all the commandments of the Lord. As the narrative develops, the title recurs frequently (1.15, 16, 25, 28, 32, 38) and is established as a common designation for God.

Against this background, Elizabeth's addressing Mary as "the mother of my Lord" (tou *kuriou mou*) is quite striking (1.43). Most commentators understand "Lord" to be a messianic title here, and sometimes reference is made to Lk. 2.11; 20.41-44 (cf. Acts 2.34-36), where the titles "Messiah" and "Lord" occur together. But such an interpretation is alien to the immediate context. Luke has already used the title repeatedly, but only with reference to God. One may wonder, therefore, if Luke intends to identify Jesus as God. But that interpretation is ruled out by the simple observation that Luke has made a clear distinction between the two in 1.32, where the angel promised that the Lord God would give David's throne to Jesus. The effect of Luke's language is instead to introduce an ambiguity. Jesus is the Lord, yet distinguished from him. In this way, Jesus appears in Luke's Gospel in the closest proximity to God. Jesus and God share the same name.

Luke's desire to show Jesus as the Lord can be observed also in the way he edits his sources. When Luke tells the story of the Sabbath controversy (6.1-5), he omits an essential part of the argument, according to both Mark and Matthew. In contrast to Mark, Luke does not include the point that has general application: that the Sabbath was made for human beings, not vice versa (Mk 2.27). In contrast to Matthew, he does not explain that Jesus' actions conform to the universally applicable principle that mercy is more important than sacrifice (Mt. 12.7). Instead Luke moves directly to the clincher: "the Son of Man is lord of the Sabbath" (Lk. 6.5). By editing the story in this way, the weight of the argument depends more directly on the title "Lord" and its applicability to Jesus. In a Jewish context, the Lord of the Sabbath would be thought to be God. Jesus thus takes God's place as the Lord.

Not only the use of the same designation for God and Jesus, but also the structure of Luke's narrative contributes to his picture of Jesus as equal to God. Luke's presentation of John the Baptist and his role as a forerunner is a case in point. When the Baptist is introduced, he is the one who will bring the children of Israel back to the Lord their God, as he will go before the Lord (1.16-17). John here appears to be identified as the messenger announced in Mal. 3.1, the messenger God sends to prepare his way (cf. Lk. 7.27). This messenger may be interpreted as Elijah, who appears in Mal. 4.5 with a similar mission, and Luke also specifies that John will go "with the spirit and power of Elijah" (1.17). Zechariah also proclaims regarding John that he will go before the Lord and prepare a way for him (1.76). In this respect, he fulfills the prophecy in Isa. 40.3-5 (Lk. 3.4-6), which speaks of the messenger that prepares the way for the Lord.

In Luke's narrative, however, John is presented as the forerunner, not of God, but of Jesus. Implicitly, Luke thus identifies Jesus as the Lord of Mal. 3.1 and Isa. 40.3-5. Jesus is the Lord who comes after the eschatological prophet has done his preparatory work.

Having introduced this careful ambiguity in the use of the Lord title in his infancy narrative, Luke maintains it throughout his Gospel. When Jesus programmatically announces the year of the Lord's favor (4.18-19), he refers to Isaiah's announcement of a Jubilee year (Isa. 61.2), and the Lord in question is of course the God of Israel. But as Luke's story unfolds, the prophecy finds its fulfillment in the ministry of Jesus himself (cf. 7.22).

In the same way, Jesus tells his disciples to pray to the Lord of the harvest that he send workers to the field (10.2). As Jesus speaks of this Lord in the third person, it is natural to assume that he refers to someone other than himself, and that the disciples are urged to pray to God. In Luke's narrative, however, Jesus is the one who calls workers.

Finally, in the story of the triumphal entry, Jesus instructs two of his disciples to bring him a colt. If anyone questions them, they shall answer that its Lord has need (19.31, 34). Jesus is not directly identified as this Lord, but the only character in Luke's story who has any need of the colt is he.

Who Is This Lord?

Once this pattern is observed it can shed some light on a passage where Luke may appear to describe Jesus as dependent on God for his ability to heal.

According to the common translation of Lk. 5.17, "the power of the Lord was with him (Jesus) to heal" (NRSV). On this translation, "Lord" unequivocally refers to God the Father. However, this translation is not the only possible way to understand the Greek text. Rowe has presented a good case for a different translation: "the power of the Lord was present to heal him [the paralytic]." On this understanding of the grammar, the genitive *kuriou* ("of the Lord") in the phrase "power of the Lord" does not refer to God, but to Jesus.[3]

If Lk. 5.17 refers to Jesus' own power, the verse would cohere with the overall picture that is painted of his miracles in Luke's Gospel. Jesus never prays for the power to perform miracles. The power is immediately available to him, presumably because this power is inherently his own. The contrast with the miracles performed by the disciples in Luke's second volume corroborates this interpretation. Luke usually explains that these miracles take place in the name of Jesus (Acts 3.6; cf. 9.34) or as an answer to prayer (Acts 9.40; 28.8; but see also 14.9-10). The implication seems to be that the disciples are dependent on an outside power in a way that Jesus was not.[4]

However, the difficulty of taking the pronoun "him" (*auton*) as the object in Lk. 5.17 is that it leaves the text with no noun to which this pronoun can refer. The paralytic is not introduced until the next verse. Based on Lukan style, Kavin Rowe provides an explanation for this pronoun as forward-referring, equivalent to the Semitic proleptic pronoun. But Rowe finally dismisses this explanation and wisely interprets the verse as another instance of Lukan ambiguity.[5]

God or Jesus?

While Luke frequently refers to Jesus as "the Lord," he never unequivocally refers to Jesus as "God." But he repeatedly refers to God with an ambiguity that compares to his use of the title "Lord." On several occasions, he mentions God where his narrative has prepared the audience for a mention of Jesus. When Jesus has liberated the demoniac from the Gerasene region he instructs him to return home and proclaim how much God has done for him (8.39a). In Luke's next sentence, he informs us that the demoniac proclaimed how much Jesus has done for him (8.39b). There is a close parallelism in these two phrases in v. 39, but where Jesus says "God," Luke says "Jesus." The implication may be nothing more than that Jesus, as God's servant, performs the works of God. But if Luke's use of the title "Lord" is a guide, there may be an intentional ambiguity here as well.

The crippled woman who is healed on the Sabbath presents us with a similar example. Jesus calls her, tells her that she is set free from her ailment and makes her stand up straight (13.12-13). The woman's response is to praise God (13.13). God has not appeared in the story at all – Jesus is the woman's benefactor. Again, the story is perfectly compatible with the understanding of Jesus as God's servant, but it may also be read in light of Luke's penchant for Christological ambiguity.

A more carefully crafted ambiguity occurs in the story where Jesus' disciples proved unable to drive out a demon and Jesus forced it into submission. All the witnesses were amazed at the greatness of God (9.43a). The reference to God is unexpected, as Luke's story has not mentioned God directly, only the unparalleled authority of Jesus. In the next sentence, Luke observes that "everyone was amazed at all that he was doing" (9.43b). Luke here uses a singular verb (*epoiei*) without making the subject explicit. At the syntactical level, the subject must be supplied from the previous sentence, where the only singular noun is God (*theou*). At the narrative level, however, the subject is Jesus, who does the works that cause amazement. A connection between Jesus' works and God's greatness is therefore presupposed by Luke, but it remains unexplained. At the historical level, there is no indication that the witnesses understood Jesus as more than a divine agent, but at the narrative level, the connection between Jesus and God may be closer.

Son of God from his conception

Although the connection between Jesus and God is very close, Luke also shows Jesus to be a character distinct from God. His chief tool in so doing is the Son of God metaphor.

Like Mark and Matthew, Luke uses the Son of God title as an authoritative title for Jesus. The angel that comes to Mary introduces Jesus as the Son of God (1.32, 35), and the heavenly voice makes the same announcement at Jesus' baptism and transfiguration (3.22; 9.35). Jesus obliquely attributes this title to himself in the parable of the wicked tenants (20.13), accepts it at his trial (22.70) and refers to himself as the Son (10.22). The demons acknowledge him to be God's Son (4.41; 8.28), and the devil challenges him to demonstrate that he is (4.3, 9).

Even more than Matthew, Luke uses the infancy narrative to establish the significance of Jesus' sonship. In Luke's account, the Son of God title is connected directly with the virginal conception (1.26-38). As Raymond

Brown correctly observes, the parallels between the annunciation of Jesus' birth and that of John the Baptist require that an actual virginal conception is being described. Jesus is consistently given epithets that supersede those given to John. This build-up would fall flat if the climax of the annunciation was simply that a young woman would conceive. Elizabeth's pregnancy was understood to be miraculous because of her old age and her previous barrenness. Mary's pregnancy must be a greater miracle: a virginal conception.[6]

However, the combination of the ideas of divine sonship and virginal conception is unknown in the surviving Jewish literature. In this literature, the title Son of God can be applied relatively broadly. When the king or a messianic figure is called son of God, the meaning of the title is functional. This Son of God is given a function that will be executed through an exceptional divine empowering (cf. 2 Sam. 7.14; 1 Chron. 17.13; 22.10; 28.6; Pss. 2.7; 89.27; **4Q174** 1.11-13; **4Q246** 2.1, 5-9; *Testament of Levi* 4.2; 18.6). Also, when the term is used for humans more broadly, that is, for the people of Israel, sonship is something that is vested in them, not something that is inherently theirs (cf. Jer. 31.9; Hos. 11.1; **Sirach** 4.10; *Jubilees* 1.23-25).

The Lukan infancy narrative is steeped in biblical imagery and Luke's annunciation story betrays close parallels to a scroll from Qumran, 4QAramaic Apocalypse (**4Q246**). This text describes an eschatological character and announces that "he will be great over the earth" (4Q246 1.7), "he will be called son of God, and they will call him son of the Most High" (4Q246 2.1) and "his kingdom will be an eternal kingdom" (4Q246 2.5). The similarities with Luke's Gospel (cf. Lk. 1.32, 33, 35) are so striking that some scholars think that Luke was dependent on 4Q246. Whatever the relationship may be, however, Luke introduces an element in his narrative that is unparalleled in 4Q246 and indeed in all the known references to divine sonship in Second Temple Judaism. Luke connects Jesus' sonship to the annunciation of his birth and to his conception. The angel that comes to Mary refers to the holy one to be born and says that he shall be called God's Son (1.35). Raymond Brown correctly concludes, therefore, that Luke in 1.35 combines the images of the Messiah and the Son of God in a way that goes beyond early Jewish expectation. Divine sonship is not tied to function and attributed to a king in connection with his coronation and his role as a ruler. Instead, Luke describes the begetting of God's Son in Mary's womb. It is an act of God's Spirit and his divine sonship refers to who he is from his conception.[7]

Announcing the one who is more than a prophet

Luke understands Jesus' birth as more than the birth of a prophet. His description has overtones of God's own coming to the world. This view of Jesus is reflected in the epithets that are given to him before his birth, as can be most clearly appreciated when the annunciation of Jesus' birth is compared to that of John the Baptist. There is extensive parallelism between these two annunciations, and the effect is to show how Jesus is greater than John. Whereas John the Baptist will be great before the Lord (1.15a), Jesus will be great without qualification (1.32a). John will be filled with the Holy Spirit from his mother's womb (1.15c), but Jesus' conception itself is a creative act of the Holy Spirit (1.35b). John will prepare a people that is ready for the Lord (1.17e), but Jesus will rule the house of Jacob forever and there will be no end to his kingdom (1.33). John is consecrated to **Nazirite** abstinence (1.15a), but Jesus is "holy" from his birth (1.35b).

To be great without qualification (1.32; cf. 1.15) is God's exclusive prerogative in the Scriptures of Israel (e.g. Pss. 48.1; 86.10; 135.5; 145.3). The greatness of human beings is always qualified. A person may be a great man (2 Sam. 19.32), great among human beings (Esth. 10.3), or even great before God (Gen. 10.9; cf. **Sirach** 48.22), but not great in and of him or herself. In contrast to John (1.15), Jesus has no need to be filled with the Holy Spirit as his union with the Spirit begun at his conception (1.35). Because of his inherent holiness, he does not have to be sanctified or consecrated.

The precise significance of the word "holy" in 1.35 depends on the understanding of the syntax. Two translations are possible. Most modern translations understand the grammar like the NRSV: "therefore the child to be born will be holy; he will be called Son of God." The other option is found in the NIV: "So the holy one to be born will be called the Son of God." The first translation is based on the assumption that the word "holy" (*hagion*) is the predicate of the verb "to be born" (the participle *gennomenon*), whereas the second translation understands the word "holy" as part of the subject, "the holy one to be born" (*to gennomenon hagion*).[8] If "holy" is understood as part of the subject, that may fit Luke's logic better. He explains why Jesus is the Son of God: it is because he is conceived by the Holy Spirit and because he is holy. On either translation, however, the inherent holiness of Jesus is underscored.

An Ambiguous Introduction

If the hymns in Luke's first two chapters show Jesus at the same level as God, they also prepare the audience for an understanding of Jesus' ministry in the same light. When the song of Mary (Lk. 1.46-55) is read in light of Luke's narrative as a whole, we observe a similar kind of ambiguity as we have seen in connection with the title "Lord." Mary magnifies the Lord and rejoices in God, her savior (1.46-47). In the immediate context, her praise is directed to God. The titles "Lord" and "Savior" obviously refer to the Father. As Luke's story progresses, however, Jesus is the one who emerges as Lord and Savior. Luke routinely refers to Jesus as the Lord, and his portrait of Jesus focuses on his function as savior.

Mary continues to extol God as the mighty one (*dunatos*), whose name is holy (1.49). The last of these divine characteristics recalls the angel's address to Mary, where Jesus is introduced as the holy one who will be born (1.35). The adjective "mighty" recurs towards the very end of Luke's Gospel, where the disciples on the way to Emmaus call Jesus a mighty prophet (24.19). Interestingly, the divine epithet "mighty" is here coupled with the idea of Jesus as a servant of God.

As Mary details the great works of God, she emphasizes how he has brought down the powerful and exalted the lowly (1.51b-53). In the context of Luke's narrative, she introduces the central reversal of values motif, a motif that will be a chief characteristic of Jesus' ministry (6.20-26; 7.36-50; 10.21; etc.). God is finally praised for remembering his mercy (1.54-55), and, once again, in Luke's narrative Jesus is the one who performs acts of mercy throughout his ministry (4.18-19; 7.22; etc.).

One of the narrative purposes of Mary's song, therefore, is to highlight the ambiguity that Luke has already introduced through his attribution to Jesus of the title "Lord." Mary's song introduces a number of important Lukan themes and provides a conventional Scriptural background for understanding them: God is Lord and savior, he is mighty and holy. He turns the values of the world upside-down and he shows mercy to his people. Luke's story then shows that the one who fills this role is Jesus. We see here the first indication that Luke presents Jesus as the one who carries out God's visitation on earth.

The picture of Jesus as interchangeable with God is quickly juxtaposed with the picture of Jesus as God's servant. The next song in Luke's infancy narrative, the song of Zechariah (1.68-79), directs praise to God for what he is doing through his agent, the mighty savior he has raised up in the house of his servant David (1.69). The savior he refers to is of course Jesus, who is described with conventional messianic imagery. He saves Israel from their enemies, according to the covenant with Abraham (1.72-75).

These two seemingly conflicting images, of God's own intervention and his dispatch of a deliverer, are combined in the angels' proclamation to the shepherds in the field: "to you is born this day in the city of David a Savior, who is the Messiah, the Lord" (2.11). For the first time, Jesus is now called Messiah (Gr.: *christos*). This title is coupled with the title with which the audience is already familiar: "Lord." Jesus is a Messiah who is also Lord (cf. 20.41-44; Acts 2.36).

Instead of seeing Luke qualifying the picture of Jesus as the Messiah, many scholars argue that the coupling of the titles "Messiah" and "Lord" shows that Luke uses "Lord" as a messianic title. A precedent for this double title may be found in the **Psalms of Solomon**. According to *Psalms of Solomon* 17.32, "their king shall be the Lord Messiah." If this indeed is the correct reading of *Psalms of Solomon* 17.32, the Greek *kurios* ("Lord") corresponds to the Hebrew *adon* (not the divine name, Yahweh) and is used as a royal title (cf. p.16). But Luke's Gospel has provided another interpretive context for reading the *kurios* title: as the name of God. In his portrayal of Jesus, Luke has already gone beyond messianic expectations (1.32, 35, 43; cf. below on pp. 122-23). If the title *christos kurios* is read in the context of Luke's own narrative world, therefore, it is best understood as another way in which Luke expands the connotations of the Messiah.

Zechariah's Dawn

This merging of the image of God himself with the image of the Messiah is anticipated in the song of Zechariah (Lk. 1.68-79). Zechariah concludes his song by observing that "the dawn from on high" has visited us (1.78).[9] To identify the referent of this "dawn" is one of the most challenging problems in the interpretation of Luke's Gospel. The search for the exact background for Zechariah's image has proved elusive. Many commentators have observed that the Greek word *anatole* (usually translated "dawn") is used in the **Septuagint** to render the Hebrew *tsemach* ("branch"), which is a messianic title in Jer. 23.5; 33.15; and Zech. 3.8; 6.12 (cf. Isa. 4.2). The metaphor is dependent on the prophecy of the shoot in Isa. 11.1. In the **Dead Sea Scrolls**, the branch is an established title for the Messiah (**4Q161** 8–10.18; **4Q174** 1.11; **4Q252**

5.3-4). It is possible, therefore, that Luke invokes the messianic image of the Davidic branch.

However, the **cognate** verb *anatello* is also used in the Balaam prophecy, when Balaam announces the star that will rise (*anatellei*) out of Jacob. This star also became established as a messianic image (*Testament of Levi* 18.3; **CD** 7.18-19; **1QM** 11.6), and this image may be more appropriate in Luke's context. The qualifier "from on high" (*ex hupsous*) is consistent with the understanding of *anatole* as a heavenly light, and the following verse promises that light will be given to those who sit in darkness. There is also evidence that Jeremiah's and Balaam's prophecies were combined, as the referent was understood to be the same (*Testament of Judah* 24.1, 6). As an established messianic symbol, the *anatole* may have a mixed background, therefore.

But the verb *anatello* is also frequently used in the **Septuagint** in connection with the eschatological salvation of the Lord, who will cause the sun to rise (*anatelei*) over those who fear his name (Mal. 4.2). With reference to the restoration of Israel, Isaiah promises that new things, glory, righteousness, and praise, will spring forth (Isa. 42.9; 43.19; 44.4, 26; 45.8; 60.1; 61.11; 66.14). Isaiah 60 uses the verb *anatello* for the rising of the glory of the Lord (v. 1) in parallelism with the rising of the Lord (v. 2). Luke's expression is therefore well fitted to depict the eschatological coming of the Lord himself.

This interpretation of the *anatole* may be confirmed by the fact that Luke uses the verb "to visit/inspect" (*episkeptomai*) with "dawn from on high" (*anatole ex hupsous*) as the subject. When *episkeptomai* (or *episkopeo*) is used for heavenly visitations in the **Septuagint**, the subject is always God. The verb denotes his visitation of human beings for the purpose of judgment or salvation.[10] Luke's coupling of *anatole* with the prepositional phrase "from on high" (*ex hupsous*) also points in this direction. Whereas Balaam's star was to rise out of Jacob and the messianic branch out of David, Zechariah's *anatole* comes from on high.

There are three plausible backgrounds for Zechariah's image, therefore. It may go back to a messianic symbol like the Davidic branch or the star from Judah, but it may at least equally well go back to the eschatological sunrise that God himself will bring. As we have seen, Luke is fond of ambiguities in his portrait of Christ. The best interpretation of Zechariah's "dawn" must therefore be that this is another ambiguous metaphor. It is an image that evokes God's eschatological intervention on earth, but also has messianic overtones. In Luke's story, the dawn is of course Jesus (cf. 2.32), who soon will be introduced as simultaneously Lord and Messiah (2.11).

God's Visitation

We can confirm this interpretation of Zechariah's "dawn" as an ambiguous metaphor when we consider Luke's continued use of the visitation theme. After Jesus' raising of the widow's son at Nain, the crowd concluded that a great prophet had risen and that God had visited (*epeskapsato*) his people (7.16). This reaction resembles the verdict of the disciples on the way to Emmaus (24.19). Jesus is seen as a prophet, but described with terminology that was normally reserved for God ("mighty;" cf. p. 125).

This inherent tension is heightened in Jesus' own words. When he approaches Jerusalem he pronounces judgment on the city because they did not know the time of their visitation (*ton kairon tes episkopes sou*; 19.44). Jesus' words contain an allusion to Jer. 6.15 **LXX**, where the prophet predicts regarding Jerusalem: "they shall perish in a time of visitation" (*en kairo episkopes auton apolountai*; cf. Jer. 10.15 LXX). The visitation to which Jeremiah refers is the visitation of God, as the Hebrew text makes explicit. In Luke's story, however, the visitation is that of Jesus, whose visit was announced six verses earlier (19.38). As he enters Jerusalem, it becomes evident that the people of Jerusalem do not recognize him. Implicitly, the visit of Jesus is the visit of God. Luke is filling in his picture of Jesus as the one who carries out God's visitation on earth.

Jesus as the Divine Lord's Presence on Earth

In accordance with this view of Jesus, Luke portrays him as the divine Lord who is now present on earth. His majesty is revealed in the story of Peter's call to become a fisher of people (5.1-11). As a call narrative, this story is in some important ways similar to Isaiah's throne vision (Isa. 6.1-13). The encounter with the greatness of the Lord/Jesus (Isa. 6.1-4; Lk. 5.4-7) provokes an expression of uncleanness/sinfulness (Isa. 6.5; Lk. 5.8), which is followed by a word of reassurance (Isa. 6.7; Lk. 5.10b) and a commission (Isa. 6.8–10; Lk. 5.10b). The similarities are merely suggestive and the pericope contains no explicit Christology. But Peter's declaration demands an explanation. He shows an awareness that his sinfulness makes him unfit for the company of Jesus. As the parallels with Isaiah's throne vision show, the character whose holiness makes him unapproachable for sinners is God. What Isaiah saw in his vision of the heavenly glory, Peter saw in real life on Lake Galilee. In Jesus, the heavenly Lord is thus brought down to earth.[11]

Salvation and Faith

Luke's portrait of Jesus' ministry can be read in the same light. God's inter-action with human beings on earth now takes place through Jesus. The acts of God insofar as they relate to human beings are performed by Jesus. Chief among these acts is the work of salvation, which Luke connects with Jesus to a much greater degree than the other Synoptic Gospels do. In Luke's Gospel, Jesus is not merely an agent of salvation; his role in salvation goes beyond that of bringing it. Salvation is connected with the person of Jesus himself. When Simeon exclaims that he has seen God's salvation he does not refer to any acts of deliverance comparable to the exodus from Egypt or the redemption brought through the judges. He has seen God's salvation when he has seen the baby Jesus (2.30). Although Jesus is frequently portrayed as granting salvation by his works of healing and forgiveness (6.9; 7.50; 8.36, 48, 50; 18.42; 19.10; 23.35), salvation is more than a gift that Jesus dispenses or a work that he performs. In the story of the ten people with a skin disease, all ten were cleansed, but only one was told that he was saved (17.19). He was saved when he returned to Jesus to give thanks. The salvation of the sinful woman in Simon's house is connected with the forgiveness of her sins (7.48), but salvation and forgiveness are not equated in Luke's story. Jesus commends the woman for the great love that she has showed him (7.44-47), and this love is part of the context for understanding what it means that she is saved (7.50). Both of these examples show that salvation is not a gift that is transmitted through a fleeting encounter with Jesus; salvation entails a relationship with him.

Closely connected with Luke's understanding of salvation is his concept of faith. More clearly than the other Synoptic Gospels, Luke ties faith to the person of Jesus. Although he does not include the reference to faith in the saying about causing the little ones to stumble (compare Lk. 17.2 and Mk 9.42; Mt. 18.6), his narrative highlights the connection between faith and the person of Jesus. The hemorrhaging woman was commended for her faith after she touched the edge of Jesus' cloak (8.44, 48). The sinful woman in Simon's house demonstrated her faith through her affection for Jesus (7.44-50). The Samaritan with the skin disease was told that he was saved when he returned to Jesus to thank him (17.19). One would not do full justice to these stories if one simply said that faith here means to believe that God is able to do something through Jesus. The object of faith in these examples is not so much God as it is Jesus himself. Accordingly, the criminal on the cross expresses a trust that is directed to the person of Jesus (23.39-43).

When Luke describes the person of Jesus as the object of saving faith, he places Jesus squarely in a role that Jews normally would have reserved for Yahweh. In the Scriptures of Israel, the faithful believed in God himself (Gen. 15.6; Isa. 43.10; Jon. 3.5; Dan. 6.23).[12] Conversely, the rebellious were censured for not believing in God (Num. 14.11; 20.12; Deut. 1.32; 9.23; 2 Kgs 17.14; Ps. 78.22).[13] Those who are condemned suffer this fate because they did not believe in God (*1 Enoch* 63.7–8; 67.8, cf. **Philo**, *On the Sacrifices of Cain and Abel* 70).

When the angels in the infancy narrative hail Jesus as savior (2.11), therefore, the primary background must be seen in the use of this epithet for God himself.[14] The term only occurs in one other instance in the Gospel of Luke, where it refers to God (1.47). In the Scriptures of Israel, human beings may be called saviors, but their salvation is of a political kind (Judg. 3.9, 15). As can be seen from the examples cited above, Luke's concept of salvation is more comprehensive. As savior, therefore, Jesus fulfills the role of God. God's saving interaction in the world now takes place through Jesus.

Jesus Takes God's Place

When Jesus appears on earth as the Lord, it follows that he possesses powers and performs tasks normally thought to be God's exclusive prerogative. From the Synoptic tradition, Luke has included a number of elements where Jesus appears in the role of God. He inaugurates God's kingdom (11.20; 17.21; cf. pp. 38-40, 90-91),[15] exercises authority over evil (10.19; cf. pp. 41-44), forgives sins (5.20; 7.48; cf. p. 45), has power over nature (8.24), issues a call that may be compared to God's call of the prophets (9.60; 14.26; cf. pp. 94-96) and has specific knowledge of the future (10.13-15; 19.30-31; 22.10-12, 34). His name takes the place of God's name, as the disciples cast out demons in his name (9.49; 10.17) and are persecuted because of his name (21.12, 17). Repentance and forgiveness of sins will also be proclaimed in his name (24.47; cf. also p. 49). In addition, Luke applies divine epithets to Jesus, such as "horn of salvation" (1.69; cf. Ps. 18.2) and "bridegroom" (5.34; cf. Hos. 2.19-20; Isa. 54.5-6; Ezek. 16.8; see also pp. 48-49).

Resurrection

A more ambiguous description of Jesus' powers is provided in connection with the resurrection. Luke usually explains Jesus' resurrection as an act of God. In the book of Acts, this idea is made explicit (Acts 2.24, 32; 3.15; 4.10

etc.), and it probably lies behind the use of the passive voice in the expression "be risen" (*egerthenai/egerth*; Lk. 9.22; 24.34). However, Luke also describes the resurrection as Jesus' own activity (Lk. 18.33; 24.7, 46; cf. Acts 10.41; 17.3).[16] The implication is probably that Jesus rose by his own power.

As the power to raise the dead is the prerogative of God (***Joseph and Aseneth*** 20.7; ***Shemoneh Esre*** 2; cf. **Tobit** 13.2; **Wisdom of Solomon** 16.13), Jesus' powers are thus described as matching those of God. Although Luke does not use the resurrection to demonstrate Jesus' identity, his description of it may presuppose an understanding of Jesus as equal to God. This presupposition also shines through when he refers to the resurrection as the Messiah entering into "his glory" (24.26). Luke has Jesus' heavenly glory in mind, and it is telling that he can refer to this glory as Jesus' own. In the Septuagint, the word *doxa* has a wide range of use, but when it denotes heavenly glory, that glory is always God's.[17] God gives glory to human beings, both in the present (1 Kgs 3.13; 1 Chron. 29.12) and in the eschatological future (Ps. 73.24), as well as to the Son of Man (Dan. 7.14).[18] But this glory is never described as their own. In contrast, Jesus enters into his own glory.

Worship

After Jesus' resurrection, Luke also shows how the believers respond to him in the way they would respond to God, by falling down in worship (Lk. 24.52). Unlike Matthew, however, Luke gives no indication that worship was an element of the disciples' response to Jesus before his resurrection. In his account, the disciples are not prompted to worship Jesus until he is lifted up to heaven.

Jesus as God's servant

Despite this emphasis on Jesus taking the place of God, Luke has not shied away from portraying him as God's servant, who is subordinate to him. The Father confers a kingdom on Jesus before Jesus confers it on his disciples (Lk. 22.29). Likewise, Jesus is frequently seen praying to the Father (3.21; 5.16; 6.12; 9.18, 28-29; 10.21-22; 11.1; 22.32, 40-45; 23.34, 46). On the common translation of 5.17, God gives Jesus the power to heal (but cf. p. 121). However, Luke has not included the saying about the ignorance of the Son (cf. Mk 13.32/Mt. 24.36) nor the one where he defers to the Father to decide who will sit at his right and left hand (cf. Mk 10.40/Mt. 20.23).

Prophet

The prophetic aspects of Jesus' ministry receive much more attention in Luke's Gospel than in the other Synoptics.[19] These aspects are introduced in the infancy narrative, which demonstrates a considerable interest in prophetic inspiration. When the angel Gabriel announces the birth of Zechariah's son, he paints this son as an Elijah-like character who will be filled with the Holy Spirit and set apart for the Lord (1.15-17). Later, Elizabeth is also filled with the Holy Spirit and enabled to provide insights regarding the son that her cousin Mary carries in her womb (1.41-45). When Zechariah and Elizabeth's son is born, prophetic inspiration appears to have been at work in giving him his name (1.59-63). Subsequently, the Holy Spirit fills Zechariah and makes him prophesy regarding John and Jesus (1.67-79). Later on, through divine revelation and the guidance of the Holy Spirit, Simeon recognizes Jesus as Israel's savior (2.25-32). The prophet Anna also speaks about the child Jesus (2.36-38).

With all this emphasis on prophecy and the Holy Spirit, it is noteworthy that Jesus himself is not directly associated with the Holy Spirit and with the gift of prophecy. Jesus is conceived as the Holy Spirit comes, not on Jesus, but on Mary (1.35). The child is holy in himself, not by virtue of the indwelling Holy Spirit (1.35). While the infancy narrative is steeped in prophetic motifs, Jesus does not emerge as a prophet. Instead, he is presented as the object of the prophetic messages. This theme recurs toward the end of the Gospel. In the resurrection appearances, Luke's Jesus claims that his own person is the focal point of all the prophets (24.27, 44). In the beginning and the end of the Gospel, the prophets appear as servants of Jesus and point to his significance.

When his public ministry begins, however, Jesus' own function fits within prophetic categories. At his baptism, the Holy Spirit descends upon him as a dove (3.22). Following this experience, Jesus is full of the Holy Spirit and is led by him into the wilderness (4.1). Still filled with the power of the Spirit, Jesus returns to Galilee (4.14) and makes his programmatic speech in Nazareth (4.16). He now defines his ministry with strong affinities to that of the prophets, as he appropriates for himself the prophecy of Isa. 61.1-2 and claims that the Spirit of the Lord is upon him to proclaim the message of the Lord (4.18-19). In the discourse that follows, Jesus explicitly uses a prophetic paradigm to explain his own actions, as he observes that no prophets are accepted in their home towns (4.24). He goes on specifically to compare himself to Elijah and Elisha (4.25-27).

The parallels between Jesus on the one hand and Elijah and Elisha on the other are highlighted by Luke on several occasions. In the story of the healing of the Roman centurion's servant (7.1-10), Jesus extends his healing ministry to a Gentile, like Elijah (cf. 1 Kgs 17.1-16) and Elisha (cf. 2 Kgs 5.1-14) had done before him. In contrast to Matthew (Mt. 8.5-13), Luke emphasizes that the Gentile was well regarded by the Jews (Lk. 7.2, 4-5) and that the Jewish elders interceded for him (Lk. 7.3-5). This portrait of the Gentile supplicant has clear parallels in the picture of the Aramean commander Naaman known from the Elisha traditions (2 Kgs 5.1-3). As Naaman did not meet his healer (2 Kgs 5.5-10), so is the centurion's servant healed from a distance (Lk. 7.10; cf. 2 Kgs 5.14). In the following story, which is unique to Luke, Jesus' ministry benefits a woman and her son (cf. Lk. 7.11-17; cf. 4.25-26), again mirroring the ministries of Elijah (1 Kgs 17.17-24) and Elisha (2 Kgs 4.18-37). Once this connection is established, a more remote parallel to Jesus' feeding miracle (Lk. 9.10-17) can be detected as well (1 Kgs 17.1-16; 2 Kgs 4.42-44).

Luke's Jesus also shows some signs that his self-understanding is comparable to that of the prophets. He expresses an awareness of being sent (4.43), and Luke shows him busying himself with the teaching of the word of God (5.1).

Like Mark and Matthew, Luke also associates Jesus with Moses and Elijah in the account of his transfiguration. In comparison with the other Synoptists, however, Luke has a more pronounced Moses **typology**. He mentions that Moses and Elijah were speaking of Jesus' exodus (Gr.: *exodon*), which he would fulfill in Jerusalem (9.31; cf. Exod. 19.1; Num. 33.38; 1 Kgs 6.1; Pss. 104.38; [ET: 105.38]; 113.1 **LXX** [ET: 114.1]). When the heavenly voice immediately afterwards alludes to Deut. 18.15 (Lk. 9.35), Jesus is identified as the prophet like Moses.

The following "travel narrative" (9.51–19.44) may be compared to Deuteronomy's account of Moses' journey towards Canaan, an account that focuses on Moses' instructions to his people, rather than on his itinerary. In a similar fashion, the journey to Jerusalem serves Luke as a useful framework for Jesus' instructions. Like Moses, Jesus brings a prophetic message of repentance to a rebellious people.

With the note regarding his exodus (9.31), Luke has connected Jesus' ministry as the new Moses with his death in Jerusalem. His journey is interpreted in the same terms: as a prophet, he goes to Jerusalem to face his death

(13.33). Accordingly, his opponents are seen as the descendants of those who killed the prophets of old (11.47-48).

In the course of Luke's narrative, however, doubts are cast upon the appropriateness of classifying Jesus as a prophet. It is a title that is associated with those who are outsiders to the Jesus movement. The crowds hail Jesus as a great prophet (7.16; 9.8), and the disciples inform Jesus that the crowds think of him as Elijah or one of the ancient prophets (9.19).[20] Simon the Pharisee is reported to be harboring doubts as to whether Jesus could be a prophet (7.39), and the soldiers dare him to prophesy (22.64). After the resurrection, the disciples esteem Jesus as a prophet (24.19), but this evaluation is associated with the ignorance they display before Jesus explains the Scriptures to them (24.25-27).

Jesus himself intimates that he is much more than a prophet. John the Baptist, he says, was more than a prophet (7.26), the final messenger before God's coming (7.27). Yet the least in the kingdom of God is greater than John (7.28). By implication, the one who brings this kingdom, Jesus, should be seen in a different category altogether. When the disciples tell him about the verdict of the crowds – that Jesus is a prophet – Jesus apparently wants them to go further and prods Peter to make his confession that Jesus is the Messiah of God (9.20). Jesus later compares himself to the prophet Jonah (11.29), then adds that something greater than Jonah is present (11.32).[21]

Through his redactional activity, Luke also reveals that there is more to say about Jesus than that he is a prophet. The story that is richest in allusions to Elijah and Elisha, the passage where Jesus raises the widow's son in Nain (7.11-17), is also the passage that contains the first unambiguous redactional reference to Jesus as "the Lord" (7.13). With this touch, Luke implies that Jesus is more than a prophet.[22]

This conclusion also follows from the fact that Jesus is described as the sender of prophets. In the Sermon on the Plain, Jesus explicitly compares his disciples to the prophets of old (6.23, 26). When he responds to the warning regarding Herod's intentions to kill him, he asserts that "it is impossible for a prophet to be killed outside of Jerusalem" (13.33). In the context of Luke's narrative, the statement is unmistakably self-referential. Elaborating on this statement, Jesus exclaims: "Jerusalem, Jerusalem, the city that kills the prophets and stones those who are sent to it! How often have I desired to gather your children together as a hen gathers her brood under her wings, and you were not willing!" (13.34; cf. 11.49). This reference to "how often" is difficult to fit into Jesus' ministry and is more naturally understood in light of the preceding mention of the prophets (cf. pp. 112-113). Jesus appears to identify his own attempt to gather Jerusalem's children with the sending of the prophets in the past. Jesus is not only the prophet that has to die in Jerusalem, but is also the head of all the prophets sent to her.

Jesus as the sender of prophets is a model that also helps explain his relationship to his disciples. He sends out the twelve and authorizes them to proclaim his message and to do the same works that he has done (9.1-6). Luke even seems to extend his Elijah **typology** to apply to the disciples. When Jesus' delegates are rejected in Samaria, they respond in Elijah-like fashion. They desire "to command fire to come down from heaven and consume them" (9.54; cf. 2 Kgs 1.10-14), but Jesus disapproves of this desire. The following passage reports some of Jesus' demands to his would-be followers (Lk. 9.57-62). He will not allow any concerns to take higher priority than the imperative to follow him, not even the duty to bury one's parents (9.60). The radical nature of Jesus' demands compares to God's call of the prophets in the Scriptures of Israel (cf. pp. 94-96). Moreover, as Jesus shares the fate of the prophets in going to his death (13.33), so does he send his disciples to lose their lives (9.24; 17.33).

In empowering his disciples, Jesus takes on a role that matches the role of God in sending and inspiring his prophets. John the Baptist announced that Jesus would baptize with the Holy Spirit (3.16), and shows Jesus on the giving – rather than on the receiving – end with regard to the Holy Spirit. This claim corresponds to the Scriptural picture of God as the one who gives the Spirit to his servants (Exod. 31.3; 35.31; Num. 11.17, 25, 29; Isa. 42.1; 44.3; Ezek. 36.27; 37.14; 39.29; Joel 2.28-29).[23]

With associations of prophetic inspiration, Jesus promises his disciples that the Holy Spirit will teach them how to defend themselves when persecuted (Lk. 12.12). The Olivet discourse contains a parallel statement regarding inspiration at the time of trial. In Luke's version of the discourse, the source of inspiration is not the Holy Spirit (as it is in Mk 13.11), but Jesus (21.15). Accordingly, the Gospel closes with a promise that Jesus will send what the Father promised (24.49), a promise that in light of Luke's second volume cannot refer to anything other than the Holy Spirit (Acts 2.33). Jesus thus has a role that is equal to that of the Father; he has the authority to grant the Spirit and he views the Spirit as representing himself.

Luke's use of prophetic motifs is ambiguous. Jesus is both painted as a prophet and as a sender of prophets. He can refer to himself as a prophet and understands his career as a prophetic one. At the same time, he is more than a prophet. As the Lord and as the one who brings the kingdom of God, he stands in a different category than the prophets do. He is empowered and led by the Holy Spirit, but he is also the one who bestows the Spirit on his own delegates.

Son of God

The picture of Jesus as a prophet shows him to be dependent upon God, and so does the Son of God title. Luke repeatedly exploits this metaphor, but he also shows Jesus' filial relationship to his Father as somewhat of an enigma. He thereby ties in with another theme in his Gospel: the failure of witnesses to grasp Jesus' true identity.

In the infancy narrative, Luke has included the story about Jesus' visit to the temple as a twelve year old. The story climaxes with Jesus' comment that he had to be in his Father's house (2.49). Sonship is here seen in relational terms. The purpose of the story, however, is to show that Jesus' true identity remains a puzzle to his family (2.50). Even though he was announced as Son of the Most High (1.32) and Son of God (1.35) before his birth, the implications of this sonship are not fully grasped by his parents.

While in the temple, Jesus demonstrates his unique wisdom (2.46-47). Some interpreters have even seen this trait as a manifestation of the person-ified divine Wisdom (cf. **Sirach** 24.3-12). Such a conclusion is unwarranted, however, as the precociousness of the child was a common theme in biogra-phies of great personalities. The closest parallels are found in the Egyptian story of Setmo Chamois and **Philo**'s account of Moses. Setmo Chamois, the son of Ramses II, surpassed all his teachers at the age of twelve.[24] Philo reports that teachers were brought in from near and far to teach Moses, but they were unable to add anything to his own wisdom (*On the Life of Moses* 1.21).[25] Luke's narrative as a whole shows that a regal or prophetic understanding of Jesus is inadequate, but this particular story about his endeavors in the temple merely serves to heighten the sense of wonder and puzzlement regarding his identity. Luke continues to develop this theme as his story leads up to the transfigu-ration and Peter's confession (cf. 4.22, 36; 5.21; 7.16, 39, 49; 8.25; 9.7-9, 18-19).

In all the Synoptic Gospels, Jesus is seen to be to the Son of God at his baptism, and Luke is no exception (3.22). Here, sonship is given a messianic interpretation (cf. below on p. 138). Immediately following the baptism, Luke includes his version of Jesus' genealogy (3.23-38). Even though divine sonship is not referred to explicitly in the genealogy, it is implied when Luke concludes the list of successive fathers with "Adam of God" (Gr.: *Adam tou theou*; 3.38). Divine sonship is here understood on the basis of creation, and the tracing of Jesus' descent to Adam and God's creation serves to connect him with humanity universally, not only the Jewish people.

After the genealogy, Luke continues with the temptation narrative (4.1-13). In agreement with the Matthean version, so does Luke's narrative presuppose a relational understanding of sonship. Jesus' filial obedience to and dependency upon the Father are now put to the test (cf. p. 104). As long as Luke focuses on these relational aspects, his ideas have much in common with traditional Jewish thinking. In a Jewish context the title "son of God" usually refers to the king or a coming savior figure, such as the Messiah (cf. p. 3). Accordingly, Luke also gives the Son of God title a messianic interpretation. When he reports that the demons called Jesus "the Son of God," Luke explains that they knew him to be the Messiah (4.41).

The Transfiguration

In the story of the transfiguration, however, the connotations of Jesus' divine sonship move beyond messiahship, as they do in the other Synoptic Gospels (cf. pp. 65-67). Luke's version preserves the basic themes that are found in Mark's account, but there is also considerable material that is unique to Luke (cf. p. 133). Unlike Mark, but more subdued than Matthew, Luke refers to the changed appearance of Jesus' face (9.29), possibly recalling the shining face of Moses (Exod. 34.29). Luke's description of Moses and Elijah is also more lofty, as he observes that they appeared in glory (9.31). Their glory is apparently not at the level of Jesus', however, because only the glory of Jesus is mentioned when Luke tells us what the three disciples were seeing (9.32). In Luke's version, the voice from heaven sounds: "this is my Son, my Chosen; listen to him!" (9.35). Like in Mark and Matthew, the first phrase alludes to Ps. 2.7 and the last phrase to Deut. 18.15. Luke alone refers to Jesus as the chosen one, and the Scriptural background may be Isa. 42.1. As in the other Synoptic Gospels, the transfiguration account associates Jesus' divine sonship with the preeminent agents of God: the anointed king, Isaiah's Servant of the Lord, and Moses.

Luke's special emphasis in the transfiguration account thus falls on elements that compare Jesus to other servants of God. But he has not omitted the features that hint of Jesus as something more than even these distinguished servants. The appearance of Moses and Elijah is associated with the eschatological intervention of God, but Jesus, not God, is the one who is seen in this **epiphanic** event.

Most importantly, however, Luke's use of the Son of God title must be understood on the basis of the infancy narrative, where the title is introduced. Luke's close association of this title with Jesus' conception (cf. pp. 122-123) shows that he has interpreted the title in light of his view of Jesus as the one who shares God's name and carries out God's visitation on earth. At the same time, Luke invests the title with messianic significance and uses it to show that Jesus is God's servant.

Messiah

Even though the messianic connotations are only one aspect of Luke's understanding of sonship, "Messiah" is an important title for him, second only to the title "Lord." Jesus is introduced as the Messiah by the angels in the field (2.11) and confessed as such by Peter (9.20). Jesus himself appears to accept the title at his trial (22.67). After his resurrection, his mission is explained in terms of messiahship (24.26, 46). Luke's narrative is also rich in messianic imagery. Beginning in the infancy narrative, the angel Gabriel draws on central messianic themes when he tells Mary that Jesus will be given the throne of his ancestor David (1.32; cf. 2 Sam. 7.12-13, 16) and reign forever (1.33; cf. 2 Sam. 7.13, 16; Pss. 89.4, 29; 132.12; Isa. 9.7). Zechariah praises God for raising up a savior in the house of David (1.69; cf. 2 Sam. 7.26; 1 Chron. 17.24), in accordance with his promise through the prophets (1.70). His deliverance is described in political terms (1.71, 74), mirroring common messianic expectations (***Psalms of Solomon*** 17.23-27). These political expectations are reinterpreted in Luke's story, however. Jesus' salvation is of a different kind – it brings God's new creation (4.18-19; 7.22).[26] Other messianic themes include the fact that he is born in David's city, Bethlehem (2.4, 11), and fulfills the messianic prophecy in Mic. 5.2. Like Mark and Matthew, Luke also shows Jesus to be the Messiah at his baptism, when the heavenly voice alludes to Ps. 2.7 and combines the themes of Messiah and Son of God (cf. pp. 61-64). Jesus' self-identification as the anointed one of Isa. 61.1-2 (Lk. 4.18-19) may also be intended messianically. At his triumphal entry (19.35-38), Jesus' actions are a fulfillment of the messianic prophecy in Zech. 9.9. Psalm 118.26 is also attributed to him (19.38). When a regal Psalm is used eschatologically like this, it has messianic overtones.[27]

Luke also repeatedly makes use of the messianic theme that Jesus is the son of David (1.32, 69; 2.4, 11; 18.38, 39). This theme is obviously important to Luke, and he has included Jesus' genealogy to establish that Jesus is descended from David (3.23–38). But Luke's view of Jesus as God's Son means that Jesus' genealogy must be qualified. It was only according to what "was supposed" (Gr.: *enomizeto*) that Joseph was Jesus' father (3.23). Further explanation is superfluous, as the infancy narrative has informed the audience about the nature of Jesus' relationship with Joseph.

The infancy narrative has already made it clear that Jesus is a Messiah who is also Lord (2.11). When Luke's story moves towards its climax in Jerusalem, Luke returns to this theme of correcting conventional messianic interpretations. During his last days in Jerusalem, Jesus questions the scribes regarding the Davidic descent of the Messiah. When David calls the Messiah "lord," how can the Messiah be David's son and therefore his inferior? (20.44). The implication of Jesus' question is that the origin of the Messiah is not adequately and completely explained when he is seen as David's son. He is also more than David's son. The question remains unanswered in the immediate context and the characters involved in the conversation are presumably left without an explanation. The readers of the Gospel, however, have learned the answer through Luke's infancy narrative.

Messiahship is again associated with sonship at Jesus' trial, when the members of the Sanhedrin ask Jesus if he is the Messiah (22.67). In response, Jesus applies to himself Dan. 7.13 and Ps. 110.1: "But from now on the Son of Man will be seated at the right hand of the power of God" (22.69). This statement in turn prompts the Sanhedrin to ask if he is the Son of God, a conclusion Jesus does not correct (22.70).[28] Through these Scriptural allusions, divine sonship is connected with Jesus' special relationship to the Father, and to his expected vindication by him. The allusion to Psalm 110 may also recall the former exchange where Jesus explains that the Messiah is more than a son of David (20.41-44), and the allusion to Daniel 7 invokes the image of a heavenly figure. There are thus overtones of Jesus as the Son of God being more than the conventional messianic expectations would imply. Unlike Mark and Matthew, however, Luke does not include the inference drawn by the high priest that Jesus was blaspheming (Mk 14.64; Mt. 26.65).

The Coming One

Another title with messianic overtones that Luke uses is John the Baptist's enigmatic "the coming one." As a powerful eschatological prophet, John himself is thought by many to be the Messiah (3.15). He announces the imminent judgment of God (3.7-9), but he attributes it to the coming, more powerful one (3.16). John's words appear to be meant as a denial that he himself might be the Messiah, but John never identifies this coming one as the Messiah (cf. 7.20). As for Jesus' understanding of the title, he apparently claims the role of the coming one for himself, and he does so with allusions to Isa. 26.19; 29.18; 35.5-6; 42.7, 18; 61.1 (Lk. 7.22). These Isaianic prophecies are not monolithic, but refer to God's own salvation, to the work of the Servant, and the work of an anointed one (cf. p. 90). Yet another interpretation of the title surfaces at the triumphal entry, where Jesus is greeted by the crowd as the coming one (Gr.: *ho erchomenos*; 19.38). Here, the term is part of a quotation from Ps. 118.26, used messianically (cf. p. 53). In Luke's account, therefore, the coming one is another ambiguous figure, taking elements both from God himself and from his agents.

In his development of the titles "prophet," "Son of God," "Messiah," and "the coming one," Luke has intertwined two motifs: the conventional idea of the Son as God's servant and the idea of the Son as God's equal. Like in Matthew's Gospel, the closest we come to a dissolution of this tension is the saying about the mutual knowledge of the Father and the Son (Lk. 10.22). As God's Son, Jesus stands on the divine side of the divine–human divide. At the same time, the Son is dependent on the Father and receives all things from him (cf. pp. 106-11).

The Servant of the Lord

A less ambiguous role that the Lukan Jesus also fills is that of Isaiah's Servant of the Lord. With an echo from Isa. 42.6; 49.6, Simeon announces that the newborn child will be "a light for revelation to the Gentiles" (Lk. 2.32). When Jesus goes to his death, he is conscious that he is fulfilling the fourth Servant song, as he declares: "this scripture must be fulfilled in me, 'And he was counted among the lawless'" (Lk. 22.37; cf. Isa. 53.12).

In the book of Isaiah, the Servant songs find an echo in Isa. 61.1, where the prophet confesses that "the spirit of the Lord is upon" him (cf. Isa. 42.1). This prophecy from Isaiah becomes an essential passage in Luke's portrait of Jesus. Jesus quotes from it at length in his programmatic sermon in Nazareth (Lk. 4.18-19), and alludes to it repeatedly (Lk. 6.20-21; 7.22).

Jesus and wisdom

The Son of God metaphor is thus Luke's most important tool for showing Jesus in close proximity to God while at the same time maintaining his distinct identity. But Luke also has other tools that he uses less explicitly, such as his much-debated application of wisdom language to Jesus.

Like Matthew, Luke connects Jesus with the theme of wisdom when he includes the saying about something more than Solomon's wisdom (11.31) and the saying about Jesus' exclusive knowledge of the Father (10.22). In Luke's version of the saying about the justification of wisdom (7.35) the implications are not immediately as clear as they are in Matthew. According to Luke, "wisdom is justified by all her children" (7.35). This version is often thought to be vague compared to Matthew, as the Lukan version may be understood as identifying Jesus and John as the children of Wisdom. But the context favors a different interpretation. There is an important parallel to v. 35 in v. 29, where the people who were listening, including the tax collectors, are said to justify God. This deed is demonstrated in their accepting the baptism of John. When the issue of justifying God or God's wisdom recurs in v. 35, those who justify God's wisdom are most likely the same group as those mentioned in v. 29. It is not Jesus and John, therefore, but the people and the tax collectors that must be identified as the children of wisdom. They are the ones who accepted God's wisdom as it was communicated to them through John and Jesus. God's wisdom, then, is closely associated with Jesus and John. But even though the saying presupposes a close connection between Jesus and wisdom, there is no identification of Jesus with wisdom here. The saying does not distinguish between John and Jesus, and they are both seen as exceptional spokespersons of God's wisdom.

The saying that comes closest to identifying Jesus with wisdom is the saying about the mother hen (Lk. 13.34-35). As in Matthew's version, Jesus exclaims: "how often have I desired to gather your children together as a hen gathers her brood under her wings, and you were not willing!" (13.34). Jesus now fills the role that in Jewish tradition was known to belong to God and his wisdom (see pp. 112-113). He also appears to be speaking from a perspective above history when he complains about "how often" he has tried to gather the children of Jerusalem. Luke is not explicit about this point, but the best explanation for his language may well be that pre-existence is presupposed here. Jesus' address to Jerusalem also recalls what the wisdom of God says in Lk. 11.49, about sending prophets and apostles to Jerusalem. Luke does not identify Jesus with wisdom, but Jesus is clearly more than a spokesperson for wisdom. Jesus takes wisdom's place in addressing Israel.

Jesus also appears as a character with a heavenly perspective on earthly affairs in his interaction with Peter before the passion. When Jesus predicts Peter's betrayal, he refers to his own knowledge of Satan's demands and his intercession on Peter's behalf (22.31-32). The background for the scene is the heavenly throne vision in Job 1.6-12; 2.1-6, where Satan is present before God as Job's accuser. Jesus is apparently not only privy to knowledge about the heavenly throne sessions, but present at them as well. To assume a heavenly journey on Jesus' part would be to import a foreign element to Luke's story. Jesus appears to be present in heaven and on earth at the same time. As in his use of the title "Lord" for the earthly Jesus, Luke's portrait amounts to a merging of the heavenly and the earthly Jesus. It also contributes to Luke's picture of Jesus as a heavenly being distinct from the Father.

Conclusion

Luke's picture of Jesus is characterized by ambiguity. As soon as he has established the title "Lord" as a name for God, he begins to use it as an epithet for Jesus. The heavenly Lord that is worshipped by the post-Easter community is thus explicitly identified with the earthly Jesus, who is attributed with God's name. This exalted understanding of Jesus is carried out throughout Luke's narrative, where Jesus is placed on the same level as God and is portrayed as performing the earthly visitation of the heavenly Lord. Jesus is both savior and the object of saving faith.

To some extent, the title "Lord" controls the other titles that Luke applies to Jesus. Jesus is the Messiah and the son of David, and at the same time he is David's Lord. He is both a prophet and more than a prophet; he is the one who sends the prophets and gives them the Holy Spirit for empowerment.

As "the coming one," the identity of Luke's Jesus also remains elusive. The title points both to God himself and to God's agent.

Sonship is not as predominant a metaphor for Luke as it is for Mark and Matthew. But Luke is also able to describe Jesus as a son that is both subordinate and equal to the Father. He is a son who obeys and submits to his Father, and he is a son who stands in a fully reciprocal relationship with him.

Luke moves a step further than the other Synoptics when he explicitly connects Jesus' divine sonship to his conception. The meaning of sonship for Luke is not merely to be given a special function by the Father and to stand in an intimate relationship with him. Sonship is tied to who Jesus is, not only to his mission.

As God's Son, therefore, Jesus is at the same level as the Father, equal to him in power and glory not by appointment but by virtue of who he is. As the Father's Son, he is also obedient to him and dependent on him.

Notes

1   There is some debate as to whether the use of *kurios* for Christ can be understood against this background. The problem is that all the Septuagint manuscripts that use *kurios* as a translation of Yahweh have been copied by Christian scribes. The non-Christian versions of the Septuagint testify to a diverse practice when it comes to translating or transcribing God's name, the **tetra-grammaton**, including attempts at writing out Yahweh with Greek letters and employing Greek characters that look like the Hebrew characters used to write Yahweh. It has been suggested, therefore, that the use of *kurios* to render Yahweh is a distinctly Christian practice and that it postdates the Christian identification of Jesus as Lord. This practice is often thought to have originated in the Hellenistic church and to be a result of the **Hellenization** of the gospel. Joseph Fitzmyer has shown, however, that *kurios* can be found as a way to render the biblical Yahweh in Hellenistic–Jewish sources and that the designation of God as Lord (*mare*) is attested in Aramaic (*A Wandering Aramean: Collected Aramaic Essays* [Missoula, MT: Scholars Press, 1979], 119–27).

2   C. Kavin Rowe, *Early Narrative Christology: The Lord in the Gospel of Luke*, BZNW 139 (Berlin: De Gruyter, 2006).

3   The accusative pronoun in the purpose or result clause *eis to iasthai auton* is ambiguous. Most versions and commentators understand the pronoun as the subject of the verb *iasthai*, resulting in the translation "in order for him to heal." The pronoun "him" (*auton*) must then refer to Jesus. But the pronoun may also function as the object of the verb. In that case, the translation will be: "in order to heal him." The pronoun (*auton*) will then refer to the paralytic. Many scholars argue that *kuriou* in the phrase "power of the Lord" has to refer to God, as the **anarthrous** *kurios* always refers to the Father. In Lukan usage, however, that is not the case. The anarthrous *kurios* refers to Jesus in Lk. 2.11; 6.5; 20.44; Acts 2.36; 10.36. In addition, 1.17, 76; 3.4, and 4.19 are ambiguous. While Luke can speak of power as coming from God (1.35), he can also speak of power coming from Jesus (8.46). It would be consistent with Lukan terminology if the "power of the Lord" refers to Jesus' own power, therefore.

    The textual variants provide evidence that some of the early readers of the Gospel understood *kuriou* as referring to Jesus. Important witnesses, including Codex Alexandrinus, Codex Ephraemi, Codex Bezae Cantabrigiensis, the Majority text and the entire Latin tradition, as well as Syriac and Coptic versions read the plural accusative pronoun *autous* instead of *auton*. According to these witnesses, the meaning is that the power of the Lord (Jesus) was present to heal them. This reading is almost certainly secondary, as these manuscripts are not the oldest and the reading smoothes out the difficulty of deciding the referent of *auton*. But this reading could only originate if *kuriou* was taken to refer to Jesus. Cf. Rowe, *Early Narrative Christology*, 92–98. It should also be noted that this section of Luke's Gospel consistently uses "Lord" with reference to Jesus. After the Isaiah quotation in Lk. 4.18, the next occurrence of "Lord" with possible reference to God comes in 10.2. The next unambiguous reference to God comes in 10.21.

Moreover, the grammar of Lk. 5.17 does not favor the conventional translation. In addition to Lk. 5.17, there are ten examples of the construction *eis to* ("in order that"/"so that") followed by a **transitive** verb and an accusative pronoun in the New Testament writings. In six of these cases, the accusative pronoun must be read as the object (Mark 14.55; Rom. 1.11; 11.11; 1 Thess. 3.2; 4.9; 2 Thess. 3.9). There are only four instances where the accusative pronoun serves as the subject (Rom. 12.2; 2 Cor. 8.6; Phil. 1.10; 2 Thess. 2.11). These four cases are poor comparisons for Lk. 5.17, however. In 2 Cor. 8.6 the object is made explicit through an adjacent accusative noun. In 2 Thess. 2.11 an indirect object is included in a dative phrase. The remaining two examples both have the verb *dokimazo* ("test, examine;" Rom. 12.2; Phil. 1.10). Moreover, when the same construction takes an accusative noun instead of a pronoun, all ten examples in the New Testament writings show the noun as the object (Rom. 15.8; 2 Cor. 8.6 [cf. above]; Gal. 3.17; 1 Thess. 2.16; 3.5, 10, 13; Heb. 2.17; 8.3; 13.21). Comparable usage of the construction in Lk. 5.17 favors taking *auton* as the object, therefore.

4   I am grateful to David Pao for this observation.

5   Rowe, *Early Narrative Christology*, 97–8.

6   Raymond E. Brown, *The Birth of the Messiah: A Commentary on the Infancy Narratives in the Gospels of Matthew and Luke*, new updated ed., ABRL (New York: Doubleday, 1993), 299–301.

7   Ibid., 312.

8   In favor of the former translation, it is argued that the predicate precedes the verb *kaleomai*. That is the more common construction (cf. 1.32; 2.23), but not the only possibility (cf. Gen. 2.23; Exod. 12.16 **LXX**).

9   With respect to the **textual criticism** of Lk. 1.78, most scholars consider the future form of *episkepto* ("to visit") to be original. It has the better attestation (Vaticanus and the original hand of Sinaiticus), and the aorist form may be explained as an assimilation to 1.68, where the aorist form of *episkepto* occurs. So, Metzger, *A Textual Commentary*, 110; Joseph A. Fitzmyer, *The Gospel According to Luke (I–IX): Introduction, Translation and Notes*, AB 28 (New York: Doubleday, 1981), 388; Darrell L. Bock, *Luke*, vol. 1, BECNT (Grand Rapids: Baker, 1994), 197–98. On the other hand, the aorist *epeskepsato* is attested in the majority of witnesses, including Codex Alexandrinus, Codex Ephraemi and Irenaeus. The aorist is also the more difficult reading; one would expect the future tense to describe Jesus' visit, which has not yet occurred. As for the origin of the variant reading, it may be due to assimilation with the future tenses in v. 76 (Brown, *Birth*, 373).

10   Exod. 4.31; Num. 16.5; Deut. 11.12; Ruth 1.6; 1Kgdms 2.21 (ET: 1 Sam. 2.21); 2 Esd 2.21 (ET: Ezra 1.2); Job 35.15; Pss. 8.5 (ET: 8.4); 16.3 (ET: 17.3); 58.6 (ET: 59.5); 64.10 (ET: 65.9); 79.15 (ET: 80.14); 88.33 (ET: 89.32); 105.4 (ET: 106.4); Jer. 5.9, 29; 9.8, 24 (ET: 9.9, 25); 11.22; 15.15; 30.2 (ET: 49.8); 34.8 (ET: 27.8); 36.10, 32 (ET: 29.10, 32); 37.20 (ET: 30.20); 39.41 (ET: 32.41); 43.31

(ET: 36.31); 51.13, 29 (ET: 44.13, 29); Lam. 4.22; Ezek. 20.40; 23.21; 34.11; Hos. 4.14; Zeph. 2.7; Zech. 10.3; **Sirach** 2.14; 17.32; 46.14; **Judith** 4.15; 8.33; 13.20; *Psalms of Solomon* 9.4; 15.12.

11 In Lk. 5.8, Peter says to Jesus: "Go away from me, Lord, for I am a sinful man!" The *kurios* title here occurs in the vocative form, *kurie*, in contrast to the instances discussed above. It is commonly argued that there is a big difference between the articular use of *kurios* and the use of the word in the vocative form. Many scholars think that only the first use may possibly be associated with the divine name in the Scriptures of Israel. When *kurie* is used to address people it is thought to be much less profound, as can be seen in the many translations that simply render it "Sir." By focusing on the narrative context, however, Rowe challenges this scholarly consensus. Luke's first use of the vocative form here in 5.8 may be an indication that its connotations go beyond those of a polite address. As this story has the character of a **theophany**, it may be justified to read the vocative *kurie* in light of Luke's previous use of *kurios* as a Christological title. Building on these observations, Rowe goes on to argue that other occurrences of the vocative *kurie* (5.12; 6.46; 7.6; 9.54, 59, 61: 10.21, 40; 22.33, 38, 49) also involve ambiguity and that Jesus' and God's sharing of the *kurios*-identity resonates here as well (*Early Narrative Christology*, 82–89). The use of *kurie* in this particular story is a good indication that there may be such an ambiguity at the narrative level. Caution is necessary, however. Luke appears to be hesitant to portray the disciples as grasping the full implications of Jesus' identity. In contrast to Matthew, for example, he waits until after the resurrection to show the disciples worshipping Jesus (cf. p. 131).

12 Believing God's spokespersons goes together with having faith in God (Exod. 14.31; 19.9; 2 Chron. 20.20; *4 Ezra* 7.130; **Tobit** 14.4, cf. **Philo**, *On Agriculture* 50). But Luke's description of faith in Jesus goes beyond such faith in God's spokespersons. Luke describes a faith that is directed towards the person of Jesus, not a faith that merely accepts what he says or does as words or works of God.

13 In the literature of **Second Temple Judaism**, the emphasis on having faith in God is even stronger (**Judith** 14.10; **Wisdom of Solomon** 12.2; 16.26; **Sirach** 2.6, 8; 11.21; 32.24; *4 Maccabees* 7.21; 15.24; 16.22; *4 Ezra* 13.23; *Jubilees* 14.6; *1 Enoch* 43.4; 69.25; *2 Baruch* 48.22; *Testament of Dan* 5.13; *Letter of Aristeas* 261; **Philo**, *Allegorical Interpretation* 2.89; 3.228, 229; *On the Change of Names* 166, 177, 186, 218; *On the Life of Abraham* 262, 269; *On the Virtues* 216, 218; *On the Migration of Abraham* 43, 44; *Who Is the Heir?* 90, 92–93, 99; *That God Is Unchangeable* 4; *On the Life of Moses* 1.225, 284; 2.259; *On Rewards and Punishments* 27, 28).

14 In the **LXX**, "savior" (*soter*) is used as a title for God in Deut. 32.15; 1 Kgdm 10.19 (ET: 1 Sam. 10.19); Pss. 23.5 (ET: 24.5); 24.5 (ET: 25.5); 26.1, 9 (ET: 27.1, 9); 61.3, 7 (ET: 62.2, 6); 64.6 (ET: 65.5); 78.9 (ET: 79.9); 94.1 (ET: 95.1); Isa. 12.2; 17.10; 45.15, 21; Mic. 7.7; Hab. 3.18; **Judith** 9.11; **1 Maccabees** 4.30; *3 Maccabees* 6.29, 32; 7.16; **Wisdom of Solomon** 16.7; **Sirach** 51.1; **Baruch** 4.22; *Psalms of Solomon* 3.6; 8.33; 16.4; 17.3.

On the way to Emmaus, the disciples refer to Jesus as "the one to redeem Israel" (Lk. 24.21). In the Old Testament, the work of redeeming (Gr.: *lutroo*) Israel is also the work of God (cf. Isa. 41.14; 43.1, 14; 44.22-24; 52.3; 63.4, 9; Jer. 31.11; 50.34; Hos. 7.13; Mic. 4.10; Zech. 10.8). I am indebted to Richard Hays for this observation.

15 One of the most influential Lukan scholars in the twentieth century was the German Hans Conzelmann. He pioneered the redaction critical method and began the trend to understand the

Synoptists as theologians, not merely collectors of tradition. According to Conzelmann, Luke was profoundly influenced by the fact that Jesus' second coming had not yet happened, usually referred to as "the delay of the **parousia**." Luke's theology is therefore characterized by a three-fold salvation historical division: 1) the period of Israel; 2) the period of Jesus' ministry; 3) the period of the church. On this understanding of Luke's theology, there is little room for **realized eschatology**. Although the kingdom is made manifest in Jesus' ministry and salvation is brought near, Luke never says that the kingdom has arrived. According to Conzelmann, the kingdom remains a transcendent reality (*The Theology of St. Luke*, tr. Geoffrey Buswell, reprint, 1961 [Philadelphia: Fortress, 1982], 113–25). While Conzelmann is correct that Luke's eschatology includes an expectation of a period of the church that precedes the consummation, his presentation is one-sided and resolves a paradox that remains unresolved in Luke: the kingdom is both present and future. Conzelmann does not discuss Lk. 11.20, a verse where Jesus' works are not only seen as a demonstration of the kingdom, but as tangible proof of its presence. At the same time, Luke corrects the idea that the kingdom would appear immediately (19.11).

16 Luke uses middle, **intransitive** forms of the verb *anistemi*.

17 See Exod. 15.11; 1 Chron. 16.27; Pss. 18.2 (ET: 19.1); 56.6 (ET: 57.5); 112.4 (ET: 113.4) Isa. 63.15; **Tobit** 12.15; **Wisdom of Solomon** 9.10. The Messiah is attributed with his own glory in ***Psalms of Solomon*** 17.31, but the Messiah is here described as a purely earthly character. His glory is comparable to the glory of the great kingdoms of the earth (cf. Isa. 14.11; Ezek. 27.7, 10). In **2 Maccabees** 3.26 two mysterious divine agents are also said to have glory. They are likely heavenly beings, rather than human, but their "glory" refers to their appearance on earth in the vision, not to their heavenly glory.

18 In the wisdom literature, God's Wisdom also has glory (**Wisdom of Solomon** 9.11; **Sirach** 14.27; 24.16-17) and gives glory to human beings (Wisdom of Solomon 10.14).

19 Cf. Luke Timothy Johnson, *The Literary Function of Possessions in Luke–Acts*, SBLDS 39 (Missoula, MT: Scholars Press, 1977), 79–126; idem, "The Christology of Luke–Acts," in *Who Do You Say That I Am? Essays on Christology in Honor of Jack Dean Kingsbury*, ed. Mark Allan Powell and David R. Bauer (Louisville: Westminster John Knox, 1999), 54–59; David P. Moessner, *Lord of the Banquet: The Literary and Theological Significance of the Lukan Travel Narrative* (Minneapolis: Fortress, 1989), 47–50; J. Severino Croatto, "Jesus, Prophet Like Elijah, and Prophet-Teacher Like Moses in Luke–Acts," *JBL* 124 (2005): 454–61.

20 The crowds are not authoritative characters in Luke's Gospel. They are outsiders, ignorant of the secrets of the kingdom (8.9-10). In contrast to Mark and Matthew, who attribute the Beelzebul charge to the scribes (Mark 3.22) and the Pharisees (Mt. 12.24), respectively, Luke attributes it to some from the crowds (Lk. 11.14-15).

21 For Luke's "correction" of prophetic Christology, see Jack Dean Kingsbury, "Jesus as the 'Prophetic Messiah' in Luke's Gospel," in *The Future of Christology: Essays in Honor of Leander E. Keck*, ed. Abraham J. Malherbe and Wayne A. Meeks (Minneapolis: Fortress, 1993), 35–41.

22 Rowe, *Early Narrative Christology*, 117–21.

23 The precedence for the idea that the Messiah gives the Spirit is scant. According to ***Testament of Judah*** 24.2-3, "the heavens will be opened upon him to pour out the spirit as a blessing of the

Holy Father. And he will pour out the spirit of grace on you," but this may well be a Christian **interpolation**. Another possible Christian interpolation is found in ***Testament of Levi*** 18.8, where the Messiah gives "the majesty" (Gr.: *megalosune*) of the Lord to those who are his sons in truth forever. Cf. I. Howard Marshall, *Commentary on Luke*, NIGTC (Grand Rapids: Eerdmans, 1978), 147.

24 Bultmann, *History of the Synoptic Tradition*, 300–1.

25 Cf. also **Josephus**, *Antiquities of the Jews* 2.230-231; *The Life* 9; Herodotus 1.114-115; Plutarch, *Alexander* 5.1; Philostratus, *Life of Apollonius* 1.7.

26 Cf. I. Howard Marshall, "Political and Eschatological Language in Luke," in *Reading Luke: Interpretation, Reflection, Formation*, ed. Craig Bartholomew, Joel B. Green and Anthony C. Thiselton (Grand Rapids: Zondervan, 2005), 157–162.

27 For Luke's portrait of Jesus as the Messiah, see Darrell L. Bock, *Proclamation from Prophecy and Pattern: Lucan Old Testament Christology*, JSNTSup 12 (Sheffield: JSOT Press, 1987); Mark Strauss, *The Davidic Messiah in Luke–Acts: The Promise and Its Fulfillment in Lukan Christology*, JSNTSup 110 (Sheffield: Sheffield Academic Press, 1995); Scott W. Hahn, "Kingdom and Church in Luke–Acts: From Davidic Christology to Kingdom Ecclesiology," in *Reading Luke: Interpretation, Reflection, Formation*, ed. Craig Bartholomew, Joel B. Green and Anthony C. Thiselton (Grand Rapids: Zondervan, 2005), 294–326. These authors tend to highlight messianic references where other themes are in the foreground. For an emphasis on how messianic images are qualified in Luke, see Brendan Byrne, "Jesus as Messiah in the Gospel of Luke: Discerning a Pattern of Correction," *CBQ* 65 (2003): 80–95.

28 Jesus' answer "You say that I am" implies consent, yet stresses that the expression is not his own (Joseph A. Fitzmyer, *The Gospel According to Luke [X–XXIV]: Introduction, Translation and Notes*, AB 28A [New York: Doubleday, 1985], 1468).

Conclusion

Despite all their differences, there are some striking similarities in the portraits of Jesus presented in the Synoptic Gospels. They have all given considerable attention to the theme of Jesus acting in God's place. For Mark, this means that Jesus is the fulfillment of Isaiah's prophecies regarding the new exodus, and he is the divine warrior who defeats Satan and his army of evil spirits. Jesus' miracles show that the new creation is already a reality. For Matthew, Jesus' equality with God means that Jesus is Emmanuel, God With Us. He is personally eternally present with his disciples and his presence is the presence of God. The proper response is therefore to worship him. For Luke, Jesus' equality with God means that the earthly Jesus is also the heavenly Lord. He is present in the heavenly council while he is also present with his disciples on earth.

Even though Jesus takes the place of God, none of the Gospels leave any room for the possibility that Jesus is God the Father. Jesus not only talks about the Father, he also talks to him, and he expresses his obedience to him. All the Synoptic Gospels also see Jesus as God's servant in a number of roles that were known from the Old Testament. He is the Messiah that God would raise up, he is the prophet that God has sent, and he is the servant that would die for the people's sins. But as God's servant, his role is also quite ambiguous. He is the Messiah, the son of David, but he is also David's lord. He is a prophet, but he is also the sender of the prophets.

This ambiguity is most pronounced in the evangelists' use of the Son of God title. In each of the Synoptic Gospels, the voice of God sounds both at Jesus' baptism and at his transfiguration. The voice identifies Jesus as God's Son and associates this title with other servants of God: the Messiah, Isaac, Moses, and the servant of the Lord. But God also makes it clear that this Son now takes his place. The Son is the one to whom one should listen.

According to Mark, it is above all the crucifixion that shows what it means for Jesus to be God's Son. He is obedient to his Father and he suffers on behalf of his people. As God's Son, he also has powers that are not available to ordinary human beings. As the Son of God, he defeats the army of Satan.

However, Matthew and Luke have a broader repertoire with which to show that the Son of God is more than a servant of God. For Luke, Jesus' virginal conception shows that he was the Son of God from his conception. "Son of God" is not merely an honorary title and it does not only describe Jesus' function as God's servant. It pertains to who Jesus is. For Matthew, Jesus' divine sonship means that he is to be worshiped as God.

Both Matthew and Luke include Jesus' profound words regarding his divine sonship (Mt. 11.25-27/Lk. 10.21-22). As God's Son, Jesus has such an intimate relationship with the Father that he stands on the divine side of the divine-human divide. In this saying and elsewhere, Matthew and Luke make use of Jewish wisdom traditions to explain Jesus' intimate relationship with God. As the revealer of God's will and the sender of the prophets, Jesus takes the place that was often attributed to God's wisdom. By implication, Jesus is included in the Godhead.

All the evangelists, but especially Matthew, also take advantage of the ambiguity of the Son of Man title. The Son of Man is a humble human being, but he is also a heavenly figure who comes in glory: a glory that is equal to God's.

There is a certain tension in all of the Synoptic portraits of Jesus. Jesus is equal to God, and yet he is God's servant. The Son of God metaphor and the application of wisdom language to Jesus go some way towards resolving this tension. John's Gospel goes further, by painting Jesus as the divine Word that became a human being. The Nicene Creed goes further still, by using the terminology of Greek philosophy: Jesus is of one essence and one substance with the Father and he was incarnate and was made man.

The conceptual world of the Synoptic Gospels is very different from that of the Nicene Creed. Abstract concepts such as "essence" and "substance" play no role in these Gospels. Instead, they use the images of Jewish tradition, such as the heavenly throne, the divine warrior, creation, and new creation, to show that Jesus is God's equal. He shares God's authority, power, and glory and is worshiped like God. What the Nicene Creed expressed with the terminology of Greek philosophy, the Synoptic Gospels anticipated through their dynamic portraits of Jesus.

Glossary

1 Enoch This **apocalyptic** writing is attributed to Enoch, who did not die but was taken up to heaven, according to Gen. 5.24. *First Enoch* describes his visions, which give insights into the mysteries of the universe and the events of the future. It is a composite work, written at different times by different authors. 1) The Book of Watchers (*1 Enoch* 1–36) describes the fall of the angels, based on the story in Gen. 6.1-8. This work may be dated to sometime between 200 and 150 BCE. 2) The Similitudes (*1 Enoch* 37–71), sometimes referred to as the Parables, concern the future judgment and focus on the role of the Son of Man. Most scholars date the Similitudes to late in the first century BCE or early in the first century CE. 3) The Astronomical Book (*1 Enoch* 72–82) explains the astronomical basis for the solar calendar. Some scholars date this work to the third century BCE, whereas others opt for a date late in the second century BCE. 4) The Book of Dream Visions (*1 Enoch* 83–90) tells the story of the future (from Enoch's perspective) in the form of two visions. In the second of them (*1 Enoch* 85–90), oxen represent the patriarchs, sheep represent the people of Israel and predatory animals represent Israel's enemies. A snow-white cow with huge horns represents the Messiah. Scholars date this book to 165–160 BCE. 5) The Book of Admonitions (*1 Enoch* 91–105) takes the form of testament, in which Enoch describes the eschatological judgment. It includes the Apocalypse of Weeks (*1 Enoch* 93.1-10; 91.12-17), which divides world history into ten weeks, followed by the new creation, consisting of "many weeks without number." The Book of Admonitions may be dated to sometime in the second century BCE. 6) The Appendix (*1 Enoch* 106–107) contains fragments from another work called the Book of Noah. *First Enoch* has been preserved in Ge'ez (the ancient language of Ethiopia, often less precisely called "Ethiopic"), but fragments of all the books except the Similitudes have been found among the Dead Sea Scrolls. Fragments of Greek and Latin translations have also survived. The original language was Hebrew or Aramaic. Nothing is known about the authors, but the theology of *1 Enoch* is related to that of the Qumran community (solar calendar). It may have originated among some of the groups from which the Qumran community later developed.

1 Maccabees One of the **Apocrypha**, this book was originally written in Hebrew, probably around 100 BCE. Its title is taken from Judas Maccabeus, who is the main character in this historical work. 1 Maccabees describes the Jewish opposition to the oppression by the Greek king Antiochus IV Epiphanes and the independence that Israel enjoyed afterwards. It covers the period from Antiochus' rise to power in 175 BCE until the death of Simon Maccabeus (Judas' brother) in 134 BCE. Little is known about the author, except that he must have been a Jew who was ardently opposed to the **Hellenization** of Judea.

1Q16 This very poorly preserved scroll from Cave 1 at **Qumran** contains a commentary on Psalm 68.

1QapGen The *Genesis Apocryphon* from Cave 1 at **Qumran**, also referred to as 1Q20, is written in Aramaic. The manuscript is dated to the late first century BCE or the early first century CE, but the original work is believed to be from the second century BCE. The surviving parts contain a non-biblical story about Noah as well as an account of Noah's grandfather Methuselah's journey to heaven to meet with Enoch and discuss his daughter-in-law's alleged infidelity with a fallen angel.

1QH The *Thanksgiving Hymns* (the Hebrew word *hodayot* means "thanks") survive in two separate manuscripts (1QH^a and 1QH^b). They were found in Cave 1 at **Qumran** and are dated to the first century BCE. Imitating the biblical Psalms, the author confesses his sinfulness and praises God for his salvation. The author is persecuted by evildoers, but God has graciously chosen him to be rescued from evil and to be enlightened through God's revelation. He has been given the wisdom that places him among God's elect. The Hymns most probably stem from the Qumran community. Many scholars believe that the **Teacher of Righteousness** is the author of some of them. With their emphasis on the weakness and sinfulness of human beings as well as their dependence on God's grace in his election, the *Thanksgiving Hymns* have frequently been compared to the writings of the apostle Paul. However, the characteristic Pauline emphasis on justification by faith is missing.

1QIsa Two scrolls from Cave 1 at **Qumran** (1QIsa^a and 1QIsa^b) are copies of the book of Isaiah. The first of these contains the complete text of the book and is also known as the large Isaiah scroll. It is dated between 150–125 BCE.

The second is fragmentary and is dated to the end of the first century BCE or the beginning of the first century CE.

1QM Also known as the *War Scroll* (the Hebrew word *milchama* means "war"). Comparing the descriptions in the scroll with what is known about Roman warfare, scholars have confidently dated the original work to between 50–1 BCE. This scroll from Cave 1 at **Qumran** describes an eschatological war between the sons of light and the sons of darkness or the army of Belial (Satan). The sons of light should probably be identified as the members of the Qumran community. Their opponents include wicked Jews in addition to the Assyrians, the Philistines, the Edomites, the Moabites and the Ammonites (the Romans are probably intended as well). Most scholars understand this battle as symbolic of the community's war against evil, but it has been argued that it should be understood as an earthly battle that corresponds to the cosmic battle between the powers of light and darkness.

1QpHab The *Commentary on Habakkuk* or *pesher on Habakkuk* contains the text of the first two chapters of Habakkuk with commentary. *Pesher* is a Hebrew word that means "interpretation." In biblical studies, the term is used for a kind of exegesis that reapplies the biblical stories to contemporary or future events. In the case of 1QpHab, the judgment described in Habakkuk concerns the Liar, who defected from the community and formed his own congregation. Perhaps this Liar is identical to the Wicked Priest, who is also mentioned in the scroll. Scholars identify the Wicked Priest as one of the high priests in Jerusalem, probably Jonathan (153–143 BCE) or Simon Maccabeus (142–135 BCE). The scroll is dated to 30–1 BCE and was found in Cave 1 at **Qumran**.

1QS The *Rule of the Community* (Hebr.: *serek hayachad*) was found in Cave 1 at **Qumran**. The scroll is dated to 100–75 BCE, and the original work is believed to stem from around 100 BCE. However, most scholars are convinced that the work has combined different traditions, reflecting the development of the community. As its name indicates, the scroll is a rule book for the Qumran community and gives a good picture of the strict hierarchy and discipline they upheld. Those who wanted to join the congregation were required to swear a solemn oath that they would obey the law of Moses as it was interpreted by the community leaders. The first two years were a probation period. After the first year, all the novice's property became the possession of the community, and full membership was granted after the second year (1QS 5.1–6.23). The scroll also outlines the community's belief that the works of all human beings are predestined by God. God appoints for each person to be ruled by the Spirit of Light or the Spirit of Darkness (1QS 3.13–4.26).

1QSa The *Rule of the Congregation* (Hebr.: *serek haedah*) or the Messianic Rule is an appendix to the Rule of the Community (**1QS**). It must be dated to the time immediately after 1QS and cannot be younger than 50 BCE. The scroll describes how the congregation of Israel will be integrated into the **Qumran** community in the end times.

2 Baruch This **apocalyptic** work has survived in a Syriac translation of a Greek text. A fragment of the Greek version has been discovered among the Oxyrhynchus Papyri. The Greek in turn probably depends on a Hebrew original. The work dates to around 100 CE. It is pseudonymously attributed to Jeremiah's secretary, Baruch (cf. Jer. 36.4, 27, 32; 45.1), who laments the destruction of Jerusalem. Ostensibly, he refers to the disaster in 587 BCE, but the occasion is actually the Roman invasion of 66–70 CE. God gives Baruch insight into his plans for the future, which includes the coming of the Messiah, the judgment of the wicked and the resurrection and reward of the righteous. *Second Baruch* is counted among the **Pseudepigrapha**.

2 Enoch The **apocalyptic** work known as *2 Enoch* has come down in two versions (recensions), one shorter (referred to as manuscript A) and one longer (referred to as manuscript B). It is generally agreed that the shorter version is the more original. Both versions are preserved in a Slavonic translation. The original language may have been Greek or a Semitic language. The basic story is that of Enoch's journey to heaven, where the heavenly mysteries are revealed to him (cf. 1 *Enoch*). Usually, *2 Enoch* is dated around 100 CE, but there is a great degree of uncertainty regarding this dating. As for the provenance, we are mostly left with guesswork. *Second Enoch* may have originated within a Jewish sect that was influenced by Zoroastrian ideas and that did not conform to the traditions that are described in the *Mishnah*. The work is counted among the **Pseudepigrapha**.

2 Esdras One of the **Apocrypha**, 2 Esdras is an expanded version of what is also known as *4 Ezra*. The expansions, written in Greek and consisting of chapters 1–2 and 15–16, are Christian additions that date to the middle of the second century CE and the middle of the third century, respectively.

2 Maccabees This book, originally written in Greek, is not a continuation of **1 Maccabees**, but covers the same story as the first seven chapters of that book (the first fifteen years). Second Maccabees was written for the benefit of the Jews in Alexandria in Egypt and intended to stir them to solidarity with their fellow Jews. It attests to the hope of resurrection for the Jews that were martyred because of their faithfulness to the Mosaic law. The surviving work is a summary of an original five-volume work and can be dated to 124 BCE. Some scholars argue that the original version should be dated to not long after 160 BCE. Scholars debate whether 2 Maccabees was written by a Jew from Judea or Egypt. It is included in the **Apocrypha**.

3 Baruch The **apocalyptic** work referred to as *3 Baruch* has survived in Greek and Slavonic manuscripts. The original language was most likely Greek, but the Slavonic manuscripts are believed to preserve a more original version of the book. The work contains both Jewish and Christian ideas, and scholars are divided as to whether *3 Baruch* is a Christian work that draws on Jewish traditions or whether it is a Jewish work that has undergone Christian redaction. *3 Baruch* is pseudonymously attributed to Baruch, the prophet Jeremiah's secretary (cf. Jer. 36.4, 27, 32; 45.1). In order to answer the question of why Jerusalem was destroyed by the Gentiles, Baruch is taken on a journey to heaven, where he learns the secrets of the heavenly world. Jerusalem was punished for the people's sin, but their enemies will also be punished by God. The dating of *3 Baruch* is uncertain, but must be later than 70 CE, as the destruction of Jerusalem is an event in the past. Some scholars date the book as late as the third century CE. *Third Baruch* is counted among the **Pseudepigrapha**.

3 Enoch This apocalyptic work is pseudonymously attributed to Rabbi Ishmael, who died shortly before the Bar Kokhba revolt broke out in 132 CE. *Third Enoch* is dated to the fifth or sixth century CE. It has been preserved in Hebrew, which is the original language. The book may have originated in Babylon, among Jews who focused on mystical experiences. It tells the story of Rabbi Ishmael's heavenly journey, his visions of God's heavenly throne and chariot (Hebr.: *merkabah*) and the revelations he received from Metatron. Metatron is none other than Enoch, who has been transformed into an archangel, is seated on a heavenly throne and is even given the name "the lesser YHWH" (YHWII is God's name in Hebrew). Many scholars believe that *3 Enoch* contains different traditions concerning Metatron and that one of these traditions is critical of the high view that others give to him. *Third Enoch* is counted among the **Pseudepigrapha**.

3 Maccabees This book tells the story of a threat to Jerusalem from Ptolemy IV Philopator (221–205 BCE), the Greek king in Egypt. Ptolemy changes his mind about attacking Jerusalem when he is visited by two of God's angels. The purpose of *3 Maccabees* is to encourage faithfulness to Jewish piety. The work originated in Alexandria in Egypt in the early first century BCE. It was written in Greek and is counted as one of the **Pseudepigrapha**.

4 Ezra This apocalyptic work consists of chapters 3–14 of the book that is included in the **Apocrypha** and is known as **2 Esdras**. These chapters were originally written in Hebrew, but have been preserved in Greek. *4 Ezra* is pseudonymously attributed to Ezra, who is in exile in Babylon, where he voices his complaints to God and asks about the origin of evil. He is assured of God's justice, which includes rewards and punishments in the afterlife. In one of his visions, Ezra sees an eagle with twelve wings, three heads and twelve secondary wings. The eagle represents the Roman empire, and it will be punished by the lion, who represents the Messiah (11.1–12.39). *Fourth Ezra* 3.1 refers to the thirtieth year after the destruction of Jerusalem, which means that the work may be dated around 100 CE. *Fourth Ezra* is counted among the **Pseudepigrapha**.

4 Maccabees This book is a philosophical treatise intended to prove the thesis that "devout reason is absolute master of the passions" (1.1). Heavily influenced by Stoic philosophy, *Fourth Maccabees* was written in Greek and refers to the martyrs as examples of virtue. It is dated to sometime in the first century CE. Scholars usually associate the work with Alexandria in Egypt, but this is disputed. *Fourth Maccabees* was written in Greek and counted among the **Pseudepigrapha**.

4Q161 Also known as *Commentary on Isaiah* or *pesher on Isaiah* (4QpIsa), this scroll from **Qumran** Cave 4 is a commentary on the messianic prophecy from Isaiah 11. *Pesher* is a Hebrew word that means "interpretation." In biblical studies, the term is used for a kind of exegesis that reapplies the biblical stories to contemporary or future events. This scroll is dated to the first century BCE.

4Q169 Also known as *Commentary on Nahum*, this scroll from Cave 4 at **Qumran** is dated to 50–1 BCE. It contains the text of Nah. 1.3-6; 2.11-13; 3.1-14 with commentary. In 4Q169 3+4.i.2–3, the interpretation names two Greek kings, Demetrius and Antiochus, the former of whom failed to conquer Jerusalem. He was advised by "those who seek smooth things," which probably refers to the Pharisees. Later, the interpretation describes the judgment of Ephraim and Manasseh, probably intended as a reference to the Pharisees and the Sadducees, respectively.

4Q171 Also known as **Commentary on the Psalms**, this scroll from Cave 4 at **Qumran** is dated to 100–1 BCE. It contains the text of Pss. 37.7-40; 45.1-2; and 60.8-9 with commentary. The interpretation understands the righteous and the wicked of Psalm 37 to be the members of the sect and their opponents, respectively.

4Q174 Also known as *Florilegium* or *Midrash on the Last Days* ("florilegium" means anthology), this document from Cave 4 at **Qumran** is dated to 50–1 BCE. It strings together quotations from 2 Sam. 7.10-14; Exod. 15.17-18; Amos 9.11; Ps. 1.1; Isa. 8.11; Ezek. 44.10; Ps. 2.1; Dan. 12.10; and different verses from Deuteronomy 33. The texts are given eschatological interpretations.

4Q175 Also known as *Testimonia* or *Messianic Anthology*, this manuscript from Cave 4 at **Qumran** is from 100–75 CE and consists of quotations from Deut. 5.28-29; 18.18-19; Num. 24.15-17; Deut. 33.8-11; and the non-canonical Psalms of Joshua in combination with Josh. 6.26. No interpretation is provided, but these biblical passages probably serve as the Scriptural basis for the community's messianic beliefs. Deut. 18.18-19 announces the coming of a prophet like Moses; in Num. 24.15-17, Balaam prophecies regarding a scepter that has arisen from Israel (a royal Messiah, the Messiah of Israel); and Deut. 33.8-11 refers to a pious man who will steward the Urim and Thummim, the priestly tools for knowing the will of God (a priestly Messiah, the Messiah of Aaron).

4Q242 Also known as the *Prayer of Nabonidus*, this manuscript from Cave 4 at **Qumran** is dated to 50–1 BCE. Some scholars believe that the original work is as old as from the late third or early second century BCE, whereas others date it to the late second or early first century. It is written in Aramaic and contains the prayer of Nabunai, the king of Babylon, who recounts how he was cured from an illness thanks to a Jewish exorcist. The situation described has much in common with the story in Daniel 4, which concerns the cure of king Nebuchadnezzar. The document has generated a lot of interest among New Testament scholars because it refers to the forgiveness of Nabunai's sins. It is possible that the exorcist was the one to forgive him, but it is equally possible that the one to forgive was God. The state of the manuscript makes it impossible to know with certainty.

4Q246 Also known as 4QAramaic Apocalypse and the "Son of God" document, this scroll from **Qumran** Cave 4 is written in Aramaic and dated to 35–1 BCE. It consists of two columns and is famous because it refers to a character that is called "son of God."

4Q252 Also known as the *Genesis Commentary*, this scroll from **Qumran** Cave 4 may be dated to 100–50 BCE. It is more of a paraphrase than a commentary. The most extensive surviving fragment concerns the story of Noah.

4Q369 Also known as *The Prayer of Enosh and Enoch*, this scroll from **Qumran** Cave 4 consists of ten very poorly preserved fragments which apparently contain various prayers.

4Q381 This poorly preserved manuscript contains non-biblical psalms that were found in Cave 4 at **Qumran**. These psalms may be older than the Qumran community.

4Q403 This scroll is one of eight scrolls known as the *Songs of the Sabbath Sacrifice* or *Songs for the Holocaust of the Sabbath* (4Q400–407). These songs contain a liturgy for the angels' praise to God, assigned to the first thirteen Sabbaths of the year. The scrolls were found in Cave 4 at **Qumran** and can be dated to the first century BCE.

4Q405 *See* **4Q403**.

4Q463 This poorly preserved scroll from **Qumran** Cave 4 contains only a few lines that include a quotation of Lev. 26.44.

4Q491 This scroll from **Qumran** Cave 4 contains small parts of the text known from the *War Scroll* (**1QM**).

4Q504 This scroll from **Qumran** Cave 4 contains corporate prayers for the days of the week.

4Q521 Also known as *A Messianic Apocalypse*, this poorly preserved scroll from Cave 4 at **Qumran** dates to the early first century BCE. It mentions the Messiah and describes the end time salvation of God as a time of healing and the resurrection of the dead.

4Q534 Also known as the "Elect of God" text, this scroll from **Qumran** Cave 4 is written in Aramaic and dates to the end of the first century BCE. It describes a miraculous birth. Some scholars think the child is the Messiah, but the majority identify him as Noah.

4Q558 This scroll from Cave 4 at **Qumran** is extremely fragmentary, and hardly anything intelligible has been preserved, except for a mention of the sending of Elijah.

11Q5 Also known as 11QPs[a], this scroll from Cave 11 at **Qumran** contains seven poems in addition to canonical Psalms. These poems probably date from the third or second century BCE. Some of them are known from other sources, such as Psalm 151 from the **Septuagint** and the old Greek versions of the Old Testament.

11Q11 Also known as 11QapPs (Apocryphal Psalms from Cave 11 at **Qumran**), this very poorly preserved scroll contains some poems related to exorcism.

11Q13 Also known as 11QMelch, this scroll from Cave 11 at **Qumran** is dated to the first century BCE. It describes the Jubilee year (Deut. 15.2; Isa. 61.1) when Melchizedek will come as the deliverer of Israel and function as the eschatological judge. This Melchizedek is not identified further, but most scholars think he is the same figure as the archangel Michael. The scroll is very significant for New Testament studies, not only because the letter to the Hebrews also takes an interest in Melchizedek (Heb. 7), but because this picture of Melchizedek has several other points of contact with New Testament Christology.

11QT (11QTemple) The *Temple Scroll* from Cave 11 at **Qumran** is dated to the second century BCE. It most likely stems from the Qumran community and contains a mixture of biblical and non-biblical laws regarding the temple service, including Sabbath sacrifices and annual feasts. The scroll is not intended to be biblical interpretation, but a new revelation from God. The Qumran community believed that they lived in the last days, and 11QTemple may have functioned as something of a "divine revelation supplement" for the end times. Some scholars believe that the work was written by the **Teacher of Righteousness**.

anarthrous A noun or adjective that does not have an article.

Apocalypse of Abraham This **apocalyptic** work has survived in a Slavonic translation, but the original was probably written in Hebrew or another Semitic language. It is pseudonymously attributed to Abraham, but scholars date it between 70 and 150 CE. It consists of two parts, the first telling the story of Abraham's youth and rejection of idolatry, the second recounting his journey to heaven, guided by the angel Iaoel. The *Apocalypse of Abraham* is counted among the **Pseudepigrapha**.

Apocalypse of Moses The **Life of Adam and Eve** has survived in both a Latin and Greek version. The Greek text is usually cited as the *Apocalypse of Moses*. Strictly speaking, the *Apocalypse of Moses* is not an **apocalyptic** work, but a retelling of the biblical story of Adam and Eve. Both works probably depend on the same Hebrew original, which may be dated to around 100 CE. The *Apocalypse of Moses* is counted among the **Pseudepigrapha**.

Apocalypse of Zephaniah Preserved in fragments of a Coptic translation, this **apocalyptic** work was originally written in Greek. It is pseudonymously attributed to the prophet Zephaniah; the actual Jewish author was perhaps from Egypt and wrote sometime between 100 BCE and 175 CE. The contents concern Zephaniah's heavenly journey, during which he witnesses the eschatological judgment. The *Apocalypse of Zephaniah* is counted among the **Pseudepigrapha**.

apocalyptic "Apocalyptic" is a designation of a literary genre, characterized by a strict dualism between this world and the heavenly world and by a focus on the revelation of heavenly secrets. Apocalyptic writings often describe a heavenly journey, on which the celestial traveler is guided by an angel, who communicates secrets to him. Apocalyptics are typically set against a backdrop of crisis. The revelations provide a heavenly perspective on the crisis and show that the heavenly realities are more important than the present hardships.

Apocrypha The writings of the **Septuagint** that are not included in the Jewish and Protestant canons are known by Protestants as Apocrypha. The Greek word *apocrypha* means "hidden." Catholic Christians consider these books canonical and refer to them as deuterocanonical (Greek for "second canon"). However, different traditions (Greek, Coptic) include a different number of deuterocanonical books. Many modern English Bible translations, such as NAB, NJB and many versions of NRSV, contain translations of these books. For a thorough introduction to the Apocrypha, see David A. deSilva, *Introducing the Apocrypha: Message, Context, and Significance* (Grand Rapids: Baker, 2002).

Aquila Through the compilation of the church father Origen (185–254), four early Greek translations of the Old Testament have survived. One of these versions was translated by Aquila, who was from Sinope in Pontus (a region in the northeastern part of what is now Turkey). He converted from paganism to Christianity and later to Judaism. His relatively literal translation dates to 100–125 CE, but exists today only in fragments.

Avot One of the subdivisions of the *Mishnah* (and the *Talmud* and the *Tosefta*) is called *Avot* (sometimes spelled *Abot* and sometimes referred to as *Pirqe Avot/Abot*). The Hebrew word *avot* means "fathers," and this tractate contains the oldest traditions of the *Mishnah* in the form of ethical rules and pithy sayings.

Babylonian Talmud The Babylonian version of the **Talmud** was completed around 500 CE. An English translation is available in I. Epstein, ed., *The Babylonian Talmud*, 18 vols (London: Soncino, 1961).

Baruch One of the **Apocrypha**, Baruch is pseudonymously attributed to the prophet Jeremiah's secretary of that name (cf. Jer. 36.4, 27, 32; 45.1). Scholars have concluded that it is a composite work, but have reached no consensus regarding its time of composition. Usually, a date in the second century BCE is suggested, and Jerusalem is often believed to be the place of origin. The work has been preserved in Greek, but the original language may be Hebrew.

It contains Baruch's confession of sin and prayer for mercy on Israel's behalf in the wake of the destruction of Jerusalem. A brief overview of Israel's history follows, with a message of hope at the end.

Berakot One of the subdivisions of the *Mishnah* (and the *Talmud* and the *Tosefta*) is called *Berakot* (sometimes spelled *Berakhot*). The Hebrew word *berakot* means "blessings," and this tractate discusses rules regarding the saying of the Shema, the Jewish creed (Deut. 6.4), and some Jewish prayers.

catechetical Relating to the teaching given to a person who is preparing for Christian baptism.

CD The *Damascus Document* (occasionally referred to as Zadokite Fragments) was first discovered in a synagogue in Cairo in 1896. The designation CD is an abbreviation of Cairo Damascus. It exists in two versions (CD-A and CD-B). Various fragments discovered at **Qumran** are witnesses to a fuller version of the text. Its name stems from the repeated mention of Damascus (6.5, 19; 7.15, 19; 8.21; 19.34; 20.12), which may be code for Babylon. Some scholars believe that the origin of the Qumran community may be traced to Babylon, but this hypothesis is disputed. The work contains a moral exhortation to the initiates of the Qumran community as well as instructions on various rules of the community. There is still a scholarly debate regarding the date of the Damascus Document, most suggestions falling between 150 and 50 BCE.

cognate Derived from the same linguistic root.

conflate To combine two or more texts into one.

Dead Sea Scrolls This term is used to refer to texts that have been discovered along the north-west shore of the Dead Sea. In a more specific sense, it refers to the scrolls discovered at Qumran. *See also* **Qumran**.

Deuteronomy Rabbah This **Midrash** is not a commentary on Deuteronomy, but contains twenty-five complete and two fragmentary homilies on passages from Deuteronomy. It may be dated to around 900 CE. An English translation is available in H. Freedman and Maurice Simon, ed., *Midrash Rabbah*, 10 vols (London: Soncino, 1961).

Ecclesiastes Rabbah This **Midrash** is a commentary on Ecclesiastes. In its final form, it dates to between the sixth and eighth century CE. An English translation is available in H. Freedman and Maurice Simon, ed., *Midrash Rabbah*, 10 vols (London: Soncino, 1961).

epiphany A visible manifestation of a divine or supernatural being.

Essenes *See* Qumran.

Ezekiel the Tragedian The work of the author known as Ezekiel the Tragedian has only survived in fragments. Ezekiel the Tragedian wrote *The Exagoge* (the Greek word *exagoge* means "leading out") to recount the story of Israel's exodus from Egypt. The focus is on Moses, who has a dream where he is seated on God's throne in heaven (68–82). Ezekiel the Tragedian's work is usually dated to 200–150 BCE. Many scholars believe the author was a Jew from Alexandria, but the evidence is inconclusive. Ezekiel's *Exagoge* is counted among the **Pseudepigrapha**.

gloss A word or phrase added for the purpose of explanation.

Greek Magical Papyri Many papyrus documents from the Greco-Roman period have been discovered in Egypt. Among these are some papyri that contain magical spells, formulas, hymns and rituals. They date from the second century BCE to the fifth century CE. An English translation is conveniently available in Hans Dieter Betz, ed., *The Greek Magical Papyri in Translation, Including the Demotic Spells* (Chicago: University of Chicago Press, 1996).

Hellenistic *See* **Hellenize**.

Hellenize This term refers to the spread of Greek culture (Hellenism) throughout the Mediterranean world in the wake of the conquests of Alexander the Great.

inclusio A literary device by which a word or a phrase occurs at the beginning and the end of a section ("bookends").

interpolation A secondary insertion into a text.

intransitive A verb that does not take an object is referred to as intransitive, in contrast to a **transitive** verb.

Isaiah Targum This **Targum** is dated to the fourth century CE.

Joseph and Aseneth One of the **Pseudepigrapha**, *Joseph and Aseneth* tells the story of what led to Joseph's marriage to the daughter of a pagan priest, Aseneth (cf. Gen. 41.45). Driven by her love for Joseph, Aseneth repudiated idolatry. *Joseph and Aseneth* was written in Greek sometime between 100 BCE and 115 CE. Many scholars believe that the book was written in Egypt and was intended to clarify questions related to marrying a Gentile.

Josephus The Jewish history writer Josephus was born in 37 CE and probably died around 100 CE. He fought briefly in the Jewish revolt of 66–70 CE, but surrendered and began cooperating with the Romans. His writings were motivated by his desire to justify his actions, and he maintained that the Jewish revolt deserved to be struck down. The Romans were instruments of God's punishment of the rebels, who were not supported by the majority of the people. His account of the Jewish revolt and the events leading up to it are found in the *Jewish War*. He also wrote a fuller chronicle of Israel's history, the *Jewish Antiquities*, as well as an autobiography, *Life*, and an apology for Judaism, *Against Apion*. Because of his bias, scholars sometimes doubt the trustworthiness of his accounts. The Greek text with a parallel English translation of Josephus' works is available in the Loeb Classical Library series, published by Harvard University Press.

Jubilees This book gives an account of the revelation Moses received when he was on Mount Sinai. It amounts to a retelling of the biblical story from creation to the time of Moses. Jubilees was originally written in Hebrew, and fragments of the work have been found among the Dead Sea Scrolls. The Hebrew original can be dated to between 161–140 BCE. It was later translated into Greek and Syriac. In turn, the Greek version was translated into Latin and Ge'ez (the ancient language of Ethiopia, often less precisely called "Ethiopic"). The Ge'ez version is the only one that has survived in an almost complete form. The author of Jubilees probably belonged to a priestly family in Israel. Like the Qumran community, the author of Jubilees advocates a solar calendar. Unlike the Qumranites, however, he does not appear to have broken fellowship with the rest of the nation. The author may have been affiliated with the conservative groups from which the Qumran community also originated. *Jubilees* is counted among the **Pseudepigrapha**.

Judith One of the **Apocrypha**, the book of Judith tells the story of Judith of Bethulia. The Assyrian army, led by general Holofernes, is ready to invade Jerusalem. However, by trusting in God and the use of trickery, the widow Judith is able to decapitate the general. As a result, the Assyrians flee. The book of Judith was composed in Hebrew and has been preserved in Greek and Latin. Many scholars believe that the author was a Pharisee who wrote around 100 BCE.

Letter of Aristeas The *Letter of Aristeas* describes the origin of the **Septuagint**. The Egyptian king Ptolemy II (285–247 BCE) wants to collect all the books in the world for the library in Alexandria. To secure a Greek translation of the Scriptures of Israel, seventy-two Jews are summoned to Alexandria, where they complete the task in seventy-two days. Most of the *Letter of Aristeas* is devoted to the king's interview of the translators regarding their religion. The *Letter of Aristeas* was written and has been preserved in Greek. It is impossible to be certain about the date, but most scholars opt for 150–100 BCE. The majority also assume that the author was an Alexandrian Jew. The *Letter of Aristeas* is counted among the **Pseudepigrapha**.

Liber Antiquitate Biblicarum The book of biblical antiquities (referred to by its Latin title) has long been attributed to Philo. Scholars now agree that this attribution is incorrect, and the author is therefore called Pseudo-Philo. Pseudo-Philo wrote in Hebrew, but only a Latin translation has survived. This version depends on an earlier Greek translation. Scholars believe the author lived in the land of Israel and that he wrote around the beginning of the first century CE. *Liber Antiquitate Biblicarum* retells much of the biblical story. The work is counted among the **Pseudepigrapha**.

Life of Adam and Eve This work has survived in both a Latin and a Greek version. The Greek text is usually cited as the ***Apocalypse of Moses***. Strictly speaking, it is not an apocalyptic work, but a retelling of the biblical story of Adam and Eve. Both works probably depend on the same Hebrew original, which may be dated to around 100 CE. The *Life of Adam and Eve* is counted among the **Pseudepigrapha**.

LXX *See* **Septuagint**.

Martyrdom and Ascension of Isaiah The Martyrdom and Ascension of Isaiah is really three works: the Martyrdom of Isaiah (1.1-3.12; 5.1-16), the Testament of Hezekiah (3.13-4.22) and the Vision of Isaiah (chapters 6–11). The oldest part is the Martyrdom of Isaiah, which tells the story of Isaiah's death by being sawed in half. Both the Testament of Hezekiah and the Vision of Isaiah are Christian additions. The Testament of Hezekiah describes the end times, and the Vision recounts Isaiah's journey through the seven heavens, where he witnesses the incarnation, life, death, resurrection and ascension of the Lord. Whereas the Martyrdom of Isaiah was composed in Hebrew and later translated into Greek, the rest of the work was originally written in Greek. The Greek version was later translated into several different languages, including Ge'ez (the ancient language of Ethiopia, often less precisely called "Ethiopic"), which is the only version that has survived in its entirety. Scholars believe that the Martyrdom may have originated in Israel at the time of the persecution under Antiochus IV Epiphanes (167–164 BCE), whereas the Testament of Hezekiah may stem from the end of the first century CE and the Vision of Isaiah from the second century. The *Martyrdom and Ascension of Isaiah* is counted among the **Pseudepigrapha**.

Masoretic Text This term refers to the text of the Old Testament in Hebrew and Aramaic as it has been preserved by the Jewish scribes of the sixth to tenth centuries CE (the Masoretes). Modern scholarly editions of the Old Testament in Hebrew rely primarily on the Masoretic Text.

Mekilta This **Rabbinic Midrash** contains a commentary on various passages in Exodus. The material that went into the *Mekilta* was probably collected in the land of Israel by the end of the fifth century CE. An English translation is available in Jacob Neusner, tr., *Mekhilta According to Rabbi Ishmael: An Analytical Translation*, 2 vols. (BJS 148, 152; Atlanta: Scholars Press, 1988).

metonymy A figure of speech in which an object is referred to by something associated with it, e.g., "suit" used to denote a business associate.

Midrash The Hebrew word *midrash* means "study" or "exposition" and has become a technical term for **Rabbinic** exegetical writings, such as *Mekilta* and *Rabbah*.

Midrash Psalms The date and identity of the editor of the Rabbinic Midrash on the Psalms cannot be determined. It is probably a composite work and has been known since the eleventh century. An English translation is available in William G. Braude, tr., *The Midrash on Psalms*, 2 vols (Yale Judaica Series 13; New Haven: Yale University Press, 1959).

Midrash Rabbah The Hebrew word rabbah means "great" and has been attached to ten different Rabbinic *midrashim* (plural of *midrash*) on various biblical books. *See also* **Deuteronomy Rabbah** and **Ecclesiastes Rabbah**.

Mishnah According to traditional Jewish belief, Moses received both the written and the oral law at Mount Sinai (*Mishnah* **Avot** 1.1). Whereas the written Torah was recorded in the Pentateuch, the oral Torah was handed down to the elders and Rabbis of Israel and finally written down in the *Mishnah*, the earliest of the **Rabbinic** writings. In its final form, the *Mishnah* dates to around 220 CE, but some of its traditions are considerably older. The *Mishnah* contains legal discussions of the Rabbis of the time between 70–200 CE. The Hebrew word *mishnah* means "repetition." An English translation is available in Jacob Neusner, tr., *The Mishnah: A New Translation* (New Haven, CT: Yale University Press, 1988).

MT *See* Masoretic Text

narrative criticism This term refers to an interpretive method that focuses on the final form of the text, in contradistinction to form criticism, which focuses on individual units, and redaction criticism, which focuses on the author's integration of these units into his or her own work. Narrative criticism examines the final form of the text as a unity and does not ask about its pre-history or about how the text relates to history. Instead, narrative critics are interested in the universe that is created by the story itself, the characters as they emerge within the story and the events as they are told by the narrator.

Nazirite A person that is consecrated to God for a specific time, during which they abstain from alcohol and let their hair grow (cf. Num. 6.1–21)

parousia The Greek word *parousia* means "presence" or "coming" and is used as a technical term for the second coming of Christ.

Pesiqta Rabbati This **Rabbinic midrash** is a collection of homilies on passages from the Pentateuch and the prophets. It is dated to around 845 CE. An English translation is available in William G. Braude, tr., *Pesikta Rabbati: Discourses for Feasts, Fasts, and Special Sabbaths*, 2 vols. (Yale Judaica Series 18; New Haven: Yale University Press, 1968).

Philo The Jewish philosopher Philo, from Alexandria in Egypt, was born around 20–10 BCE and died about 50 CE. He was heavily influenced by Greek ideas, especially by the Platonic, Stoic and Neopythagorean schools of thought. Nevertheless, Philo was a faithful Jew who believed in all the basic tenets of Jewish religion, including the divine inspiration of the Bible. He believed that everything that was true in Greek philosophy had already been taught by Moses. In order to demonstrate this, he interpreted the Bible allegorically. The Bible stories were not really about historical events, but pointed to philosophical truths. Inspired by Plato's view of ideas as the true reality, Philo saw spiritual realities behind all created things. The highest of these spiritual entities, or ideas, is the Logos (Greek for "word" or "idea"), which is the root of all the others. For Philo, the Logos is God's reason, his agent in creation, and the archangel through whom he communicates with the world. Most of his works take the form of commentaries on the books of the Pentateuch. The Greek text with an English translation of Philo's many writings is available in the Loeb Classical Library series, published by Harvard University Press.

Pirqe Rabbi Eliezer This Rabbinic work is a narrative midrash that describes the events from creation to Israel's forty years in the wilderness. An English translation is available in Gerald Friedlander, tr., *Pirkê de Rabbi Eliezer (The Chapters of Rabbi Eliezer, the Great): According to the Text of the Manuscript Belonging to Abraham Epstein of Vienna* (2nd ed.; Judaic Studies Library SHP 6; New York: Hermon, 1965).

post-exilic Dated after Israel's exile in Babylon (587 CE).

Psalms of Solomon Eighteen psalms, pseudonymously attributed to Solomon, have been preserved in Greek and Syriac manuscripts. Their original language was probably Hebrew. The psalms were written in response to the Roman invasion of Jerusalem in 63 BCE and probably date to around the middle of the first century BCE. Traditionally, scholars have believed that the *Psalms of Solomon* were written by a Pharisee and thought of the work as the most important document that has survived from this Jewish group. However, this view has been challenged lately. Some modern scholars have argued that the *Psalms* originated among the **Essenes**, among another group closely related to them, or among an otherwise unknown group. Nevertheless, others, with good reasons, still argue that the *Psalms* originated within a group closely related to the Pharisees, if the writer was not a Pharisee himself. The author understands the Roman invasion as God's punishment for the rampant sin and ungodliness in Israel. Nevertheless, he holds out hope for the future. God will send his Messiah (chapter 17), who will bring salvation to his people. The *Psalms of Solomon* are counted among the **Pseudepigrapha**.

Pseudepigrapha A diverse body of literature from Second Temple Judaism is commonly referred to as the Pseudepigrapha, as many of these writings were written pseudonymously. An English translation is conveniently available in James H. Charlesworth, ed., *The Old Testament Pseudepigrapha*, 2 vols (New York: Doubleday, 1983–1985).

Qumran In 1947 a straying sheep led a Bedouin shepherd boy to what is considered the most important manuscript discovery of modern times. Seeing a hole in one of the cliffs north of Khirbet Qumran on the north-west shore of the Dead Sea, the boy threw a stone into it and heard it make a peculiar sound. It turned out that the cave contained large terracotta jars used to store scrolls. Since then, eleven caves have been discovered that contained different kinds of manuscripts. Some of these manuscripts are copies of Old Testament books, and some are copies of works that are otherwise known. In addition, these discoveries have brought to light a number of works that were previously unknown. Although the identity of the Qumran community continues to be debated among scholars, there is relatively broad agreement that these caves contained the library of the Essenes, a Jewish group that is known from the writings of **Philo** and **Josephus**. The Qumran library is also referred to as the **Dead Sea Scrolls**. Many of these writings give insights into the beliefs and practices of this ascetic community. Led by the **Teacher of Righteousness**, they separated from the rest of the Jewish community, whom they considered to be apostate. They disagreed with the Jerusalem establishment about matters of legal interpretation and rejected the Jerusalem high priests because they did not belong to the high-priestly line of Zadok (cf. 1 Chron. 6.53). They also advocated the use of a solar as opposed to a lunar calendar. As a result, they also rejected the religious festivals that other Jews celebrated since they did not celebrate them at the proper times. A record of the community's history is found in the *Damascus Document* (**CD**), and their strict discipline is laid out in the Community Rule (**1QS**). A reliable and relatively accessible translation of the non-biblical Dead Sea Scrolls is Geza Vermes, tr., *The Complete Dead Sea Scrolls in English* (Penguin Classics; London: Penguin, 2004). Although now dated, a very good, accessible introduction to Qumran and the Dead Sea Scrolls is Joseph A. Fitzmyer, *Responses to 101 Questions on the Dead Sea Scrolls* (New York: Paulist, 1992).

Rabbinic literature "Rabbinic Judaism" is used as a designation for the form of Judaism that emerged after the destruction of the Jerusalem temple in 70 CE. A vast body of literature belongs to Rabbinic Judaism, including legal discussions (***Mishnah***, ***Talmud***, ***Tosefta***) and biblical exposition (**Midrash**). Since the destruction of the temple represented a watershed moment within Judaism, many scholars argue that Rabbinic Judaism is quite different from earlier forms of Judaism and that the Rabbinic literature therefore is of little relevance to New Testament studies. Others emphasize the conservative nature of Rabbinic traditions and maintain that this literature may be used judiciously to cast light on the Judaism of Jesus' time.

realized eschatology The New Testament attests to the belief that the fulfillment of God's promises regarding the last times (eschatology) has already taken place in Jesus Christ. This conviction is referred to as realized eschatology.

Sanhedrin The *Sanhedrin* is one of the subdivisions of the *Mishnah* (and the *Talmud* and the *Tosefta*). The name refers to the Jewish legal council, and the tractate discusses its organization and procedures.

Second Temple Judaism The "Second Temple" refers to the temple that was rebuilt under Ezra in 516 BCE and later expanded by King Herod around 19 BCE. Second Temple Judaism is the term that is used for Judaism in the period from 516 BCE to 70 CE and must be clearly distinguished from Rabbinic Judaism (*see* **Rabbinic literature**). The literature from the Second Temple period includes the **Apocrypha**, the **Pseudepigrapha** and the writings from **Qumran**, as well as the writings of **Josephus** and **Philo**.

Septuagint The oldest surviving translation of the Old Testament from Hebrew to Greek is known as the Septuagint. The Greek word *septuaginta* means "seventy" and refers to the seventy-two translators that according to Jewish tradition were responsible for the translation (*see* **Letter of Aristeas**). Scholars believe that the work was begun in the third century BCE, but that most of the books were translated in the second century. The Septuagint contains books that are not included in the Jewish and Protestant canons. Protestants refer to these books as the **Apocrypha**. An English translation of the Septuagint is avaliable in *A New English Translation of the Septuagint and the Other Greek Translations Traditionally Included Under That Title* (ed. Albert Pietersma and Benjamin G. Wright; New York: Oxford University Press, 2007).

Shekinah The Hebrew word *shekinah* means "dwelling" and is used as a technical term for the presence of God, especially his presence above the Ark of the Covenant in the Holy of Holies.

Shemoneh Esre According to **Mishnah Berakot** 3.3; 4.1, 3, every Jew was required to pray these eighteen prayers daily (the Hebrew *shemoneh esre* means "eighteen"). Many of these prayers probably date from the period before the fall of the temple (70 CE). *Shemoneh Esre* has survived in a Babylonian version that actually contains nineteen prayers.

Sibylline Oracles "Sibyl" is a designation for a prophetess in the ancient world. The apocalyptic work known as *Sibylline Oracles* is a collection of twelve books written in Greek and of various origins. Modern versions rely on two manuscripts with different systems for ordering and numbering these books. As a result, the twelve books are numbered 1–8 and 11–14. Originally one Jewish composition, books 1 and 2 have undergone extensive Christian redaction. The Jewish version was probably written in Phrygia (in what is now Turkey) around the turn of the era, and the Christian redaction may date to around 150 CE. Book 3 was probably written in Egypt during the period 163–145 BCE. It takes a very positive view of the Greek king in Egypt, perhaps motivated by a desire to show that Jews and Gentiles can coexist harmoniously. The fourth book originated as a Jewish composition around 300 BCE, but the surviving version has undergone a Christian redaction that dates to around 80 CE. Dating to around 100 CE, book 5 is a Jewish work from Egypt. In stark contrast to book 3, it represents an extreme within Judaism in terms of its hostility towards Gentiles. Book 6 is a Christian hymn to Christ and must be dated sometime in the second or third century CE. The collection of Jewish–Christian oracles found in book 7 dates to the same period. Book 8 is another Jewish work with Christian additions. The oldest parts date to around 175 CE. Books 11–14 tell a continuous story from Noah to the Arab invasion (in the seventh century CE). They were probably written by Jews in Egypt, but contain Christian additions. Books 11 and 14 cannot be dated with any degree of certainty, but book 12 may have been written shortly after 235 CE and book 13 around 265 CE.

Similitudes *See 1 Enoch.*

Sirach The Jewish sage Jesus son of Eleazar son of Sirach is the author of this collection of wisdom sayings (Sirach 50.27). Commonly referred to as ben Sira, the author wrote in Hebrew between 196 and 175 BCE. His grandson translated the work to Greek sometime after 132 BCE (prologue). In form and content his work may be compared to the book of Proverbs. Many scholars believe that Sirach represents a theological outlook that is close to that of the Sadducees. The work is included in the **Apocrypha**.

Soṭah The *Sotah* is one of the subdivisions of the *Mishnah* (and the *Talmud* and the *Tosefta*). The Hebrew word *sotah* means "to stray" and the tractate discusses the procedures for dealing with an unfaithful wife (cf. Num. 5.11-31).

Symmachus Through the compilation of the church father Origen (185–254), four early Greek translations of the Old Testament have survived. One of these versions was translated by Symmachus, who is identified as an Ebionite in ancient sources. The Ebionites were a Jewish–Christian sect that did not believe in the divinity of Jesus Christ. Symmachus' more idiomatic translation is dated to 150–175 CE, but exists today only in fragments.

Talmud Rabbinic legal discussions after the time of the *Mishnah* are contained in the *Talmud*, which exists in two versions, the *Babylonian Talmud* and the *Jerusalem Talmud*. The Hebrew word *talmud* means "learning."

Targum The Hebrew word *targum* means "translation" or "interpretation." This term refers to Aramaic translations of the Old Testament. These translations have the form of a paraphrase and therefore provide an insight into how the Scriptures were interpreted. The Aramaic text and English translations of the Targums are published in the series The Aramaic Bible by Michael Glazier.

Targum Pseudo-Jonathan Originally known as the Jerusalem Targum, this **Targum** was mistakenly attributed to Jonathan ben Uzziel. It was composed in the land of Israel, but its date is uncertain. Scholars have variously dated the final product to sometime between the eighth and the thirteenth centuries.

Teacher of Righteousness One of the early leaders of the Qumran community, the Teacher of Righteousness was a priest who was believed to provide an authoritative interpretation of Scripture. His identity is unknown, but many modern scholars believe he may be the author of some of the *Thanksgiving Hymns* (**1QH**).

*Testament of Benjamin See **Testament of the Twelve Patriarchs**.*

*Testament of Dan See **Testament of the Twelve Patriarchs**.*

*Testament of Issachar See **Testament of the Twelve Patriarchs**.*

*Testament of Levi See **Testament of the Twelve Patriarchs**.*

Testament of Moses Sometimes called the *Assumption of Moses*, this pseudonymous work purports to contain the last words of Moses. In predictive form, it tells the story of God's people until the end of the world, when the kingdom of God and the new creation will appear. The *Testament of Moses* has survived in a Latin translation that depends on a Greek version, but the original language was probably Hebrew or possibly Aramaic. The original work probably dates to 7–30 CE. Some scholars have argued that the author belonged to the Pharisees, others that he was an **Essene**. The Testament of Moses is included in the **Pseudepigrapha**.

*Testament of Naphtali See **Testament of the Twelve Patriarchs**.*

*Testament of Simeon See **Testament of the Twelve Patriarchs**.*

Testament of the Twelve Patriarchs There is some debate among scholars whether the *Testaments of the Twelve Patriarchs* should be considered a Jewish or a Christian work, but the majority agree that it is a Jewish work that contains many Christian additions. It is included in the **Pseudepigrapha**. Modeled after Genesis 49, this work takes the form of testaments written by Jacob's twelve sons. The Testaments have been preserved in Greek, but some scholars believe that the original language was Hebrew. The Jewish version of the *Testaments* probably dates to the second century BCE and may have been written in Syria.

Testament of Zebulon *See* **Testament of the Twelve Patriarchs**.

tetragrammaton Formed from the Greek words *tetra* ("four") and *gramma* ("letter"), *tetragrammaton* is a technical term for the divine name as it occurs in the Hebrew Bible. As Hebrew is written without vowels, the name of God is written YHWH. The original pronunciation was most probably Yahweh (not Jehovah), but when the Bible was read in the synagogue the name was considered too holy to be pronounced. Instead, the reader substituted the word *adonai* ("Lord").

Textual criticism None of the original manuscripts of the biblical writings have survived, only copies that have been made by hand. The oldest complete manuscripts of the New Testament are known as Codex Sinaiticus and Codex Vaticanus. They are dated to the fourth century CE. The more than five thousand surviving manuscripts differ in numerous places. Most of these differences are so minor that they do not even effect the translation, but some are more substantial. Many modern Bible translations use brackets around parts of the text that are omitted in certain manuscripts. Other versions relegate such elements to footnotes (see, e.g., Mt. 6.15b; Mk 16.9-20; Jn 7.53–8.11). Textual critics attempt to determine what is likely to be the original text. They use external and internal criteria. External criteria concern the weighing of the manuscripts. A reading is more likely to be original if it is found in older and better manuscripts and if it is attested to in manuscripts from different traditions. Internal criteria concern the likelihood of a scribal change in the text. A reading is less likely to be original if it can be explained as a scribal deviation from another attested reading. For an accessible introduction to textual criticism, see J. Harold Greenlee, *Introduction to New Testament Textual Criticism* (rev. ed.; Peabody, MA: Hendrickson, 1995).

Theodotion Through the compilation of the church father Origen (185–254), four early Greek translations of the Old Testament have survived. One of these versions was translated by Theodotion from Ephesus. Theodotion's relatively literal translation is dated to 150 CE, but exists today only in fragments. Some quotations, particularly from the book of Daniel, follow the same form as Theodotion. Scholars therefore discuss on what earlier versions Theodotion's translation may be based.

theophany A visible manifestation of a divine being.

Tobit One of the **Apocrypha**, Tobit tells the story of the family of Tobit, who maintain their piety while in exile in Nineveh. The angel Raphael leads Tobit's son Tobias to Media, where he meets the beautiful and virtuous Sarah. However, Sarah is cursed: she has had seven husbands, but they have all died on their wedding night. With Raphael's help, Tobias is able to lift the curse, and he and Sarah are united in marriage. The purpose of Tobit is to encourage faithfulness to Jewish piety. Tobit was originally written in Aramaic or Hebrew, probably between 250 and 175 BCE. There is no scholarly agreement regarding its place of origin.

Tosefta A collection of Rabbinic legal discussions modeled after the *Mishnah*, the *Tosefta* is traditionally dated to a time shortly after the completion of the *Mishnah*. However, some modern scholars believe it may be much younger, although some insist that it contains traditions that are even older than the *Mishnah*. The Aramaic word "tosefta" means "additions." An English translation is available in Jacob Neusner, tr., *The Tosefta: Translated from the Hebrew with a New Introduction*, 2 vols (Peabody, MA: Hendrickson, 2002).

transitive A verb that takes an object is called a transitive verb, in contradistinction to an **intransitive** verb.

typology This term is used for a method of interpretation by which certain events, persons and institutions in the Old Testament may be understood as types that correspond to antitypes in the New Testament. For example, Paul explains that Adam was a type of Christ (Rom. 5.14).

Wisdom of Solomon One of the **Apocrypha**, this work belongs to Jewish wisdom tradition (compare with Proverbs). Pseudonymously attributed to

David's son, Solomon, it was written in Greek, probably by a **Hellenized** Jew in Alexandria in Egypt sometime between 50 BCE and 50 CE. It contains polemic against Egyptian paganism.

Bibliography

Allison, Dale C., Jr. *The New Moses: A Matthean Typology*. Minneapolis: Fortress, 1993.

Barker, Margaret. *The Great Angel: A Study of Israel's Second God*. London: SPCK, 1992.

Bauckham, Richard J. *God Crucified: Monotheism and Christology in the New Testament*. Grand Rapids: Eerdmans, 1999.

—. *Jesus and the God of Israel: God Crucified and Other Studies on the New Testament's Christology of Divine Identity*. Grand Rapids: Eerdmans, 2008.

—. "Jesus and the Wild Animals (Mark 1:13): A Christological Image for an Ecological Age." In *Jesus of Nazareth: Lord and Christ: Essays on the Historical Jesus and New Testament Christology*, ed. Joel B. Green and Max Turner. Grand Rapids: Eerdmans, 1994, 3–21.

—. "The Son of Man: 'A Man in My Position' or 'Someone.'" *JSNT* 2 (1985): 23–33.

Blackburn, Barry. *Theios Anēr and the Markan Miracle Traditions: A Critique of the Theios Anēr Concept as an Interpretative Background of the Miracle Traditions Used by Mark*. WUNT II/40. Tübingen: Mohr Siebeck, 1991.

Boccaccini, Gabriele, ed. *Enoch and the Messiah Son of Man: Revisiting the Book of Parables*. Grand Rapids: Eerdmans, 2007.

Bock, Darrell L. "Blasphemy and the Jewish Examination of Jesus." In *Key Events in the Life of the Historical Jesus: A Collaborative Exploration of Context and Coherence*, ed. Darrell L. Bock and Robert L. Webb. WUNT 247. Tübingen: Mohr Siebeck, 2009, 589–667.

—. *Luke*. Vol. 1. BECNT. Grand Rapids: Baker, 1994.

—. *Proclamation from Prophecy and Pattern: Lucan Old Testament Christology*. JSNTSup 12. Sheffield: JSOT Press, 1987.

Brenton, Lancelot Charles Lee, tr. *The Septuagint Version of the Old Testament*. London: Bagster and Sons, 1844.

Broadhead, Edwin K. *Teaching with Authority: Miracles and Christology in the Gospel of Mark*. JSNTSup 74. Sheffield: JSOT Press, 1992.

Brown, Raymond E. *The Birth of the Messiah: A Commentary on the Infancy*

Narratives in the Gospels of Matthew and Luke. New, updated ed. ABRL. New York: Doubleday, 1993.

—. *The Death of the Messiah: A Commentary on the Passion Narratives in the Four Gospels*. Vol. 2. ABRL. New York: Doubleday, 1994.

Bultmann, Rudolf. *History of the Synoptic Tradition*. Tr. John Marsh. Oxford: Blackwell, 1963.

Byrne, Brendan. "Jesus as Messiah in the Gospel of Luke: Discerning a Pattern of Correction." *CBQ* 65 (2003): 80–95.

Casey, Maurice. *The Solution to the "Son of Man" Problem*. LNTS 343. London: T & T Clark, 2007.

Chae, Young S. *Jesus as the Eschatological Davidic Shepherd: Studies in the Old Testament, Second Temple Judaism, and in the Gospel of Matthew*. WUNT II/216. Tübingen: Mohr Siebeck, 2006.

Charlesworth, James H., ed. *The Messiah: Developments in Earliest Judaism and Christianity*. Minneapolis: Fortress, 1992.

Chilton, Bruce D. *The Isaiah Targum*. The Aramaic Bible 11. Wilmington, DE: Glazier, 1987.

Christ, Felix. *Jesus Sophia: Die Sophia-Christologie bei den Synoptikern*. ATANT 57. Zurich: Zwingli, 1970.

Collins, John J. *The Scepter and the Star: The Messiahs of the Dead Sea Scrolls and Other Ancient Literature*. ABRL. New York: Doubleday, 1995.

Conzelmann, Hans. *The Theology of St. Luke*. Tr. Geoffrey Buswell, 1961. Philadelphia: Fortress, 1982.

Croatto, J. Severino. "Jesus, Prophet Like Elijah, and Prophet-Teacher Like Moses in Luke–Acts." *JBL* 124 (2005): 451–65.

Davies, W. D. and Dale C. Allison, Jr. *A Critical and Exegetical Commentary on the Gospel According to Saint Matthew*. Vol. 1. ICC. Edinburgh: T & T Clark, 1988.

—. *A Critical and Exegetical Commentary on the Gospel According to Saint Matthew*. Vol. 2. ICC. Edinburgh: T & T Clark, 1991.

—. *A Critical and Exegetical Commentary on the Gospel According to Saint Matthew*. Vol. 3. ICC. Edinburgh: T & T Clark, 1997.

Dunn, James D. G. *Christology in the Making: A New Testament Inquiry into the Origins of the Doctrine of the Incarnation*. 2nd ed. Grand Rapids: Eerdmans, 1989.

Ebeling, Hans Jürgen. *Das Messiasgeheimnis und die Botschaft des Marcus-Evangelisten*. BZNW 19. Berlin: Töpelmann, 1939.

Evans, Craig A. *Mark 8:27–16:20*. WBC 34B. Nashville: Thomas Nelson, 2001.

Fenton, J. C. "Matthew and the Divinity of Jesus: Three Questions Concerning Matthew 1:20–23." In *Papers on the Gospels.* Vol. 2 of *Studia Biblica 1978,* ed. Elizabeth Anne Livingstone. JSNTSup 2. Sheffield: JSOT Press, 1980, 79–82.

Fitzmyer, Joseph A. *The Gospel According to Luke (I–IX): Introduction, Translation and Notes.* AB 28. New York: Doubleday, 1981.

—. *The Gospel According to Luke (X–XXIV): Introduction, Translation and Notes.* AB 28A. New York: Doubleday, 1985.

—. *A Wandering Aramean: Collected Aramaic Essays.* Missoula, MT: Scholars Press, 1979.

Fossum, Jarl E. *The Name of God and the Angel of the Lord: Samaritan and Jewish Concepts of Intermediation and the Origin of Gnosticism.* WUNT 36. Tübingen: Mohr Siebeck, 1985.

France, R. T. *The Gospel of Matthew.* NICNT. Grand Rapids: Eerdmans, 2007.

—. *Jesus and the Old Testament: His Application of Old Testament Passages to Himself and His Mission.* London: Tyndale, 1971.

Frankemölle, Hubert. *Jahwebund und Kirche Christi: Studien zur Form- und Traditionsgeschichte des Evangeliums na ch Matthäus.* NTAbh 10. Münster: Aschendorff, 1974.

García Martínez, Florentino and Eibert J. C. Tigchelaar, ed. *(1Q1–4Q273).* Vol. 1 of *The Dead Sea Scrolls Study Edition.* Leiden: Brill, 1997.

Gathercole, Simon J. *The Preexistent Son: Recovering the Christologies of Matthew, Mark, and Luke.* Grand Rapids: Eerdmans, 2006.

Gerhardsson, Birger. *The Mighty Acts of Jesus According to Matthew.* Scripta Minora Regiae Societatis Humaniorum Litterarum Lundensis. Lund: Gleerup, 1979.

—. *The Testing of God's Son (Matt. 4: 1–11 & par.): An Analysis of an Early Christian Midrash.* ConBNT 2. Lund: Gleerup, 1966.

Gnilka, Joachim. *Das Matthäusevangelium.* Vol. 2. HTKNT I/2. Freiburg: Herder, 1988.

Grindheim, Sigurd. *God's Equal: What Can We Know About Jesus' Self-Understanding?* LNTS 446. London: T & T Clark, 2011.

Gundry, Robert H. *The Use of the Old Testament in St Matthew's Gospel with Special Reference to the Messianic Hope.* NovTSup 18. Leiden: Brill, 1967.

Gurtner, Daniel M. *The Torn Veil: Matthew's Exposition of the Death of Jesus.* SNTSMS 139. Cambridge: Cambridge University Press, 2007.

Hahn, Ferdinand. *The Titles of Jesus in Christology: Their History in Early Christianity.* New York: World, 1969.

Hahn, Scott W. "Kingdom and Church in Luke–Acts: From Davidic Christology to Kingdom Ecclesiology." In *Reading Luke: Interpretation, Reflection, Formation*, ed. Craig Bartholomew, Joel B. Green and Anthony C. Thiselton. Grand Rapids: Zondervan, 2005, 294–326.

Hannah, Darrell D. *Michael and Christ: Michael Traditions and Angel Christology in Early Christianity*. WUNT II/109. Tübingen: Mohr Siebeck, 1999.

Harris, Murray J. "The Translation of *Elohim* in Psalm 45:7–8." *TynBul* 35 (1984): 65–89.

Head, Peter M. "A Text-Critical Study of Mark 1.1: 'The Beginning of the Gospel of Jesus Christ.'" *NTS* 37 (1991): 621–29.

Heil, John Paul. *Jesus Walking on the Sea: Meaning and Gospel Functions of Matt 14:22–33; Mark 6:45–52 and John 6:15b–21*. AnBib 87. Rome: Biblical Institute Press, 1981.

—. *The Transfiguration of Jesus: Narrative Meaning and Function of Mark 9:2–8, Matt 17:1–8 and Luke 9:28–36*. AnBib 144. Rome: Editrice Pontificio istituto biblico, 2000.

Hengel, Martin. *The Charismatic Leader and His Followers*, ed. John Riches, tr. James C. G. Greig. 1981. New York: Crossroad, 1996.

—. "'Sit at My Right Hand!' The Enthronement of Christ and the Right Hand of God and Psalm 110.1." In *Studies in Early Christology*. Edinburgh: T & T Clark, 1995, 119–225.

—. *Studies in Early Christology*. London: T & T Clark, 2004 (1995).

—. With the collaboration of Daniel P. Bailey. "The Effective History of Isaiah 53 in the Pre-Christian Period." In *The Suffering Servant: Isaiah 53 in Jewish and Christian Sources*, ed. Bernd Janowski and Peter Stuhlmacher, tr. Daniel P. Bailey. Grand Rapids: Eerdmans, 2004, 75–146.

Holladay, Carl R. *Theios Aner in Hellenistic-Judaism: A Critique of the Use of This Category in New Testament Christology*. SBLDS 40. Missoula, MT: Scholars Press, 1977.

Hurtado, Larry W. and Paul L. Owen, ed. *Who is This Son of Man? The Latest Scholarship on a Puzzling Expression of the Historical Jesus*. LNTS 390. London: T & T Clark, 2010.

Johnson, Luke Timothy. "The Christology of Luke–Acts." In *Who Do You Say That I Am? Essays on Christology in Honor of Jack Dean Kingsbury*, ed. Mark Allan Powell and David R. Bauer. Louisville: Westminster John Knox, 1999, 49–65.

—. *The Literary Function of Possessions in Luke–Acts*. SBLDS 39. Missoula, MT: Scholars Press, 1977.

Kee, Howard Clark. "The Terminology of Mark's Exorcism Stories." *NTS* 14 (1968): 232–46.

Kingsbury, Jack Dean. *The Christology of Mark's Gospel*. Philadelphia: Fortress, 1983.

—. "Jesus as the 'Prophetic Messiah' in Luke's Gospel." In *The Future of Christology: Essays in Honor of Leander E. Keck*, ed. Abraham J. Malherbe and Wayne A. Meeks. Minneapolis: Fortress, 1993, 29–42.

—. *Matthew as Story*. 2nd ed. Philadelphia: Fortress, 1988.

Kittel, Gerhard and Gerhard von Rad. 'δοκέω κτλ.' In *TDNT* 2: 232–55.

Kupp, David D. *Matthew's Emmanuel: Divine Presence and God's People in the First Gospel*. SNTSMS 90. Cambridge: Cambridge University Press, 1996.

Luz, Ulrich. *Matthew 8–20*, tr. Wilhelm C. Linss. Hermeneia. Minneapolis: Fortress, 2001.

—. *Matthew 21–28*, tr. James E. Crouch. Hermeneia. Minneapolis: Fortress, 2005.

Malbon, Elizabeth Struthers. *Mark's Jesus: Characterization as Narrative Christology*. Waco, TX: Baylor University Press, 2009.

Marcus, Joel. *Mark 1–8: A New Translation with Introduction and Commentary*. AB 27. New York: Doubleday, 2000.

—. *Mark 8–16: A New Translation with Introduction and Commentary*. AB 27A. New Haven: Yale University Press, 2009.

Marshall, I. Howard. *Commentary on Luke*. NIGTC. Grand Rapids: Eerdmans, 1978.

—. "Political and Eschatological Language in Luke." In *Reading Luke: Interpretation, Reflection, Formation*, ed. Craig Bartholomew, Joel B. Green and Anthony C. Thiselton. Grand Rapids: Zondervan, 2005, 157–77.

Mason, Eric F. *"You Are a Priest Forever": Second Temple Jewish Messianism and the Priestly Christology of the Epistle to the Hebrews*. STDJ 74. Leiden: Brill, 2008.

Matera, Frank J. *The Kingship of Jesus: Composition and Theology in Mark 15*. SBLDS 66. Chico, CA: Scholars Press, 1982.

Metzger, Bruce M. *A Textual Commentary on the Greek New Testament*. 4th revised ed. New York: United Bible Societies, 1994.

Moessner, David P. *Lord of the Banquet: The Literary and Theological Significance of the Lukan Travel Narrative*. Minneapolis: Fortress, 1989.

Mowinckel, Sigmund. *He That Cometh*, tr. G. W. Anderson. New York: Abingdon, 1954.

Neusner, Jacob, tr. *The Mishnah: A New Translation*. New Haven, CT: Yale University Press, 1988.

A New English Translation of the Septuagint and the Other Greek Translations Traditionally Included Under That Title, ed. Albert Pietersma and Benjamin G. Wright. New York: Oxford University Press, 2007.

Nolland, John. *The Gospel of Matthew*. NIGTC. Grand Rapids: Eerdmans, 2005.

—. "No Son-of-God Christology in Matthew 1.18–25." *JSNT* 62 (1996): 3–12.

Norden, Eduard. *Agnostos Theos: Untersuchungen zur Formengeschichte religiöser Rede*. 1913. Darmstadt: Wissenschaftliche Buchgesellschaft, 1974.

Peterson, David. *Engaging With God: A Biblical Theology of Worship*. Downers Grove: IVP, 2002.

Porter, Stanley E., ed. *The Messiah in the Old and New Testaments*. McMaster New Testament Studies. Grand Rapids: Eerdmans, 2007.

Räisänen, Heikki. *The "Messianic Secret" in Mark's Gospel*, tr. Christopher Tuckett. Studies of the New Testament and Its World. Edinburgh: T & T Clark, 1990.

Rowe, C. Kavin. *Early Narrative Christology: The Lord in the Gospel of Luke*. BZNW 139. Berlin: De Gruyter, 2006.

Segal, Alan F. *Two Powers in Heaven: Early Rabbinic Reports About Christianity and Gnosticism*. SJLA 25. Leiden: Brill, 1977.

Snodgrass, Klyne. *The Parable of the Wicked Tenants: An Inquiry into Parable Interpretation*. WUNT 27. Tübingen: Mohr Siebeck, 1983.

Strauss, Mark. *The Davidic Messiah in Luke–Acts: The Promise and its Fulfillment in Lukan Christology*. JSNTSup 110. Sheffield: Sheffield Academic Press, 1995.

Suggs, M. Jack. *Wisdom, Christology, and Law in Matthew's Gospel*. Cambridge, MA: Harvard University Press, 1970.

Tuckett, Christopher M. "Messianic Secret." In *ABD* 4: 797–800.

Twelftree, Graham H. *Jesus the Exorcist: A Contribution to the Study of the Historical Jesus*. WUNT II/54. Tübingen: Mohr Siebeck, 1993.

Van Unnik, W. C. "Dominus Vobiscum: The Backgound of a Liturgical Formula." In *New Testament Essays: Studies in Memory of Thomas Walter Manson, 1893–1958*, ed. A. J. B. Higgins. Manchester: Manchester University Press, 1959, 270–305.

Vermes, Geza, tr. *The Complete Dead Sea Scrolls in English*. New York: Penguin, 1997.

Watts, Rikki E. *Isaiah's New Exodus in Mark*. WUNT II/88. Tübingen: Mohr Siebeck, 1997.

—. "Jesus' Death, Isaiah 53, and Mark 10:45: A Crux Revisited." In *Jesus and the Suffering Servant: Isaiah 53 and Christian Origins*, ed. William H. Bellinger and William R. Farmer. Harrisburg, PA: Trinity Press International, 1998, 125–51.

Weeden, Theodore J. *Mark – Traditions in Conflict*. Philadelphia: Fortress, 1971.

Wrede, William. *The Messianic Secret*, tr. J. C. G. Greig. Cambridge: James Clarke, 1971.

Yarbro Collins, Adela. *Mark: A Commentary*. Hermeneia. Minneapolis: Fortress, 2007.

—. "Mark and His Readers: The Son of God Among Jews." *HTR* 92 (1999): 393–408.

Ziegler, Joseph, ed. *Isaias*. Vetus Testamentum Graecum. Auctoritate Academiae Scientiarum Gottingensis Editum 14. Göttingen: Vandenhoeck & Ruprecht, 1983.

Ziesler, J. A. "Matthew and the Presence of Jesus (1)." *Epworth Review* 11, no. 1 (1984): 55–63.

Index of References

The Old Testament

In the index, all references to the Bible are cited according to the English numbering of the verses, even in those cases where the text may refer to the numbering in the Hebrew or Greek versions.

44.29 145
45.1 154, 155, 160
49.8 144
50.34 145

Lamentations
4.22 145

Ezekiel
1.1 61
1.4–28 23, 79
2.1 23, 55
2.3 23, 55
2.6 23, 55
2.8 23, 55
3.1 23, 55
16.8 49, 130
20.5 78
20.40 145
23.21 145
27.7 146
27.10 146
32.7–8 77
32.7 79
34.1–6 12
34.4–8 102
34.5 102
34.11–16 102
34.11 145
34.12 102
34.17–22 102
34.22 114
34.23–24 9
34.23 102
34.25–31 9
36.27 135
36.29 114
37.14 135
37.23 82
37.24–28 9
39.29 135
44.10 157

Daniel
2.34–35 116
2.37 77
2.44–45 116
3.25 3

3.28 77
4.30 77
6.22 77
6.23 130
7 24
7.2–8 23
7.9 67
7.13–14 18, 23, 64, 65, 91, 108, 109
7.13 25, 50, 55, 56, 69, 86, 139
7.14 23, 58, 86, 109, 131
7.15–28 23
7.17 23
7.19–20 23
7.23–26 23
7.27 23, 50, 58, 108
9.24 9, 11
9.24–27 9
9.25–26 2, 9, 10
9.25 9, 10
9.26–27 10
9.26 9, 10
10.13 20, 24
10.21 20, 24
12.1 24
12.10 157
12.3 79

Hosea
1.7 114
2.18 76
2.19–20 49, 130
4.14 145
7.13 145
11.1 3, 62, 100, 104, 108, 123
13.4 114
13.5 108

Joel
2.10 77, 79
2.28–29 135
2.31 77, 79
3.1–12 91
3.2 91
3.15 77, 79

Amos
3.2 108
7.8 47

Apocrypha

The New Testament

Index of Subjects

Index of Modern Names